Painted by A.Dickinson.

Eng.d by W.Warner.

Benjamin Lundy

THE

LIFE, TRAVELS AND OPINIONS

OF

BENJAMIN LUNDY,

INCLUDING HIS

JOURNEYS TO TEXAS AND MEXICO; WITH A SKETCH
OF CONTEMPORARY EVENTS, AND A NOTICE
OF THE REVOLUTION IN HAYTI.

COMPILED

UNDER THE DIRECTION AND ON BEHALF OF HIS CHILDREN.

NEGRO UNIVERSITIES PRESS
NEW YORK

Originally published in 1847
by William D. Parrish, Philadelphia

Reprinted 1969 by
Negro Universities Press
A DIVISION OF GREENWOOD PUBLISHING CORP.
NEW YORK

SBN 8371-2179-5

PREFACE.

In preparing a history of the life and opinions of Benjamin Lundy, as well as of cotemporary events connected with the anti-slavery cause, the compiler has in general abstained from the introduction of his own opinions in reference to the matters recorded. In the very few instances of a departure from this rule, he has been solicitous to avoid giving offence to any class of emancipationists, and not to offer his own views on points respecting which the different classes are at issue. It has been suggested, however, since the succeeding pages were printed, that a remark written in reference to an observation made by Lundy on "political action," might be understood differently from what was intended. He will therefore state, that the term "political action," as used by himself, was intended to signify any kind of action, by petitions, resolutions, editorials, lectures or otherwise, aimed expressly at effecting a change in the laws, the constitution or the political relations of the country, or any part of it.

The notice of the Haytien revolution is appended to the volume, both because it is an abridgement of one of Lundy's works, and because the main facts of that revolution, which have been much misunderstood, are of interest, as illustrating the only instance recorded in history of a supposed successful insurrection of slaves.

CONTENTS.

THE LIFE OF BENJAMIN LUNDY.

~~~~~~~~~~~~~~~~~~~~~~~

CHAPTER I.

Introductory Statement.

It has, perhaps, been too often the province of Biography to record the achievements of the heroes of the sword—of those whose principal distinction arose from the torrents of blood they had caused to flow, from the number of widows and orphans they had made, and from the extent of the countries which they had devastated or enslaved, with no better motive than that principle of self-aggrandizement which actuates the thief, the robber and the pirate.

Our enterprise is of a different character. Its purpose is to record the deeds of a hero of the soul—of one who toiled incessantly, and patiently endured every privation in order that he might heal the wounds which tyranny had inflicted ; that he might bind up the hearts which avarice had rent; that he might sanctify the rights of consanguinity, that he might secure to labour its just reward ; to virtue its due protection, to the rights of man their full enjoyment, to human intellect its freedom of expansion, to life the shield of just laws ; and that he might elevate his race to a more full conformity to that religion which teaches peace on earth and good will to men.

As BENJAMIN LUNDY was principally known through his devotion to the cause of emancipation, we will, before entering on his personal history, give a brief account of the previous state of that cause in the United States of America.

The first Anti-Slavery publication ever issued in North America, is said to have been a tract written by Ralph Sandiford, in 1729. .The next was written by Benjamin Lay, and published by Dr. Franklin, at Philadelphia, in 1737. As Dr. Franklin was printer of one of the earlier tracts, so he became at an early period president of the first Society established in America expressly to promote emancipation, viz. the Pennsylvania Abolition Society, which received an act of incorporation from the State Legislature, and which is still in active existence.

From the period of the publication of Lay's tract, the anti-slavery doctrine continued to spread, until at length it manifested itself as the sentiment of the country at large, in the declaration, signed by all the members of the North American Congress of 1774, that they would not engage in the slave trade themselves nor lease their vessels to others for that purpose. Slavery was extinguished by provisions of the State Constitutions adopted in Massachusetts in 1776, in New Hampshire in 1792, and in Vermont in 1793. Laws for gradual abolition were passed by the State Legislatures, in Pennsylvania in 1780, in Rhode Island and Connecticut in 1784, in New York in 1799, and in New Jersey in 1804. Laws favouring voluntary emancipation by the owners of slaves, were passed in Delaware in 1787, in Maryland in 1796, in Kentucky in 1798, and in Tennessee in 1801. The national congress in 1787, conformably to the request of Virginia, who had relinquished her claims to the territory north-west of the Ohio river, passed an ordinance prohibiting the introduction of slaves into that territory, and thus the region of country which now composes Ohio, Indiana, Illinois, Michigan and Wisconsin, became permanently free.

During the revolutionary war, viz., from 1776 to 1783,

the slaves who enlisted in the army were emancipated; and at that time, as well as subsequently, up to the year 1789, fugitive slaves escaping from one state to another, were held to be free, in conformity to the law of Moses, and the international code of civilized nations.

When the Convention of 1788 assembled to revise the articles of confederation existing between the states, it was found that every state except North Carolina, South Carolina and Georgia was opposed to the toleration of the African slave trade, and North Carolina would probably have readily yielded the point; but at the ultimate settlement of the question, the extreme northern States, in consideration of the concession by the extreme south to Congress of the privilege of passing navigation acts, for the benefit of northern ship-owners, coalesced with Carolina and Georgia, and effected, in opposition to the votes of Pennsylvania, New Jersey, Maryland, Delaware and Virginia, the insertion of a clause in the Constitution, by which the continuance of the slave trade was authorized, in such states as should choose to permit it, for the period of twenty years longer, viz., until 1808. The Convention also conceded to each state, for the slaves contained within its limits, a representation in Congress, in the proportion of five slaves to three freemen. It likewise inserted, in the Constitution, a provision for the return to each state of persons held to labour or service by its laws, and escaping to other states. This provision was construed by the framers of the Constitution, by Congress and by the Judiciary, as applicable to fugitive slaves. The propriety of this construction, however, has recently been disputed by a considerable number, but it has received the sanction of a late unanimous opinion of the Supreme Court of the Union.

It will thus be seen, that the cause of slavery gained some practical advantages in the adoption and construction of the Constitution; while, on the other hand, Congress obtained the power of prohibiting the importation of slaves altogether, after the year 1808, which it did not before possess, and the amendatory clause of the Constitution authorized three-fourths of the states, by means of an alteration of that instrument, to extinguish slavery entirely throughout the country :—a power which has hitherto been unproductive of utility.

Directly after the adoption of the Constitution, petitions were sent to Congress by the Pennsylvania Society and others, asking that body to exert its full constitutional power for the abolition of Slavery. These petitions were referred to a committee, who reported, that the national government had no power to interfere for the extinction of slavery within the limits of any state of the confederacy. The report, to this |effect, was adopted with unanimity. From that time the energy of anti-slavery action evidently declined, and it seemed ultimately to have been almost extinguished in the high excitement of the conflict between the two great political parties of the country, insomuch that in the year 1810 there were scarcely any abolition societies still in existence, and the very few that remained confined their operations principally to the defence, in courts of justice, of free people of colour, against unfounded claims to their services, and to the improvement of their condition, by education and other means ; and even in these departments, the efforts made were altogether inadequate to the objects in view.

The lethargy into which the nation had sunk, in reference to the great question of slavery, was at length dissipated, by a renewed agitation, in which BENJAMIN LUNDY, the subject of this memoir, may be justly considered the pioneer, as well as one of the most energetic, indefatigable and self-sacrificing actors.

The following narrative of his life has been compiled partly from letters written by him to a friend, and partly from his publications and other sources. The materials would doubtless have been more ample, had it not been for the destruction of a portion of his papers, in the conflagration of the Pennsylvania Hall at Philadelphia, in May, 1838.

The compiler has generally adopted the use of the first person in the narrative, in consideration of the fact that it is principally taken from Lundy's own account, and nearly in his own words; yet his language has been varied and corrected condensed or modified, in a manner similar to what it may be presumed he would have done himself, had he revised for publication what had been hastily composed for the perusal of a friend.

CHAPTER II

Narrative of Lundy to the period of the commencement of his Anti-Slavery labours.

My native place (says Lundy) was the county of Sussex, New Jersey. Both my parents, as also their ancestors and most of their connexions, were members of the religious Society of Friends. Their families came originally from England and Wales. My great grandfather settled at Buckingham, Bucks county, Pennsylvania, at an early period. He was a preacher, and one of the principal founders of the Friends' meeting at that place, as he was also of the meeting at Plumstead, Bucks county, Pennsylvania, and of that at Handwich, Sussex county, New Jersey; so that it was said of him, that he had been mainly instrumental in establishing three " churches in the wilderness." He had removed to each place, successively, in the commencement of its settlement. It was at Handwich that my father and myself were born. The date of my birth was the 4th of the first month, (January,) 1789.

My mother, whose maiden name was Shotwell, died when I was about five years of age, leaving me an only child. About two years after her decease my father married again.

During my mother's life I had been to school and learned to read a little. After my father's second marriage, I attended school again for a few weeks, and began to try to write before I was eight years of age. I went again for a short time, when at the age of sixteen, to learn arithmetic. This is all the schooling I ever had.

I had an unquenchable thirst for knowledge, and was, withal, very ambitious, insomuch that when my father hired men to work on his farm, I laboured with them, much too hard for my physical frame, in order to convince them, that though a mere boy, I could do the work of the largest and strongest man. By this means, I partially lost my hearing, and otherwise injured my health. In this, I was alone to blame, as my father often cautioned me against it.

At the age of nineteen, my health continuing to decline, I concluded to travel a while. Accordingly, I went to Maiden Creek, in Berks county, Pennsylvania, thence to Mount Pleasant, Ohio, and thence to Wheeling, Virginia, where I remained four years, during which period I served an apprenticeship at the saddler's trade, and worked at it for eighteen months as a journeyman.

While at Wheeling, I paid little attention to any thing but the mechanical business in which I was engaged. But during my stay there, my faculties were developed, my character became known to myself, and the principles that have since guided me in my public labours were formed and fixed.

My father, while I was at home, had been very strict in restraining me with respect to dress and amusements; but when I found myself free from his control, I felt a strong disposition to indulge my youthful propensities in these matters. I was settled, too, among a worldly minded people, most of whom cared little for my future welfare. The man with whom I lived, was a regular gambler; and my only associates were wild, fashionable

youths, "*clever*"* enough, but thoughtless and fond of
frivolous sport. For my own part, I had some concern
for the future, and, upon reflection, I resolved to check
my unreasonable propensities, before it should be too
late. I kept on my plain dress, attended regularly the
meetings of our religious Society, shunned every species
of gambling and frolicking, and spent most of my leisure
in reading instructive books.

It was in this situation that I first became acquainted
with the wrongs of the slave. Wheeling was a great
thoroughfare for the traffickers in human flesh. Their
"*coffles*" passed through the place frequently. My
heart was deeply grieved at the gross abomination; I
heard the wail of the captive; I felt his pang of distress; and the iron entered my soul.

On leaving Wheeling I returned to Mount Pleasant,
Ohio, where I became acquainted with William Lewis
and his sisters, one of whom I afterwards married.
Here I published, anonymously, my first poetical effusion. It was an answer to a tirade of a bachelor against
matrimony. After remaining two years at Mount Pleasant I went home to New Jersey, and spent eight or ten
months there. My father urged me to stay in his vicinity and pursue my trade, offering me some assistance,
which he could not well render at a distance. Upon
inquiry, however, I concluded that I could do better at
the West, though without aid.

I accordingly returned to Ohio, was married, and
went to St. Clairsville, ten miles west of Wheeling, and
there set up my business. I began with no other means
but my hands and a disposition for industry and economy. In a little more than four years, however, I
found myself in possession of more than three thousand
dollars worth of property, beyond what was necessary
to pay the moderate amount which I owed.

I had then a loving wife and two beautiful little
daughters, that it was real happiness to possess and to

---

*The word *clever* is here used in the American sense of *amiable*.

cherish : I was at peace with my neighbours, and knew
not that I had an enemy ; I had bought a lot and built
myself a comfortable house; all my wants and those of
my lovely family were fully supplied ; my business was
increasing, and prosperity seemed to smile before me.

CHAPTER III.

Narrative from the commencement of Lundy's Anti-Slavery labours
in Ohio, to his removal to Tennessee.

I had lamented the sad condition of the slave, ever
since I became acquainted with his wrongs and sufferings. But the question, " What can I do ?" was the
continual response to the impulses of my heart. As I
enjoyed no peace of mind, however, I at length concluded that I *must* act ; and shortly after my settlement
at St. Clairsville, I called a few friends together, and
unbosomed my feelings to them. The result was the
organization of an anti-slavery association, called the
Union Humane Society.* The first meeting, which was
held at my own house, consisted of but five or six persons. In a few months afterwards, the Society contained
nearly five hundred members, among whom were most
of the influential preachers and lawyers, and many
respectable citizens of several counties in that section of
the state.

I also wrote an appeal on the subject of slavery,
addressed to the philanthropists of the United States,
and circulated five or six copies in manuscript. I
was urged to publish it by some of my friends, and by
persons from a distance whom I met at the Yearly Meeting of the Society of Friends, held at Mount Pleasant.

* This was in the year 1815, when Lundy was at the age
of 26.

I consented, on condition that it should appear with a *fictitious signature.* Since that time my modesty has much worn off.*

Soon after this occurrence, proposals were issued by Charles Osborne, for publishing a paper at Mount Pleasant, to be entitled the Philanthropist. He stated in his

---

* The address or circular here alluded to was dated, in the printed copies, one of which is now before me, "St. Clairsville, 1st mo. 4th, 1816," being Lundy's birth day, on attaining 27 years.

After an introduction in which he urged the impolicy of stopping short at the abolition of the African slave-trade, as the seeds of the evil system had been sown in our soil, and were springing up and producing increase, he proposed, 1. That societies should be formed wherever a sufficient number of persons could be induced to join in them. 2. That a title should be adopted common to all the societies. 3. That they should all have a uniform constitution, "varying only on account of necessity, arising from location." 4. That a correspondence should be kept up between the societies, that they should co-operate in action, and that in case of important business, they should choose delegates to meet in general convention.

This plan, it will be seen, is nearly the same as that which was in efficient operation twenty years afterwards, and then embraced nearly 1000 anti-slavery societies.

At the conclusion of the address, which was signed "Philo Justitia," the writer stated that he had had the subject long in contemplation, and that he had now taken it up, fully determined, for one, never to lay it down while he breathed, or until the end should be obtained. The first alternative of this determination he accomplished; the second will be perfected by his successors.

A note appended to the printed circular stated, that since the circular was drawn up, a number of societies had been formed in various parts of Ohio, each taking the name of "The Union Humane Society;" and that a constitution had been formed, calculated to embrace all the societies which existed, or might thereafter be established.—[ED.

prospectus, that he should discuss the subject of slavery in the columns of the paper. The idea now occurred to me, that I might act efficiently for the cause of emancipation—that I could select articles, (for I did not think of writing myself,) and have them published in the Philanthropist, and that I could also get subscribers to the publication. Engrossed with these thoughts, I went to work with alacrity.

My leisure moments were now fully employed. When I sent my selections to Charles, I sometimes wrote him a few lines. After he had published the Philanthropist a few months, I was surprised at receiving from him a request that I should assist in editing it. The thought that I could do such a thing had not then even occurred to me. But on his repeating the request, I consented to try ;—and from that moment, whenever I have thought that something ought to be done, my maxim has been, though doubtful of my ability—" *try*." Although I resided ten miles from the office, and was extensively engaged in other business, I continued, for some time, to write editorial articles for the paper.

At length, Charles proposed to me to join him in the printing business, and to take upon myself the superintendence of the office. After some deliberation, I consented to accept the offer, and, with that view, prepared to diminish my other business. I discharged some of my workmen, and took a portion of the articles which had been made in my shop, to Missouri, in order to sell them. I returned in about six months, when finding business more dull than before, I determined to break up my establishment at St. Clairsville, altogether, and remove to Mount Pleasant.

With that view, I then took all the articles from my shop, put them in a boat, and accompanied by my three apprentices, started again for Missouri. We proceeded down the Ohio river, my boys working at their trade in the boat, while I steered it in the current. In going up the Mississippi, the boys assisted the boat hands in row-ing. It was late in the fall of 1819 when I arrived at St. Louis.

At this time the famous " *Missouri question*," being that of the toleration or prohibition of slavery in the Constitution of the proposed new State of Missouri, which was to be formed out of the Louisiana territory, had begun to agitate the American Union. I was on the great scene of discussion, and in the midst of those whose interests were most involved. My feelings prompted me to engage in the controversy. I devoted myself sedulously to an exposition, in the newspapers of Missouri and Illinois, of the evils of slavery. The contest, which was long and severe, terminated in our losing the day. Congress decided that the people of Missouri might form a Constitution, without restriction as to slavery, which was accordingly done; and at the next session of that body, the State with her slave Constitution, was admitted as a member of the Union.

After this event, I returned home, a distance of 700 miles, on foot, and in the winter season. I had lost, at St. Louis, some thousands of dollars, and had been detained from home a year and ten months. The tide of misfortune to me, was caused by the utter stagnation of business, which at that time overspread the whole country, and occasioned the sacrifice of property to an incalculable amount.

Before I left St. Louis, I heard that, as I had staid from home so much longer than had been anticipated, Charles Osborne had become quite tired of the employment of editor, and had sold out his printing establishment to Elisha Bates, and also that Elihu Embree had commenced the publication of an anti-slavery paper, called " The Emancipator," at Jonesborough in Tennessee. I therefore made up my mind to settle with my family in Illinois. But on my way home I was informed of the death of E. Embree; and as E. Bates did not come up to my standard of anti-slavery, I determined immediately to establish a periodical of my own. I therefore removed to Mount Pleasant, and commenced the publication of the Genius of Universal Emancipation, in January 1821.

E. Bates published my prospectus, and also the first number of my paper. I afterwards had my printing done at Steubenville, Ohio, a distance of twenty miles. I went to and from that place on foot, carrying my papers, when printed, on my back. I had begun the work without a dollar of funds, trusting for success to the sacredness of the cause; nor was I disappointed. In four months from the commencement, my subscription list had become quite large.

When the friends of the deceased Elihu Embree heard of my paper, they urged me to remove to Tennessee and use the press on which his had been printed. I assented; and after having issued eight monthly numbers of the "Genius" in Ohio, I started for Tennessee. I travelled, in going there, eight hundred miles, one-half on foot, and the rest by water. On my arrival, I rented the printing office, and immediately went to work with the paper, laboring myself at the mechanical as well as the editorial department. I thus learned to be a printer, by carrying on the trade, without having ever served an hour's apprenticeship. In a short time, in addition to publishing "The Genius of Universal Emancipation," I established a weekly newspaper, and a monthly agricultural work.

CHAPTER IV.

Narrative from Lundy's settlement in Tennessee in 1821, until his removal thence to Baltimore in 1824.

While thus engaged in the midst of a slaveholding region, I was often threatened in various ways. On one occasion two ruffians came a distance of thirty miles to demand some concession respecting an article that had been inserted in the Genius. They asked me into

a private room, shut the door, and with deadly weapons
undertook to enforce their demand. They found themselves mistaken in the person with whom they had to
deal, and the owner of the house hearing the dispute,
came in and released me from confinement. Often the
bullies vapoured around me with bludgeons, in such a
manner, that the sparing of my life might seem to have
been providential.

  I had not taken my family along with me at first, but
after a few months trial I removed them to Tennessee,
where I continued to reside for nearly three years.
During this period I went to Philadelphia, a distance of
six hundred miles, to attend " the American Convention for the Abolition of Slavery," performing the journey
on horseback, in the winter season, and at my own
expense. I was the first delegate that ever attended
the Convention from any portion of the country as far
south as Tennessee. On this occasion I became personally acquainted, for the first time, with some of the
abolitionists east of the Allegheny mountains.

  " The Genius of Universal Emancipation" had now
obtained a pretty wide circulation in the United States.*
As it was the only anti-slavery paper in America, I concluded to attempt the transfer of its publication to one
of the Atlantic cities, hoping thereby to extend its influence still more widely, and secure for it a better support. In going to Philadelphia to attend the Convention,
I had made a few acquaintances in Baltimore, and had
suggested to them the measure of transferring the paper
to that city. They gave me but slight encouragement,
as most of them were very little interested in the subject
of emancipation. Acting, however, on my before mentioned maxim, of " trying," I resolved to make the
experiment. Having arranged my business in Tennes-

  * In a letter dated 3d month 16th, 1823, Lundy said: "My
paper circulates well. If any person had told me when I commenced that I should be as successful under all my disadvan-
tages as I have been, I could not have believed them."

see, I shouldered my knapsack and set out for Baltimore, on foot, in the summer of 1824.

I proceeded through the south-western part of Virginia into the State of North Carolina, where I had some family connections. On this occasion, I delivered at Deep Creek, North Carolina, my first public lecture on the subject of slavery.* I shall never forget the incidents of that meeting. It was held by the side of a fine spring, in a beautiful shady grove near the Friends' Meeting House at Deep Creek, after the meeting for worship had closed. The audience signified their approbation of the lecture, by appointing another meeting for me to be held in the meeting house on a subsequent day. The second meeting having been publicly advertised, was attended by many persons, besides members of the Society of Friends; and before its adjournment, an anti-slavery or abolition society was organized. I afterwards, during that visit to North Carolina, held some fifteen or twenty anti-slavery meetings at various places. My discourses were similar to all that I have since delivered in other parts of the United States, and as ultra orthodox in anti-slavery sentiment as any of modern times.

I embraced every opportunity of obtaining an audience. At one time I went to the raising of a house, and lectured to the persons who were there assembled. At another I called a meeting at a place where there was to be a militia muster. The captain and some of his men attended, as did also a number of "Friends" who resided in the vicinity. It was quite amusing to see the intermingled plain and military dresses, while I was reminding the wearers of them of the principles of Christian humanity, and of civil liberty, as based upon eternal justice. At this meeting an anti-slavery society, consist-

* This was probably the commencement of the system of lecturing on the subject of emancipation, which has since been so extensively and effectively pursued in the United States.— ED.

ing of fourteen members, was formed. The captain of militia was chosen president, and a member of the Society of Friends, secretary. One of my meetings was at Raleigh, the seat of government of North Carolina. Before I left the State, there were some twelve or fourteen anti-slavery societies organized.

On departing from North Carolina I again entered Virginia, and travelled through the middle section of that State, holding numerous meetings, and effecting the organization of several anti-slavery societies.

CHAPTER V.

Narrative from Lundy's removal to Baltimore till his return from a visit to New England in 1828.

I then went, through a part of Maryland, to the city of Baltimore, where the friends of the cause received me civilly, but coolly enough. They wished me success, but entertained strong doubts of my attaining it. I nevertheless engaged a printer, made arrangements to save expense by working for him a portion of the time as a journeyman, and issued the first Baltimore number of the "Genius," in the tenth month (October) 1824, it being No. 1 of Vol. 4, and the 44th monthly number from the commencement; some interruptions of the regular publication having previously occurred.

I soon made acquaintances, increased my subscription list, brought my family from Tennessee, and got a printing office for myself. In about a year after my commencement at Baltimore, I changed the paper from a monthly publication to a weekly.

In the latter part of 1825, I visited the Island of Hayti. The occasion of my journey was this. When I passed through North Carolina, as before stated, a gentleman who held eleven slaves agreed to give them

up to me in consideration that I should take them where
they could enjoy their rights. I had sent them to Hayti,
and as other American slaveholders proposed to follow
the example of the gentleman alluded to, I now repaired
to Hayti myself to make arrangements with the government of that country for the settlement of any emancipated slaves which might be sent thither. Being detained there much longer than I had anticipated, my
views of earthly happiness were clouded before my
return, by news of the decease of my loved and cherished
bosom companion, which was brought me by a vessel
that arrived the day before that on which I was to sail
for home.

I returned to Baltimore with a heavy heart. On our
arrival the vessel was ordered to perform quarantine,
and the persons on board were forbidden to land until
the next day. I persuaded the captain, however, to go
on shore with me at night, that I might see my little
orphan children. We rowed a small boat several miles
to the shore. I hastened to my dwelling, but found it
deserted. All was lone and dreary within its walls.
I roused some of the neighbours, but they could tell me
nothing about my children. I returned with the captain
before day-light to the vessel, and the next day obtained
legal permission to land. On further inquiry, I found
that my little ones were scattered among my friends.
But " home with all its pleasures" was gone. The soul
that once animated it had been called to the realms of
eternal felicity, and I was left to mourn over the desola-
tion that remained.

I collected my children together, placed them with
friends in whom I could confide, and renewed my vow
to devote my energies to the cause of the slave, until
the nation should be effectually roused in his behalf. I
relinquished every prospect of the future enjoyment of
an earthly home until that object should be accomplished.

I still continued to publish my paper weekly at Baltimore. Many warm friends of the cause were added to
those that I had found there, and we established several

anti-slavery societies. A very capable, intelligent and philanthropic young man (William Swain) joined me, and became assistant editor. He was one of my North Carolina converts. About that time, Elizabeth M. Chandler* also began to write for me. She thought nothing about slavery then, but wrote on other subjects, until her feelings were awakened by reading the paper.

In 1828, I made a journey to the middle and eastern States, for the purpose of lecturing and obtaining sub-scriptions to "The Genius." I took Philadelphia in the way, where I called a meeting to consider the sub-ject of encouraging the use of free-labour products, being the first meeting of that kind ever held in Ame-rica. At New York I formed a slight acquaintance with Arthur Tappan and a few others. I found Wm. Goodell at Providence, Rhode Island, and endeavoured to arouse him; but he was at that time 'slow of speech" on my subject.

At Boston I could hear of no abolitionists resident in the place. At the house where I staid, I became ac-quainted with William L. Garrison, who was also a boarder there. He had not then turned his attention particularly to the anti-slavery question. I visited the Boston clergy, and finally got together eight of them, belonging to various sects. Such an occurrence, it was said, was seldom if ever before known in that town. The eight clergymen all cordially approved of my object, and each of them cheerfully subscribed to my paper, in order to encourage, by their example, the members of their several congregations to take it. William L. Garrison, who sat in the room and witnessed our pro-ceedings, also expressed his approbation of my doctrines. In the course of a few days afterwards, we had a public meeting, which was attended by most of the eight cler-gymen, together with a large audience. After I had finished my lecture, several clergymen addressed the meeting. They concurred in my views, except one of

*Author of a volume of poems on slavery and other subjects.

them, who said something a little like opposition. I
forthwith challenged him to a public debate on the spot,
which he declined. Wm. L. Garrison shortly afterwards wrote an article on the subject for one of the daily
papers.

I also visited New Hampshire, Maine and New York,
after which I returned home, having, during my tour,
considerably increased my subscription list, and, as I
have since learned, scattered the seed of anti-slavery in
strong and luxuriant soil. While casting it by the way-
side, and on the mountains covered with flint and gla-
ciers, (for it was then the very winter of philanthropy,) I
could not know on what ground the good seed fell.
But time and the vivifying sun of free discussion have
fructified it in such a manner as to demonstrate that my
labour was not in vain.*

---

* Lundy left a journal or memorandum of the journey to the
eastern States, above briefly described. The following is the
substance of some of the principal incidents contained in it.

1828. *May* 1st. I started from Baltimore. 2d. Saw on the
road a negro with an iron yoke or collar on his neck. 4th. Held
my first meeting this day at the close of Friends'. meeting.
10th. I attended a meeting of the Anti-Slavery Society at Ken-
net Square, Pennsylvania. 13th. Arrived at Burlington, New
Jersey, and went thence to my father's residence, where I spent
the 14th. 18th. Reached the house of Evan Lewis in West-
chester, New York, and held an anti-slavery meeting there on
the 19th, it being the fifth meeting of the kind since I left home.
20th. Saw this morning a cotton factory at New Rochelle, near
which were fifteen or twenty boys from eight to fourteen years
of age, all at play, hopping and jumping. They went to work
at the ringing of the factory bell. This is the way the Yankees
get rich :—no idlers out of the cradle ! 27th. I delivered my
seventh lecture at the close of a meeting of the District Association of Presbyterian Ministers, held near Bridgeport, Connecticut. I lodged at the house of one of the number, where I
found kind people. 30th. At New Haven I held my eighth
meeting, which was a large one, and included some members
of the Legislature.

June 6th. I had a very large meeting of men and women at
Hartford, Connecticut. 9th. Had a large meeting at Brooklyn,
Connecticut, where I tarried at the house of George Benson, a

After my return, my assistant editor, William Swain, returned home to North Carolina, having staid with me about six months. He shortly afterwards established a weekly newspaper in North Carolina, in which he treated

zealous friend of Emancipation as well as of the Peace Society: 11th. I had a good sized meeting at Norwich, Connecticut, but it was attended only by men. The people here are all too politic, and will do nothing for our cause. 16th. Attended Friends' Yearly Meeting at Newport, Rhode Island, and on the 20th, held at that place my twelfth anti-slavery lecture. It was attended by few and they were all men. Sectarianism nearly closes up my way here, I being but a moderate Quaker. 23d. Arrived at Providence, and on the 24th attended a meeting of the Abolition Society of that place. 28th. At New Bedford, Massachusetts, I had a small meeting, it being Saturday evening; on the following afternoon, however, I had a large meeting of men and women. Found liberal people in this town.

July 3d. I sailed to Nantucket. During my stay on the Island I held two meetings, the second of which was well attended by men and women. On the 7th I sailed for Portland, where I arrived on the 9th, having sailed one hundred and ninety miles and been sea-sick, as well as becalmed on the way. I held a large meeting in the Presbyterian meeting-house on the 10th. The people of Portland seem in general to be cool calculators. 15th. At Portsmouth, New Hampshire, I held a very large meeting in the Baptist meeting-house of Rev. B. Stow. 18th. At Newburyport, Massachusetts, I had a small meeting in the Court House. 21st. At Andover I held a meeting before a committee of the College of that place, and in the evening another meeting which was large. 24th. At Salem, Massachusetts, I held a very large meeting in the Congregational meeting-house. 27th. At Lynn I had a respectable meeting, in the Unitarian meeting-house. Many Friends were present. 31st. At Boston, whence I went again to Lynn, with a communication on the subject of slavery, for the Methodist Conference.

August 1st. I am making arrangements for a meeting in Boston, which are embarrassed by there being too many other meetings, as negroes are every where and always the last to be thought of or noticed. 4th. At Charlestown, Massachusetts, I held a meeting in the Rev. Mr. Hay's vestry room. 6th. I visited Brighton, and saw the Rev. Noah Worcester, the patriarchal advocate of the cause of Peace. 11th. Held a meeting in Boston at which a committee was appointed to form an Anti-Slavery Society. 12th. Held another meeting in Charlestown, where a

much of slavery and emancipation, until he was silenced
by that malignant spirit which has finally driven us all
from the slave country.

Seed, however, has been sown in that gloomy region,
which is living and germinating ; nor will all the fire of
oppression ever be able to destroy it, how much soever
its growth may be checked for a season.

CHAPTER VI.

Events from November, 1828, to removal to Washington in 1830
including visits to Hayti and Texas, and thence till Lundy's removal to Philadelphia, and his second visit to Texas in 1833.

In November, 1828, I visited New England a second
time, and applied to William Lloyd Garrison to assist me
in editing the Genius of Universal Emancipation. But

committee was chosen to propose a plan for a Society. 20th.
At Worcester, I had a large meeting of men and women in the
Town Hall. On the 22d I walked from Leicester to Springfield,
a distance of forty-five miles, being the greatest walk I have
accomplished in a single day. On the 24th, I had a large meeting at Springfield, in the Unitarian meeting-house of Rev. Mr.
Peabody. There appears to be harmony among the various
religious professors here. On the 25th I arrived at Northampton, after 9 o'clock in the evening, and called at three taverns
before I could get lodgings or polite treatment.
September 6th. At Albany I made some acquaintances.
Philanthropists are the slowest creatures breathing. They think
forty times before they act. 14th. Arrived at Lockport, where
I had a large evening meeting in the Court House. Having
visited the Falls of Niagara on the 14th, I came on the 19th to
Buffalo, where I had a small meeting.
October 5th. At Utica I had a meeting in the Presbyterian
meeting-house, which was so crowded that many could not get
in. 14th. At Albany I held a meeting for coloured people in
the meeting-house of Rev. N. Paul. 19th. At Poughkeepsie I
held my forty-third meeting. 25th. I reached home at Baltimore.

he was at that time conducting a paper in Vermont from which he could not then disengage himself.

Soon after I had published the account of the sending of eleven slaves to Hayti, a young man came to see me from the lower part of Virginia, and asked my counsel and assistance in forwarding to that Island eighty-eight slaves, of which he was the holder. I complied with the request, and they were all settled there, perfectly free. I also persuaded the "Friends," in the State of North Carolina, to send to Hayti one hundred and nineteen slaves who were under their care, and who could not be emancipated, according to the laws of that State, except by migrating beyond its limits.

In the winter of 1828-9, I was assaulted and nearly killed in Baltimore by the slave-trader Austin Woolfolk, for commenting on his conduct. The judge before whom he was tried, said from the bench, that I "got nothing more than I deserved," and he sent my paper to the grand jury, charging them that several passages in it were libellous. The jurors, however, could not agree with him, and returned the paper without finding a bill of indictment against me.

In the Spring of 1829 I went a second time to Hayti, taking with me twelve more emancipated slaves, which a man in Maryland had given up to me for the purpose.

After my return from Hayti, William Lloyd Garrison joined me at Baltimore in the editorship of the "Genius." I then set out again on a tour to lecture, but I was soon obliged to return, on account of the imprisonment of Garrison, for writings published in the paper. Being less guarded in his language than myself, he was soon placed between grated walls. The attempt to indict me had been made several times without success. It was remarked by one of the oldest editors, that though more severe than Garrison, I so selected my words that they could not be construed into libels.

When the release of Garrison was obtained by the payment of his fine, he left Baltimore, and the paper fell again under my exclusive management. I found that I could not publish it weekly without an assistant, and therefore restored it to its original form of a monthly paper. It had been issued weekly for a period of about four years.

At length the spirit of tyranny in Maryland became too strong and malignant for me. My language was forcibly construed into libels, and some half-dozen prosecutions threatened me with a long imprisonment. I was actually in prison a few days, and finally concluded that I could do more good without the walls. I therefore avoided persecution, by removing to Washington city, at which place the paper was published for some length of time. While there, I had a sharp controversy with several editors, and was freely threatened by some individuals, but the authorities were more friendly to me than in Baltimore. We organized a respectable anti-slavery society in the District of Columbia, and, at one time, obtained the signatures of more than eleven hundred of the inhabitants to petitions to Congress for the abolition of slavery there. I should have mentioned before, that after I settled in Baltimore, I succeeded in changing the place of sitting of "The American Convention for the Abolition of Slavery," &c., to Baltimore, and, at the next succeeding session, to Washington. After its meeting at the latter place, it never assembled again to transact business.*

In the years 1830 and 1831, I found it necessary to travel considerably in order to obtain subscribers for my paper. I took a part of the type, &c., along with me, and had the printing done in different places ; but the nominal place of publication was still Washington. I also, during those years, visited both Canada and Texas. I wished to see the condition of the coloured people in Canada, and to establish a settlement of that class of population in Texas, with a view to the culti-

---

* The Convention spoken of, had been chosen usually every second year for a long period. Its dissolution was disapproved of by Lundy.

vation of sugar, cotton and rice by free labour. This tour was commenced in the winter of 1830–31. I travelled mostly on foot in Canada in the coldest of the winter, and in Louisiana and Texas in the hottest of the summer, going in disguise in the Southern country, as my life would otherwise have been endangered. My labours, for eighteen months of the time, were truly arduous; but I considered that the sufferings of the slave were greater than my own. I remembered him in the bonds of toil as bound with him.

I returned home in the summer of 1832, without having been able to stay in Texas long enough to accomplish my object. Having consequently to go there again, I engaged Evan Lewis to conduct the paper in my absence. The publication office was then in Philadelphia, where I had formed several acquaintances, among whom were Abraham L. Pennock, Dr. Jonas Preston, the Doctors Atlee, (father and son,) Thomas Shipley, Thomas Earle Isaac Barton and others. My acquaintance with Dr. Parrish and his sons was limited.*

CHAPTER VI.

Journey of Lundy from Philadelphia to Nashville, Tenn., and thence to New Orleans on his way to Texas a second time, in 1833.

Having completed my arrangements, and, through the kindness of Dr. Joseph Parrish, received medicine and prescriptions to guard against the cholera, which was at that time raging fearfully in the south-west, I set out again for Texas and Mexico on the 7th of 5th month, (May) 1833.

The following are the principal events and observations of my journey, taken from a journal kept at the time, and from my recollections of occurrences.

* In page 21, Lundy speaks of forming acquaintances with others engaged in the cause.

1833.—*May* 5th.* At Cincinnati, Ohio, I had a respectable meeting in the evening, which passed resolutions approving my conduct, my plans of Texan colonization, &c.   24th. We proceeded by steamboat down the Ohio river, stopping at Evansville and Henderson, in Indiana, which have improved but little since I saw them 12 years ago. We passed Shawneetown, Illinois, which, though a beautiful place, yet improves but slowly, by reason of inundations. ` 26th. We went up the Cumberland river to Clarksville, Tennessee, 65 miles below Nashville, where we stopped awhile to land freight, &c. The country about Clarksville is a great tobacco region, and contains many slaves.   27th. We reached Nashville, where I went on shore and took lodgings with my old friend Thomas Hoge, Jr. Esq. 28th. I rose this morning quite unwell. There is much alarm in town to-day on account of the cholera, and the court has adjourned in consequence of it. There were twenty or more cases of the disease, and several deaths reported. 29th. I went on foot three miles into the country to see a coloured man about going to Texas.

June 4th, 1833. I stayed with my friend William Bryant, one of the best of men, waiting for a colored man named William Nickens, who has gone some distance, and who is much interested in my Mexican enterprise.   6th. I am quite clear of the cholera myself, though many others are afflicted.   11th. This cholera is an extraordinary disorder. It attacks with the ferocity of a tiger, keeps its hold like a bull dog, and as soon as it is conquered returns again to the charge. As to who or what are its agents, I believe no two agree, that pretend to *know*. I may therefore venture to give my opinion. It is that the cause of the disease is poisonous animalculæ floating in the atmosphere, and taken into the system with our breath. These animalculæ, being

*This journal was much of it written presumably for the information of colored people, or others who might contemplate settling in Texas, or its vicinity. It is deemed sufficiently interesting to be embraced in this volume.

too minute for discovery, it is impossible to know with
certainty and precision how the malady assails us, or
how to guard against it.   It has been said, that " it is a
strange, curious and quite uncommon disorder, and
there is no possibility of ascertaining the cause of it." But
the ague is also a very curious disorder, baffling the
learned to discover the precise causes of its periodical
returns, and its alternations of cold and heat.   Yet we
have ample evidence of its being produced by inhaling
the dense and infectious atmosphere of deep vallies,
marshes, or stagnant waters, charged with putrid miasma
and sickening animalculæ.   The animalculæ which
cause the one disease, may be more poisonous than
those which produce the other, and of an entirely different nature.   Hence the variety in the modes of operation and the different degrees of malignity observable in
the character of the two disorders.—14th. I witnessed
a fight between an old man and a boy ; the old man's
head was cut in several places by a club.   He got a
pistol to defend himself.   This is appropriate business
for Nashville.

On the 15th I had a smart attack of the cholera,
which yielded at once to camphor and laudanum.   At
5 o'clock, P. M., I held a meeting of coloured people, at
which resolutions favourable to my enterprise were adopted.   18th. I made a knapsack, mended my clothes, and
prepared to resume my journey.   26th. I engaged a deck
passage on board the steamboat Jefferson for Smithland,
Kentucky.   Nickens, the coloured man who was to go
with me, did not come.   We put off about 1 o'clock,
and I bade adieu to some very kind friends at Nashville.
During the month that I have passed in this place and
its vicinity, I have been confined a large portion of the
time by the cholera.   27th. We are stopped, waiting for
freight.   To relieve the irksomeness of the delay, I
study Spanish.   30th. We arrived at the mouth of the
Ohio river, where those of us who were bound down
the Mississippi, went on shore to wait till we could des-
cry a boat going that way, in order to take passage.

At the end of two hours we saw a boat bound down; went on board and found her to be the North Alabamian.

July 1st, 1833. We stopped at Memphis, Tennessee, for half an hour, where I formed an acquaintance with the post master, who appeared to be a sociable and clever man. 2d. We passed the mouth of the Arkansas river. The country on the banks of the Mississippi below the Arkansas' mouth, is inundated in many places. I would not reside here long, for all the land and money in these parts. We stopped to take in some wood, the hands being obliged to wade the inundated shore in order to obtain it. A poor little house was visible with a family in it, and not a rod of dry ground in sight. Men were floating cypress logs from a back swamp up to the banks of the Mississippi, in order to raft them to New Orleans. Musquitoes abound here by millions. 3d. We arrived at Petit Gulf in the State of Mississippi. The principal products here are cotton and musquitoes. July 4th. At 12 o'clock the captain hoisted the national flag, and ordered 24 rounds from a small field piece, in honor of the anniversary of American Independence. There are here, negroes in great numbers, who have not yet realized the enjoyment of the rights proclaimed on the day so celebrated. The captain purchased a slave for $150, after which we put off from the place. 5th. We arrived at New Orleans.—The river is up to the levee, and the streets are watered by sluices, which suffer a portion of the current to pass through them. Were free passage given to it, the city would be instantly submerged. 7th. The Sabbath is the great market day at New Orleans. Many stores are open, and business of various kinds is transacted.

CHAPTER VII.

Passage from New Orleans to Brazoria, Texas.

1833. *July* 8th. I took passage for Brazoria, Texas, in the schooner Wild-Cat. We put off from New Orleans a little after sunset, being towed by the steam towboat which is to take us along one hundred miles to the mouth of the Mississippi. Just at dark we passed the ground of the celebrated battle of Jan. 8th, 1815. 9th. We arrived at the mouth of the Mississippi, where the pilot left us, and we put to sea.

15th. We find the dews at sea very light—an instance of the adaptation of things to ends, as heavy dews would be of no use here. Behold the economy of nature! When it does not rain at night, our passengers all sleep on deck, where they find it more pleasant and wholesome than in the close cabin. 16th. Calm as a Sabbath morning in Boston! Our captain, who is an experienced sailor, and who has often traversed these regions, says that he never before witnessed so protracted a period of calm and head winds. Before retiring for sleep we discovered a very distinct light to the north, even with the horizon, supposed to come from prairies on fire, in Louisiana or Texas.—I had an argument with a Missouri-Texan on the subject of slavery.

18th. We entered the mouth of the Texan river Brazos. The water of the river here is of a real vermilion colour. For the first few miles from the sea, the river is bordered with marshes or plains, destitute of wood; above these, timber of various kinds abounds, among which the live oak is very common. I saw, this morning, a young alligator walking along the shore.

Since the argument that I held yesterday with the pro-slavery man, our captain seems to be somewhat discourteous. He ordered me to-day to the most unpleasant part of the deck. I thought at first that he was well satisfied with the castigation received by my opponent;

but he now says that complaint was made about myself, a deck passenger, occupying a place that the cabin passengers wished to appropriate to themselves. He is, in fact, an impudent drunken fellow.

19th. The boat lay-to at the shore until 8 o'clock, A. M., enabling me to take a short ramble on shore. No settlement was near.* The soil here is exceedingly rich. There are innumerable vines, and a profusion of long dangling moss, every where in the woods. I saw some rocks, all of which were of a kind that I was before unacquainted with.   20th. We are said to be six or eight miles below Brazoria.   The soil continues black on the surface, with a reddish, or in some places a whitish loam beneath. It is all alluvial, no rocks being perceptible. The banks of the river are of the perpendicular height of ten or twelve feet above the water. We heard, in the night, the cry of a panther, on the opposite side of the river.   21st. At about 2 P. M., we formed a party, consisting of two gentlemen, a lady and her son, and myself, to leave the vessel and walk by land to Brazoria, a distance of three and a half miles. The live oak is here the monarch of the forest. One that we saw was six or seven feet in diameter near its roots. They spread out in branches not far from the ground, and are very umbrageous.   After a wet and muddy walk, in the course of which we saw a grape vine six inches in diameter, we reached Brazoria at about four o'clock. The population of this place is about one hundred and fifty, of whom a very few are mechanics; but there are plenty of lawyers and doctors. The cholera prevails here at present to an alarming extent. 24th. The schooner, which we left two days since, arrived to-day, and I made sale of some things that I could not take along in my contemplated journey.

* The description of the soil and face of the country were noted by Lundy, with a view to publishing the results of his observations for the information of settlers.

CHAPTER VIII.

Journey from Brazoria to San Felipe de Austin, and stay at the
'latter place.

July 26th. I left Brazoria early in the morning, in
company with two young men from Kentucky, to travel
on foot to San Felipe de Austin. We saw great numbers of cattle on the prairie, the land of which is very
rich, but subject to inundation. It has been nearly all
overflowed lately. The cattle here are very fine, but
they are shy, and indeed, half wild. We found some
lagoons, abounding with flags and bulrushes, where we
saw numbers of cranes and herons. A shower which
overtook us on the way, drenched us thoroughly, and we
were obliged to wade a good deal through the water.
Our day's journey terminated at the house of Alexander
Hodge, an old settler on Oyster Creek, and a clever
man. The land here is cane-bottom, producing seventy-
two and a half bushels of corn to the acre if planted with
a stick, and seventy-six bushels if ploughed. 27th. We
continued our route as far as the house of David Tally,
a non-slaveholding emigrant from Hopkinsville, Kentucky, with a clever family. He is opposed to the
recent hasty acts of some prominent persons* in Texas.
On our journey, to-day, we met with an alligator lying
dead in the road. 28th. Our kind host, D. Tally,
refuses any compensation for our lodging. I wrote him
Dr. Parrish's prescription for the cholera, and gave the
lady of the house some camphor, which is a scarce article
here. Mr. Tally's son, a small boy, being about to go on
an errand, twenty miles along my road, I received and
accepted a kind invitation to ride with him. The heat
of the sun to-day almost blistered my neck and hands.
We saw, on the prairie, very fine cattle, some horses,
and two fine deer. At one of several houses that we

---

* Alluding, probably, to the measures for forming a state
government for Texas, separate from Coahuila.

passed on the edge of the prairie, we obtained some
bread and milk, and took some of the milk along with
us, for quenching thirst, it being better for that purpose
than water.   At 5 P. M., we reached the house of Wm.
Stafford, half-way from Brazoria to San Felipe. Stafford
was originally from Tennessee and once a Quaker. His
family are genteel people : his house has good accom-
modations, and is more of a public one than is common
in these wild regions.   He is an industrious man, formerly a blacksmith, and now a maker of ploughs, wagons,
&c.   He has on Oyster Bayou, a mill for grinding corn,
and one for manufacturing sugar.   He owns about ten
thousand acres of excellent land, ten or twelve slaves,
some horses and a large stock of most beautiful cattle.
One of his steers measures nearly four feet from the tip
of one horn to that of the other. He has a peach-
orchard, the peaches in which are now ripe, but of
small size.   I spent the 29th here, and visited the lands
and improvements.   The land is highly productive, and
sugar-cane thrives well on it, though apples will not succeed. Last spring, after the first planting, the fields were
overflowed, and the corn and cotton, together with some
of the sugar-cane, was drowned out.   It was re-planted,
and the worms cut it up.   It was planted a third time,
and now it looks promising.

Stafford thinks slavery a bad thing, but he says it is
no harm for him to hold slaves and treat them well until
all will agree to abolish the institution, and to send the
emancipated away to another country.   He treats his
slaves, in fact, so far as work is concerned, very much
like other people.   Three of his field hands are females.

I saw, here, three Indians, viz., one squaw and two
pappooses.

I take a little camphor and laudanum every day
being not yet quite free from the cholera.

July 30th.   Having agreed with a wagoner, who
encamped here last night with his family and herds on
their way to San Felipe, to take my baggage along to
that place, I set out in his company.   His wagon is

drawn by three yoke of oxen—a most unwieldy team. We spent the night at the house of James Hodge, son of A. Hodge, before mentioned. The Cayenne pepper grows wild in this vicinity. 31st. As we proceed on our way, the ground begins to change from level to slightly rolling, and we meet the peccan and other trees, among them the black-jack, which is the first I have seen. We spent the night at the house of Jesse K. Cartwright. He and his wife are kind people. They migrated hither from Nashville, Tennessee.

August 1st, 1833. We went on seven miles, when a hard rain came on and drenched us all. The wagon stopped for the day, and I shouldered my knapsack, weighing 25 lbs., took leave of the wagon, and marched on for San Felipe, which was twenty miles distant. After a while, I was overtaken by a man on horse-back, who had heard something of my medicines. He begged me to go home with him, a short distance off my road, as his wife was attacked with cholera. I complied with his request, and found the woman delirious, with cramps, &c. I gave her camphor and laudanum, applied a mustard plaster, wrote directions, and left some medicine. The husband offered me payment, which I declined: he then insisted on my taking some coffee, which I accepted. Having resumed my journey, I arrived at dusk at the house of Captain Bird, who was then from home. He came home late in the evening, and informed me that he had seen the sick woman after I left her, and that she was better. 2d. I sat out at day-break and walked six miles before breakfast; came to the Brazos-bottoms and plunged into the mud, which abounds, from the country having been recently inundated. After a most laborious and disagreeable walk of several hours, I arrived at San Felipe, and stopped at Jones' tavern. Travellers from Brazoria say that the cholera is still raging there, and many persons have left the place. 3d. I felt symptoms of another attack of cholera. 4th. Feeling a little better, I walked out towards evening. After my return I was somewhat light-headed, which is very unusual with me.   5th. An attempt was made to mob me.*   I visited Samuel Williams, who talked quite rationally.   He is no mad revolutionist. In his opinion, Texas will not very soon become a separate State.

I can hear of no opportunity to ride, or to have my baggage carried from this place on the route to Bexar, nor can I obtain any employment while waiting here. Learning, however, that some wagons are to start in that direction in a few days from a point on the Colorado, twenty-five miles distant from this town, I concluded to proceed to that point to-morrow.   There being no house on the way, and the country being a prairie destitute of shade, except for a small distance, I prepared to encamp out for one night, by providing myself with a pocket pistol and some ammunition.

CHAPTER IX.

Journey from San Felipe de Austin to San Antonio de Bexar.

August 6th.   I set out from San Felipe before daylight for Bexar, otherwise called San Antonio de Bexar. The grass was so dewy that I had occasion to stop three times before breakfast, to pour the water from my shoes and wring out my stockings.   When night came on, I laid down on the grass by the road-side, my knapsack serving for a pillow, and my small thin cloak for sheets and counterpane, while my hat, my staff, and my pistol smartly charged, lay at arm's length from my person.   Thus, under the broad canopy of heaven, with its countless stars and distilling dews, I reposed till after midnight.   But owing to the attacks of numerous

* Lundy's Journal does not explain the cause of the disposition to mob him.   It probably arose from his expressing his sentiments strongly in opposition to the project of a separation of the government of Texas from that of Coahuila.

musquitoes, the apprehension of visits from more formidable, though not more ferocious enemies, such as panthers, alligators and rattlesnakes, and the pains of fatigue, resulting from exposure to the hot sun during the day, the very idea, even, of sleep, almost forsook me.

Aug. 7th. At about one in the morning, I rose from my grassy couch, and by the light of a moon nearly in the zenith, pursued my journey. I had six miles of prairie and three of timbered land to traverse before I could reach the nearest house on the Colorado river. It was with difficulty that I could trace the road through the thick and overhanging herbage. Soon after day-light I reached the farm and house of two brothers, named Alley, where I stopped for the day. Here, on the bank of the Colorado, I saw the first rock which I have met with since entering "Austin's Colony." The two Alleys are industrious immigrants from the State of Missouri. They have never married. They purchased, however, a handsome black girl, who has several fine-looking party coloured children—specimens of the custom of some countries.

Aug. 8. Having repaired my walking shoes, I waited till after mid-day for the expected wagons, but as they did not arrive, I determined to go on alone. I proceeded up the Colorado, to the ferry of Benjamin Beeson, where I put up for the night. 9th. Rising early in the morning, I found that the ants had taken possession of my knapsack. After half-an-hour spent in dislodging them, I started before sunrise. On my way, I saw plenty of deer and wild turkeys, but no water; though there were numerous dry beds, where the streams run in wet weather. At eleven o'clock I laid down in the shade to take my dinner and siesta. I then proceeded six miles further, without water, my bottle having been drained at dinner. At length, almost famished, I took a little water, thick with mud, from a puddle, and washed my mouth. The prairie was large and beautiful, rich and rolling. I mounted an eminence and saw the most extensive, diversified and delightful landscape that I had ever beheld. To the north-west, west and south-west, far as the eye could reach, there rose on the view a country magnificently chequered with alternate prairie and wood-land, like a region thickly settled with farms and plantations. Houses alone were wanting to perfect the resemblance. Proceeding onward I came at last to a little stream, where I slaked my thirst and replenished my water-bottle. Then advancing one mile further, I arrived at 4 P. M. at the house of Joseph Thompson. There I found another beautiful stream of water, also a party of fine looking Indians encamped. I spent the afternoon in writing, &c. Unfortunately, I had, during my day's journey, broken my phial of laudanum, and lost it all—a great misfortune! The lady of the house gave me a few drops to take with me, and I, in return, gave her some ground mustard, for cholera-plasters, and wrote for her Dr. Parrish's prescriptions.

Aug. 10. I started before day-light, and travelled six miles, to Rocky Creek, where I encamped for a while. In a short time, one of the party of Indians that I had seen the evening before, came to the creek for water. He saw me, but said nothing. A quarter of an hour afterwards, a Mexican, who accompanied the Indians and could speak some English, came and invited me to their camp, where they were dressing a fine deer that they had killed. I went with him, and spent several hours of the hottest part of the day with the Indians. Their camp was pitched beneath some large trees. There, the pleasant breeze, together with Mexican sociability and Indian hospitality, rendered me exceedingly comfortable. Their party consisted of six Indian men, three Indian women, and the Mexican. The Mexican was a little lighter coloured than the rest, and was dressed better. Otherwise, there was little difference in their appearance. About noon, one of the men presented me with a piece of venison elegantly roasted. Their mode of roasting is to build a smart fire, take a stick sharpened at both ends, put the meat on one end and thrust the other end into the ground, near the fire. The venison thus prepared, would not be rejected at the table of any epicure in Washington or Philadelphia. In return for the kindness of my Indian friends, I gave them, out of my small stock of provisions, a little fried bacon and corn bread—articles of which they were entirely destitute, and which appeared to be as great luxuries to them, as their venison was to me.

At about 2 P. M., I took leave of my kind entertainers, went on my way for a few miles, and then laid down to rest under a shady tree. In a short time, two Mexicans, armed with swords and guns, passed by. They pointed first to me, then back to the Indians' camp, and hurried on their way. When I had resumed my march I overtook them, in travelling half a mile, at a place where they had stopped, and were anxiously looking back on the road by which they had come. As I approached them, one who could speak a little English, addressed me with the words: "You no carabina?" (Have you no gun?*) Knowing that my pistol would not bear that title, I shook my head. "You see the Indians," said he. I told him I had just spent several hours with them, very agreeably. He was anxious to know to what tribe they belonged. I informed him that they were Paranamies, that they were civil, friendly people, engaged in hunting wild horses, and that a Mexican from La Bahia† was one of their party. At this my inquirer seemed satisfied, but he still expressed his surprise that I carried no "carabina."

I pursued my course, over an immense prairie, destitute of shade, where I found it hot walking. A little before night, a part of the Indians, with their Mexican companion, overtook me, and we went on together to the Labaca‡ river, which is the western boundary of Austin's colony. There I put up at the house kept by

---

*Or rifle.   † Called also Goliad.—ED.

‡Otherwise called Lavaca, or La Vaca, literally "the cow."

a gentleman from Missouri, named Daniels, the Indians encamping out, near the house. I found at Daniels', the two armed Mexicans before mentioned, who had put up for the night. Having gotten over their alarm, they entered freely into conversation with the other Mexican, viz., the companion of the Indians. I found the prickly pear growing in this vicinity, being the first time that I had met with it in this country.

Aug. 11th. I sat out a little before sun-rise, forded the Labaca river and proceeded on my route. Between 9 and 10 A. M., I reached an elevation, where a most extensive and magnificent view towards the north-west, west, and south-west presented itself. The whole valley of the Guadaloupe river was spread out before me for a great distance. This vast region has to me a new aspect, viz., that of an immense wilderness, or dense forest, as level, and, with the exception of a few small spots of light prairie, as unbroken as the ocean. The difference between the country before me and that which I have just traversed, is striking in the extreme. There is a haziness in the atmosphere, arising, it is supposed, from the burning of the grass, by the Indians, at many places in their hunting grounds. I rested here a while, absorbed in reflections on the future population and policy of the country, and then descended from the lofty eminence.

After continuing my route for some distance, and until near sunset, I came to the house of Francis Berry, who was originally from Virginia, and came last from Missouri. He has no slaves, all he formerly had having run away, as he states, "to the Spaniards." He thinks himself best off without them. I have travelled this day 22½ miles, making my best days' journey since leaving Brazoria. In various places on the way, I met with a great deal of Cayenne pepper growing wild.

Aug. 12th. I left Berry's early, and proceeded 2½ miles to Gonzales, a new town laid off by the government upon a most beautiful sight. It is as yet small, containing, perhaps, twenty families. It has its regular

Ayuntimiento, Alcalde, &c.* I am obliged to wait at
this place for company, and for assistance in taking my
luggage along to Bexar, which is 76 miles distant, with
not a house on the route. The two armed Mexicans,
before spoken of, are here. A report prevailed in the
place that they had intercepted me on my way thither.
Enquiries on the subject were made of me, accompanied
by offers to apprehend them, but I corrected the mistake.
13th and 14th. Being still waiting at Gonzales for
company to Bexar, I occupied myself in mending my
shoes, and purchased a panther skin for the sum of 75
cents, to serve as a blanket

Aug. 15th. I took a walk of a mile and a half to the
house of Cyrus Fuqua, a member of the Ayuntimiento
of Gonzales, who is a cousin of the Rev. Peter Fuqua,
and, like him, is resolutely opposed to slavery. There
I saw and conversed with a Swiss gentleman, highly
intelligent and communicative.

Aug. 15th. After breakfast I left Gonzales, and crossed
the river, to join a party going to Bexar. The cartman
not being yet ready to go, I spent the day and night at
the house of Col. Green de Witt. 17th. We set out
early and proceeded seven miles to a camp ground, near
the place of —— Williams. While our teams were
resting there, I took a ramble through a field full of corn,
pumpkins, beans, melons, &c., there being a heavy
growth of each. I never saw ground better occupied
in this way. The corn was as ripe as it is in New Jersey, four months later in the season. At 2 P. M we
started again, the two armed Mexicans, before named,
having joined us, so that our party amounted to seven,
all Mexicans, and all strongly armed except myself. As
neither of the Mexicans could speak English, I had an
excellent opportunity of communing with my own
thoughts. At night, we encamped near a small stream,
where I made my bed under the cart of my travelling

* The word Ayuntimiento, translated Union, answers nearly
to council or board of public officers. Alcalde, to Justice of
Peace, or local Judge.

companions. Some of the prairie land here is good, but much of it is but second rate.

Aug. 18th. We struck our tents about daybreak and proceeded, but had gone but a few rods before one of the wheels of the cart broke. We repaired it hastily, and went on a few steps, when it broke again. We then stopped and prepared breakfast; but two of the men went on for Bexar, and one went out to hunt a deer. After breakfast, the lazy fellows who remained, laid down and took a nap; that done, they rose and went to mending the wheel again. These Mexicans are curious fellows to make carts. They construct them to carry a load for a yoke of oxen, without using a particle of iron about them. Ropes made of raw hide serve instead of chains. This is the best way to rig teams here. What could we have done, if we had been under the necessity of depending on a blacksmith? But as it was, if we broke a wheel, we could cut down a tree and mend it; if we broke a chain, we could kill an ox, or a mustang,* and make a new one. At about 10 o'clock, the man who went in search of deer returned with two.—A little before sunset the wheel was finished.

Aug. 19th. We started early and went six miles to Carizo Creek. There we stopped to wait for another cart wheel to be obtained, as our mended one proved insufficient on trial. 20th. Here we are, four days from Gonzales, and under the necessity of waiting here at least one day longer. I caught a catfish in the morning, and made a fine breakfast. Then I caught a large turtle on a very small hook, and made an excellent dish of soup from it, though without any seasoning but salt. 21st. I found three more catfish on my hooks this morning. When opened, they proved to be the fattest fish I ever saw. One of them would weigh eight or ten pounds. The three made a fine meal for our company. At 2 P. M. our new cart wheel having arrived, we set out, and went on to Galeta Creek, where we encamped for the night, and I slept soundly on my panther pallet.

* The wild-horse.

The creek had stopped running, owing to the dryness of the weather.

22d. We set off a little after daybreak, and after travelling several miles, arrived at the river Gibolo, a branch of the San Antonio. The Gibolo, where we crossed it, is merely a fine mill stream, with banks thirty or forty feet in height. We laid by there till 3 P. M., then went on some distance, to a small creek, where we encamped again. Being then within 15 miles of Bexar, and my stock of provisions nearly exhausted, I determined to go on by myself the next morning.

Aug. 23. I shouldered my knapsack and set out about daybreak, passing through a beautiful country, rich and delightful to behold: stopped at a fine stream and ate the remainder of my provisions: then replenished my gourd with water and resumed my journey. In travelling two miles further, I came in sight of the powder magazine near Bexar.* Its white cast walls were refreshing to the sight of one who had spent days in the wilderness and on prairies, without beholding a human habitation. There, too, the beautiful valley of the San Antonio river presented itself to the view, and a most grand and delightful prospect lay stretched out to the west and south-west, a vast distance. The scene had the appearance of an immense amphitheatre, within which rose the town of Bexar, appearing to good advantage, though in general but humbly built. Throughout the vast expanse before me, the woodlands and prairies were alternated in regular strips or gradations, producing an effect alike surprising and delightful.

I arrived at Bexar, otherwise called San Antonio, before noon, and stopped at the public house of John W. Smith. In the afternoon I took a walk around the town, and in the evening called on my friend Juan Antonio Padilla, with whom I had become acquainted the summer before, at Nacogdoches. He continues as favourable as ever to my project.

*San Antonio de Bexar was the site of the celebrated fortress of "the Alamo."

The town of Bexar contains about two thousand inhabitants. Many of the buildings are of stone, and very lofty, with flat roofs. The larger portion however, are mere huts, constructed principally of poles, with one end set in the ground, in the form of picket-fence. These huts are thatched with a kind of coarse grass, and are entirely destitute of floors. 24th. I rose early and walked about the town. Many of the people were stirring by daylight, while others were lying on their pallets in front of their houses, it being customary with numbers of the labouring class to sleep in the open air. I called again upon Padilla and showed him my credentials, with which he was quite pleased. He accompanied me on a visit to the authorities of the place. We went first to the political chief, and showed him my passport. He is rather a pleasant man, and speaks pretty good English. We next visited the Alcalde, who took a copy of the passport.—Then I spent the rest of the day in looking about town. There lives here, in Bexar, a free black man, who speaks English. He came as a slave, first from North Carolina to Georgia, and then from Georgia to Nacogdoches, in Texas. There his master died, and the heirs sold him to another person. This new master, being apprehended for debt, offered the slave his freedom if he would take him out of prison. The slave complied, but the master dying soon after, an attempt was made by his heirs to re-enslave the man, which however proved unsuccessful. He now works as a blacksmith in this place. I have been to converse with him, he having seen me at Nacogdoches last summer, and knowing me again when he met me here. He is highly pleased with my plans. Though he is jet-black, he says the Mexicans pay him the same respect as to other laboring people, there being no difference made here on account of colour. Padilla says it is the policy of the Mexican Government to unite all colours and treat all with respect. The Mexicans, in this region, make as good an appearance as any people; but there are very few among them that we should call white. The inhabitants of Bexar appear far better in general than those of Brazoria, San Felipe or Gonzales. They have graceful manners and honest countenances, and exhibit tokens of wealth and independence. Both men and women are fine looking people;—less vivacious than the Haytiens, but more mild and easy in their manners.

In the afternoon I went out to the fields north of the town, where I was struck with the wonderful growth of the vegetables of almost every kind known to us further north. The Indian corn is very luxuriant. The peaches are large, and of fine flavour, as well as in great abundance. Every where, in the gardens, there are fig-trees loaded with fruit. The figs keep ripening all the year. They are sold at the rate of twelve to fifteen for a six cent piece.

Aug. 25th. Sabbath morning. I walked out and found all very still in the streets, but the stores and shops were open as usual. Some of the people were at church and some at work. 26th. I have commenced providing my own board in a small but convenient room which I have rented in Bexar, and which is to serve me as a work shop.* It is reported to-day that a Mexican was killed yesterday within four miles of town by a party of Indians, probably Camanches. This tribe is very hostile to the Mexicans, but friendly to the northern Americans.

27th. I was informed early this morning, that a fellow named Morgan, who has been in Bexar for some days, had decamped. He professed to be a son of the proprietor of Morgantown, Virginia. He begged of me the loan of several articles of clothing, and two other North Americans lent him money. He was then drunk for two or three days, at the end of which he left for La Bahia (or Goliad,) without repaying loans of any

---

*Lundy mentions in one of his letters that he had great difficulty in raising money for this journey, and that he worked on the route to assist in defraying the expenses.

kind. Another of my countrymen got intoxicated yesterday, and behaved as in "the land of the free." Being complained of by the keeper of the North American tavern, he was lodged in prison. To-day he was tried and fined ten dollars. A great part of what we hear of the bad treatment of our countrymen among the Mexicans, is caused by the misconduct of such persons.

28th. At work in my shop. 29th. Being unable to get work at my trade to-day, I walked out. Saw much stone in quarries, though the surface of the ground is generally clear. Limestone is abundant in the vicinity. Lime is used in covering the roofs of most of the stone houses in Bexar. The roof is commenced by laying cedar poles horizontally across the building from wall to wall, then across these poles smaller pieces of timber are laid compactly; and over them are put stones and earth rounded up in the middle; then over the whole a coating of parget or rough-cast is laid. Around the roof, there is a sort of parapet, from which wooden spouts extend outwards, two or three feet, for carrying off the water. On some of these roofs, grass and the prickly-pear are seen growing. The roofs of the inferior houses are covered, some with shingles, some with bark laid after the manner of clap-boards, and some are thatched with a coarse grass which grows on the margins of the streams.—Going into the market to-day, I found good beef selling at two cents per pound.

Aug. 30th. There is news this morning of an attack by Indians, supposed to be Tiwaukanes, upon a horse-pen five miles from town. One man was wounded by them.—Information of recent date from Mexico says that all is going on well, that centralism is defunct, &c.*

* The two parties of federalists and centralists, the former in favour of an association of States like the American Union, as established by the Mexican Constitution of 1824, the latter in favour of the annihilation of the State governments, had existed in Mexico from the time of the expulsion of Iturbide in 1823. In 1834 Santa Anna, the then President, went over from the federal to the central party, and in 1835 the federal system was abolished, and a single central government established in its place.—ED.

31st. I purchased some provisions this morning, expecting to set out to-day for Monclova, the capital of Coahuila, and the seat of government for Coahuila and Texas. I learned that the Ayuntamiento determined yesterday to send out forty men of the " civic guard" against the Indians. The people in town are in some alarm. Not a man ventures into his field, or to a distance of a quarter of a mile to procure wood, without taking his gun along with him. It looks strange to see a man or a boy with a musket on his shoulder, driving an ox-cart. Having been disappointed in my plan of leaving town to-day, and my finances being reduced to the lowest ebb, I was obliged to sell some of my clothing. As there was no work at Bexar to be done in the saddling line, I determined to try to make and repair suspenders, in which business I had made some experiments during my apprenticeship. A company of merchants is now organizing to start for Rio Grande, Monclova, &c., in about a week. I must wait and go with them.

September 1st, 1833.—The autumn has commenced, and I am still here at Bexar. It is the part of philosophy to bear up against difficulty, disappointment and affliction, and I will do so as long as possible. I have still some resources. I have not been obliged to beg or steal, nor am I likely to be : my case, therefore, is not yet desperate.

There was not much talk in town to-day about Indians : the alarm concerning them was probably in part without foundation. In the evening I walked out of town ; found the peach trees looking better here than in the United States : the hackberry, persimmon and mulberry are abundant.

2d. Busy in my shop with making and repairing suspenders. 3d. I was called up this morning to visit a sick man. Having told the people something about the cholera, they all think me a doctor. 5th. I saw this evening a large and beautiful skin which was taken from a Mexican leopard. It is fully equal to that of the African leopard, which it much resembles.

There are at this time in Bexar many people from Austin's lower settlements, who have come here, on account of the salubrity of the place, to spend the sickly season.

6th. I had arranged to leave Bexar to-day with a company going to Monclova. It is now said, however, that they will not start in less than two weeks. What shall I do? My consolation is that there is yet hope for the virtuous and support for the industrious.

Sept. 8th. Another Sabbath. This is the day set apart in the Christian calendar as the anniversary of the birth of the blessed Virgin Mary. The bells of the old church are pealing merrily, and rockets are flying briskly. As high mass is to be performed; more *eclat* than usual is perhaps necessary, to draw the attention of the careless and merely formal professor to the high importance of the occasion.

11th. We had a fine shower to-day, a thing somewhat rare now a-days, as it is generally dry here during the summer months, though wet enough at other seasons. In the afternoon I walked out to recreate myself from the fatigue of sitting constantly in my shop for several days.

13th. News came by last night's mail that the cholera is raging in many parts of Mexico. Gen. Duran, chief of the Centralists, lately died of it. Letters received by the Ayuntimiento here from Stephen F. Austin at Mexico, state that the Mexican Congress will not accept the "Constitution of Texas"* prepared by the self-delegated convention, until they proceed constitutionally in the business.

12th. In addition to making suspenders I have now started a new branch of business, viz., the making of shot bags from panther and deer skins. Any thing for an honest livelihood, and to keep my spirits from sinking while I am pent up here.

* The Constitution by which it was proposed to erect Texas into a state distinct from Coahuila.—ED.

14th. I learned to-day that Vann, the Cherokee chief, having obtained leave from the government to arrest and take away two of his slaves who had escaped to this vicinity, delegated his authority to one Williams, who went with an assistant to a ranche* thirty miles south of this place, and having made demand of the slaves proceeded to take them. One of them resisting was shot dead by Williams; the other escaped. This event has created some excitement here. I have sold to-day a shot bag and a pair of suspenders at $1 each. Thus I am quite in funds again!

16th. A splendid ball was to have taken place here this evening, but it has been prevented by the sad news of the death, from cholera, of the Vice-Governor and Chief Justice of the State.

17th. I sold yesterday, two shot bags, and to-day I sold one to the slave-hunter Williams, before I was aware that he was the person who had shot the black man. Was it providential that this wretch should thus contribute to my support while I was engaged in the cause of freedom? Hercules will assist your wagon out of the mire, if you but put your own shoulder to the wheel.

The authorities have instituted an inquiry into the slave's death; and I learn, in the evening, that the villain, Williams, who shot him, has absconded, under the apprehension that some evidence was to be produced, which would be likely to make the trial go hard with him. It is said that he went in pursuit of the slaves, on condition of receiving one-half their value, in case he should return them to Vann.

18th. I was called on to-day to visit another sick man; also a sick woman. They persist here in considering me a doctor. I still work away, however, at suspenders and shot bags.

19th. Early this morning some Camanche Indians arrived in town, with skins, &c., to trade.—A great

---

* A hut, or farm-house.

religious parade is held here to-day. It is a sort of religious invocation to God for preservation from the cholera. There are great apprehensions, among the people, of that terrible disease; and those who can afford it, carry little bags of camphor in their bosoms, fo guard against an attack. The state of health, at present, however, is as good as I ever witnessed at any time or place. My own health has become very good.

23d. A row took place yesterday between two of our Northern Americans, or United States people. The victor was taken before the Alcalde, and upon hearing, to-day, was fined ten dollars.—A person who resides on Kimball's Creek, Texas, informs me that there is an abundance of mineral coal in that quarter, similar to that of Pennsylvania, though somewhat more sulphurous.

26th. The merchants with whom I am to go to Monclova, have engaged a team and expect to start in a few days. 28th. A man from Pittsburg, named George Pagan, stole to-day, from my room, a pair of suspenders worth $2. These Mexicans are novices in the arts of thieving, drunkenness and vagabondism, in comparison with these fellows from the North.

29th. I walked out this forenoon with Matthew Thomas, to see the cane patch, grounds, &c., of his father-in-law, Felipe Elua, a black Louisiana creole, who was formerly a slave, but who has purchased the freedom of himself and family. He has resided here twenty-six years, and he now owns five or six houses and lots, besides a fine piece of land near town. He has educated his children so that they can read and write, and speak Spanish as well as French. They are all fine looking, smart black people. He has a sister also residing in Bexar, who is married to a Frenchman. The sugar cane, of which there is a patch of about an acre on Elua's land, looks as well as that which grows in Hayti, and the land is evidently well adapted to it. The frost does not kill the roots of the plant here as it does further north, but the sprouts make their appearance in the spring, so that it is unnecessary to replant it. Besides the cane, we saw some fine looking cotton, a large patch of sweet potatoes, together with beans and other garden vegetables, the property of the same black man, and all in beautiful order.

30th. A merchant named Rubideau,* who arrived here two days since from St. Louis, where I knew something of him in 1820, and whose character and standing is considered good, proposes to buy me a horse and to pay some bills for me, and desires me to accompany him immediately to Monclova. He is a Louisiana French creole, and is now acting as agent for the Missouri fur trading company. He says he knows all about my public career. I have introduced him to my friend Padilla. There is also another person who is going from Monclova to Mexico, that offers to furnish me with money to accompany him. These offers seem certainly to be fair and friendly.

October 1st, 1833. Another month has passed, and I am still here at Bexar.—Another religious procession took place this afternoon. Its object was " to keep away the cholera," as our North Americans here say. I went out with several others to see it. At a particular part of the ceremony all in the procession knelt for a few moments. The same thing is done by the Catholic bystanders, but it is not required of strangers. The latter, however, generally stand and uncover their heads, as a mark of respect.

5th. Our company for Monclova being frightened, by reports of the cholera, have concluded to defer starting for a week or two. Rubideau is willing to go on, but he has an attack of the ague, of which I have undertaken to cure him. To-day some Shawnee and Delaware Indians arrived in town on their way to attack the Camanches. 6th. There is a very cool north wind to-day. The Mexicans are all blanketed up as they walk abroad.

* Called Robidoux in a subsequent part of the journal.

CHAPTER X.

Journey from Bexar to Monclova, via the towns of Rio Grande and
Santa Rosa.

Oct. 8th. Having heard yesterday that there is no
cholera at Monclova, our company left Bexar for that
place at one o'clock to-day. The party consists of Rubideau with his hired servant and pistol, a Mexican soldier and myself, travelling on horseback. We went on
till about ten o'clock at night, when we encamped near
a small lake, turning out our horses to pick what they
could of the short grass which has sprung up since the
recent burning of the crop, and making a fire to cook
our supper. After our repast, we laid down to sleep
under a mesquite bush.

9th. We rose at day break, and while Rubideau boiled the coffee, the servant and myself went in search of
the horses, which had strayed to some distance. I found
them and called to the man. My call was heard by
some Indian hunters, six in number, who had encamped
a little way to the south of us. They came immediately
to us, and offered us some venison if we would accompany them to their camp. We went with them and
they gave us as much as we wanted, and we, in return,
gave them some tobacco. They are the same Indians,
of the Shawnee and Delaware tribes, before mentioned
as having been at Bexar. After filling our bottles and
gourds with water from the lake, we proceeded on our
journey, and soon met four Mexicans carrying the mail.
During the forenoon we saw numbers of deer, rabbits,
wild turkeys, quails and hawks; also four wild horses,
being the first I have met with in the untamed state.
At noon we put our horses out to graze again, and my
companions took their siesta while I prepared my notes.
After resting an hour and a half, and eating some venison, we went on, passing in our way over a chain of
broken, hilly land, more resembling mountains than any
thing that I had before crossed in Texas. On the hills

there was little timber, some rock and much rubble stone and gravel. Before sunset we reached and crossed the San Miguel river, and encamped a mile or two beyond it, in a most beautiful prairie. Much of the land passed over during the day was good, but water was very scarce, every creek being totally dry.

10th. We started again, about sunrise, and passed over some land that was good, and some that was very poor, until we reached the Rio Frio, or Cold river. There we found large mesquite trees, with some undergrowth, such as I had not seen before. Among this undergrowth was a species of thorn that would be excellent for live fence, also a kind of tough wood that would answer many good purposes on a farm. The land is dark, a little sandy in spots, and to appearance exceedingly productive.

The bottom of the Rio Frio is perhaps a mile in width : its water is clear and excellent, running swiftly over a pebbly bed. Where we crossed it, by a bridge, it appeared to be a very fine mill-stream. About noon we stopped to let our horses regale themselves on some fine young grass that had grown three or four inches since the fires destroyed the summer's crop. After starting again and travelling for some distance, we came to a pond or small lake, where we shot one of a number of ducks that were swimming. They were of the same species as the common wild duck of the United States. We saw to-day a large rattle snake and a pole-cat; also a large herd of wild horses that were feeding near the road. As soon as they saw us they started off at full speed, being apparently quite as wild as deer.

11th. We proceeded this morning over some delightful plains on a good and level road. At half past nine we reached and crossed the river Nueces, which is the western limit of what is called Texas. Of course we are now in Coahuila. The weather became clear, resembling that of April or May of our Middle States, in its mildest aspect. We saw some bear and wolf tracks, and afterwards, a little off the road, two wolves trotting

away. A plain which we crossed is the most remarkable of the kind that I ever saw. It is the high table-land
between the Nueces and the Rio Grande, otherwise
called the Rio Bravo del Norte. At dark we encamped
near a mesquite bush, there being none large enough
for us to get under. So we slept in the open air, exposed
to a very heavy dew.

12th. This morning we were a long time in finding
our horses, which had strayed away, in consequence of
the grass being so young and short as to afford them
scanty picking. At ten o'clock we came in sight of the
river Bravo, and soon after of the town of Rio Grande,
situated on the Bravo, 183 miles from Bexar. Just before we crossed the river, two Mexicans who had been
hunting wild horses, arrived at the ford. They were the
first human beings that we had seen since the mail car-
riers that we met on the ninth, the day after leaving
Bexar. In the town of Rio Grande, we saw a large cypress, and many peccan, fig, mulberry, willow and hackberry trees. The population of the place, as I should
judge, amounts, at the least, to twelve or fifteen hundred
persons. They are good looking people—many of them
very light coloured. We did not alight in the town, as
Rubideau was in haste to continue our journey, and I
had been told that not an individual in the place could
speak English of such sort as would be intelligible to me.
Having proceeded three miles further, we encamped for
the night under an umbrageous live-oak.

On the 13th we set off at day-break, and went twenty-
one miles to a *ranche*. There we saw a great quantity
of land occupied as a stock farm, all of which was irrigated, and all destitute of fences. We saw on the place,
watermelons, large patches of Indian corn, forty or fifty
young kids, and large numbers of all kinds of domestic
animals. At noon we came to a village of forty or fifty
houses, all built of sun-burnt bricks. Here we stopped
for the remainder of the day to rest our horses. At the
house of our host, we found smart looking people and
handsome young women, but neither table nor chairs.

The family all sat on skins, which looked strange, especially for women clad in fine white dresses. I saw there a person from North Carolina.

Oct. 14th. We started early this morning, our entertainers charging us all three but one dollar for our fare from noon of yesterday. We passed within twelve miles of the town of San Fernando, which we concluded not to visit, and at 7 A. M., stopped at a ranche* and fed our horses on grass and green corn, while we breakfasted ourselves on roasted corn and muskmelons, which we got at the corn-tender's tent. Upon resuming our journey, we soon passed a village called Villa de Morelos, which is supplied with water by a fine stream, artificially conducted for that purpose a long distance, through an extensive plain. At a few miles from the village, there is much fine limestone in quarry : hence it is presumable that good wheat might be raised in the vicinity. The country which we passed through to-day, abounds in grass of fine quality, much of it resembling our timothy, though the seed is dissimilar. This with the weather, resembling that of June with us, reminds me of mowing time. An endless variety of plants and shrubs are now in blossom : among the rest, my pretty little " mouse-ear " bush is common. Its flower is in shape much like that of our morning-glory, but smaller and of a reddish pink colour. I plucked a few twigs with their blossoms, and placed them between the leaves of my journal. Our breakfast, dinner, and supper, to-day, were each of roasted Indian corn, with coffee added at dinner. At night, being remote from habitations, and finding no large tree near us, we encamped in the open air, made our beds on the grass, and took the dews as they came —most plentifully.

Oct. 15th. We proceeded on our way till past 11 A. M., when we stopped to rest our horses, my own being much fatigued. A couple of Mexicans whom we

---

*The word ranche seems to be used as synonymous with farm, or plantation. It literally means a hut or farm house.

met on our route northward, stopped us and gave us
some bread; which was very acceptable, as we were
tired of roasted corn. Going on again, we reached and
crossed the Sabinas river, being the first water fit for
drinking that we had found for the last twenty-four hours.
Afterwards we crossed a large branch of the same river,
and at dark encamped under a mesquite bush. We soon
found that a large force of musquitoes had got there before us. It was the first considerable body of these
ferocious insects, that we had seen since we left Austin's colony. They were on this occasion excessively
presuming and persevering in their efforts to make our
acquaintance. We lay combating them for an hour or
two, at the end of which our whole force gave way,
and left them complete masters of the field. In order
to shun them, we went on a few miles further, until we
found some cartmen encamped, and lying by their fires.
Stopping there, we soon found our remorseless foes had
pursued us : yet we maintained our ground manfully
till daybreak.

16th. We proceeded to Santa Rosa, where we arrived
in the forenoon, and put up with a gentleman from New
York, named Knauff, who practices physic. The town,
which is not healthy, contains at present about 2,500
inhabitants, 250 having recently died of the cholera.
The buildings are all either of stone or of unburned brick,
like those of the other villages passed since we crossed
the Rio Bravo.* Santa Rosa is within four miles of the
stupendous Rocky mountains, which loom so that at a distance of forty miles they appear to be within ten. Its
position reminded me strongly of that of Port-au-Prince,
in the Island of Hayti.

As our horses were much fatigued, we concluded to
rest at Santa Rosa, for a day or two. The place is
situate in 27 degrees and a few minutes north. The
fig, the peach and the quince flourish here, and produce
well. Oranges were lately cultivated, but a severe

* Or Rio Grande.

frost, about a year since, destroyed the trees. Sheep are extremely numerous in the vicinity. They are mostly of the coarse-wooled kind. The adjacent mountains are rich in minerals. Dr. Knauff showed us a piece of sulphur, in the pure state, which was cut out of a rock. It looked like a yellow crystal. Lead, copper, iron, and mineral coal are abundant; and there is a fine sulphur spring on the side of the mountain.

Santa Rosa is a fine place for the establishment of manufactures, by reason of the plentifulness of coal and water power. Good blankets are now made here from sheep's wool. Business at present is dull. There are but two regular dry goods stores in the place; but there are a large number of temporary peddling shops.

They have a kind of whiskey here, called muscal,* which is distilled from a plant called Maguey.† This liquor, which tastes like Holland gin, is retailed at about twenty-one cents a pint. Poor people cannot afford to drink much of it. I see no beastly drunkards in this country.

While at Santa Rosa, I sold my watch and paid a debt out of the proceeds.

18th. We started in the morning for Monclova. During the day we crossed the beds of two streams. Much grass and some shrubbery were seen on our route, but no timber; and we were obliged to encamp for the night in the open air.

Oct. 19th. The weather being very cool, and almost frosty, we wore our cloaks in riding until ten o'clock, A. M. We passed a fine stream with sycamores growing along its banks, and saw three teams, on their way to Monclova, carrying lumber, which is procured on the borders of the creeks in this vicinity. In the afternoon, we crossed a spur of the mountains, and went through a singular opening, called "the door," which

---

*Folsom writes it "Mexical."

†The Agave Americana, or American aloe, from the juice of which a fermented liquor called Pulque is also made.—ED.

affords passage for a fine stream.   In this narrow pass
there are some huts, containing eight or ten families,
and two caves, one or both of which are also occupied
as dwellings.   Our path ascended very gradually,
with tremendous cliffs composed of great masses of
rocks towering on either hand, and at length emerged
into a kind of cove—a spacious plain, surrounded by
high mountains.   This plain, which is not entirely level,
is nearly five miles long, and from three to four miles
wide.   It is elevated a few hundred feet above the
plain which we left on reaching the mountains.   In this
plain or cove we encamped at evening, and the wind
being high and cold, we passed a restless night.

20th.   We issued forth from the cove this morning,
through another door, and by a rocky and very difficult
path.   At eleven, A. M., we came to a small village,
seated beside a stream of water.   There we stopped to
rest our horses, and to warm ourselves, after our exposure of the night.   Then proceeding again we ascended,
ere long, an elevation from which we beheld, at the
distance of a few miles, the end of our journey—the city
of Monclova.   In the intermediate space there were a
number of fine ranches.   We soon after overtook a
company of muleteers, with fifteen or twenty mules, all
loaded with lead, from Santa Rosa or its vicinity.   Every
mule carries two cakes of lead, each cake weighing one
hundred and fifty pounds.   At near dark we reached
Monclova, and put up for the night, with a Mexican
family.

CHAPTER XI.

Residence and events at Monclova and its vicinity.

Oct. 21st.   We paid our respects to an Irish gentleman named Joshua Davis, who is a merchant in this
place, and were received by him with kindness and

hospitality. I spent the rest of the day in looking about town, and making some acquaintances. I presented my letter from J. A. Padilla of Bexar, to Santiago del Valle, the Secretary of State for Coahuila and Texas. As he could not speak English, I was obliged to take an interpreter with me, and found some difficulty in obtaining a suitable one for my purpose. In the course of the day, I met accidentally with a coloured man, who is a nephew of Robert Douglass of Philadelphia. He is much pleased with my projects, and will assist me in making some arrangements.

24th. This morning early, accompanied by Dr. Pope, I again visited del Valle, the Secretary of State. I had a long conversation with him at his own house, and found him tolerably friendly to my views. He started an objection, however, to my plan of establishing a colony of coloured people from the United States, founded on the degradation of the class from which the emigrants were to be selected ; but I explained the matter apparently to his satisfaction. He thinks I shall succeed in obtaining the necessary permission and grant of land, in case the law of 1830, which prohibits the settlement within the Mexican Republic of persons from the United States, should be repealed, but that until such repeal shall take place it will be useless to apply to the governor on the subject, as he has no power to comply with my wishes. I saw the secretary again in the afternoon at his office, in order to examine maps, &c., and he lent me some papers for my information.

There appears to be no distinction in this place as to freedom, or condition, by reason of colour. One complexion is as much respected as another.

27th. The Sabbath.—Here, as in all Catholic countries, there is little attention paid to this day. The stores and shops are all open. The people, in general, are nominal Catholics, but I am told that many of the most intelligent and influential desire the free toleration of Protestantism, which doubtless will soon take place in all parts of the republic.*   Many influential persons seldom attend church.

29th. The weather is quite pleasant, though a.little smoky, like our Indian summer. It is as warm here now as the month of May in New Jersey, and the grass is as green, and there are as many blossoms of pumpkins, &c., as there are in that state in June. I went to-day to visit the river near the town. It is a fine stream, with a considerable fall, excellent for water-works.

30th. I prepared a petition to be in readiness to lay before the governor as soon as the way shall be open, and sent it to Dr. Pope, at Saltillo, who has kindly offered to translate it for me, there being no translator at Monclova since the cholera has prevailed here. Dr. Pope was once a subscriber to the Genius of Universal Emancipation. He is now very friendly to me and my objects.

31st. To-day del Valle resigned the office of Secretary of State, in consequence, as it is said, of not being on the best terms with the acting governor.

Nov. 1st, 1833. I am still waiting at Monclova, and have become afflicted with depression of spirits, to drive away which, I must obtain some more active business.— News is received from the city of Mexico, that one branch of the general Congress has passed the repeal of the law of 1830, against the sale of lands to emigrants from the United States. The Secretary of State says that our civilized Indians will be allowed to settle in this country upon the same terms as white people, but upon none other. This probably will not suit our Cherokees and Chickasaws.

3d. Returning from a walk to-day, I saw many people collected at corners, about the principal squares, and many ladies walking in the streets. This day looks more like one of rest or cessation from business than any

---

* The realization of this expectation was prevented by a military revolution the year following, in favour of the perpetuation of an exclusive established religion.—ED.

other Sabbath that I have witnessed for some months. There are four Catholic churches at Monclova. The people who attend them appear as pious as those of other denominations in other countries.

4th. This evening I visited the governor, in company with J. Blackaller, who went as interpreter. I found the governor disposed to listen to my representations, though at first he evidently thought me one of the rash Texan schemers.* He had much to say about obedience to the laws, &c., yet he appeared liberal in wishing a change in some of the colonial regulations. I had much unofficial conversation with him, and he appointed 8 A. M., of the 7th instant, for me to call and treat with him officially.

The papers by the mail of this evening bring great news, viz: that of the passage, by the British Parliament, of the bill for the abolition of slavery in the West Indies. Huzza for the triumph of just principles! But thou, my country, with thy heavenly profession and hellish practice, the laurel with which Liberty had crowned thee is torn from thy brow by England.

> O, is there no balm in our Gilead left?
> Shall our fame to oblivion's ocean be swept?
> Shall the harps of our bards on the willows be hung,
> And the funeral dirge of our glory be sung?

5th. Good news has been received this evening from the interior of Mexico. It is that Generals Duran and Arista, the leaders of the central faction, have given themselves up, on condition that their lives shall be spared.†

I took a walk to-day along the banks of the river. The stream was as clear as crystal, and thousands of fine fish were to be seen in it, some of them eight or nine

---

* The advocates of a State Government for Texas separate from Coahuila.—Ed.

† The two generals here spoken of had been for some time at the head of an insurrection, raised for the purpose of abolishing the state governments, and establishing consolidation.

inches in length. They could be discerned perfectly at the depth of eight or ten feet, so transparent was the water. I find that apples of an excellent quality are among the products of this region. They grow best on the high lands near Saltillo. I received a present of some from my friend J. Davis. Two crops of Indian corn a year may be raised on the land here. Every thing grows in the vicinity that is found in New Jersey, and a thousand things in addition. The wheat is as good as can be produced any where in the world. Excellent sugar, made by free labour, is retailed at from 8 to 12 cents per pound. Then, the pure air of the neighbouring mountains, is perhaps the most healthy on earth.—What a country this would be for the enterprize of our industrious farmers of the North?

One of my acquaintances here informs me, that, in his opinion, Stephen F. Austin* acts a double part in every thing. He says that Austin once told him that it was necessary to practise duplicity in dealing with the Mexicans.

Nov. 7th. This morning I had my official interview with the governor, presented my credentials, and explained to him the general scope of my views. I found him frank and communicative, and still more friendly than at our former interview. He approves highly of my proposals, and assures me that he will grant me any land within his prerogative, as soon as the law of 1830 shall have been repealed. He promises to give me information of the repeal immediately on receiving it, and assures me that no other application which may be made to him shall take precedence of mine. He says that if the general Congress, now in session, should fail to repeal the law in question, the State Legislature will make a strong appeal to it in favour of the measure; and he feels sure that the professors of the various sects in religion will henceforth be admitted as settlers, without any restriction in regard to their faith. He is far more liberal

*Well known afterwards as a prominent leader of the Texan revolution.

in his views of general policy than I had been led to expect; hence I hope strongly that my errand here will not prove abortive.

In the course of the interview, I showed the governor a copy of my newspaper. He expressed a desire to have one number translated, which I assured him should be done, at least in part, if possible. He appeared highly pleased to learn what I was doing on the subject of slavery.

This evening I was informed that plenty of good sugar, produced in this vicinity, may now be had at six and a quarter cents by the single pound.

Nov. 8th. This morning I took a walk to an eminence on the south of the town. In passing along the streets, I feasted my eyes on the myriads of flowers with which the fences and the garden shrubbery were bespangled. On reaching the eminence above mentioned, I saw, to the north-west, numerous "ranches," belonging to inhabitants of the town. In various directions, stupendous peaks, and ridges of irregular and disconnected mountains towered aloft, while immense valleys and plains of the richest land, were stretched out between them.

In the afternoon I took a walk with J. Blackaller to the south of the town, in order to visit the cotton gin, and the mills for grinding wheat, &c. They are but poorly constructed. I examined the Mexican wheat at one of the mills. It is smaller than ours, but of good quality. They wash it before grinding, which is quite an unnecessary process. The buildings, saws, &c., for manufacturing and milling, were made by Don Victor Blanco, under the superintendence of Blackaller. They are now in a state of suspense, owing to a dispute which has arisen, and a suit which is pending, between these gentlemen. Blackaller states that he had been very badly treated. He is a very ingenious mechanic, and by profession a civil engineer.

9th. I got a couple of jobs this afternoon—a neat bridle to fill and a saddle to repair. This was quite cheering.

10th. I had, to-day, a sample of butter, made here by
a coloured woman from Mississippi, the article being one
that the Mexicans are not accustomed to use.   It was
white, hard and beautiful.   I also had a taste of goat's
milk, which I do not like so well as that of the cow.
Walking out to the west of the town, I saw some good
looking people; but many more who were of a dark
reddish complexion.   There is a larger proportion of
people of unmixed European descent here, than at Bexar;
but even here, a great majority are closely allied to the
original lords of the soil, as may be seen by their straight
raven hair, and the dark hue of their skins.

Nov. 11th. The weather this morning was almost
cold enough for frost.   To-day I saw a young priest or
friar, by no means a reverend looking personage, passing along the street.   As he approached the door of a
house, which he was to pass on his way, an old man,
with a beard half an inch in length, stepped forward
from the door, and bowed his head; the young ecclesias-
tic thereupon threw out his hand, with great apparent
sang-froid, and the old man kissed it.   He was doubtless happy in doing so, nor would I in the least contest
his right of choice.

12th. A young man from Tennessee gave us a single
number of the Philadelphia Saturday Evening Post,
which was of a later date than any paper we had previously seen from the United States.   Though it did not
contain much important news, yet the perusal of it was
truly refreshing to us, in this strange land.

I saw Del Valle this evening, and learned from him
that the law of 1830 is not yet repealed.   He fears that
the measure will be deferred till the January session of
the national Congress.   That body has passed some very
liberal laws, at the present session—among the rest one
for the abolition of the tithe system.   Centralism is now
completely put down, and Santa Anna is again in the
city of Mexico, and in the presidential chair.*

* During the absence of the President, in command of the
army, his place, according to the provisions of the Constitution,
had been filled by the Vice President, Gomez Farias.—ED.

I also, this evening, received an introduction to Juan
Francisec Lumbrano, a member of the Legislature of
Coahuila and Texas. He professed himself strongly
opposed to slavery, and invited me to call upon him.

13th. I changed my quarters to-day, and took board,
lodging, and a room for a shop, with J. Blackaller. I
saw, in the evening, a Mexican newspaper, entitled
" The Shade of Washington." This title is indicative
of a state of feeling now very prevalent in Mexico. I
understand, too, that Santa Anna some time since pledged
himself to follow in the footsteps of Washington. Thus
far he appears to have redeemed his pledge. The military, it is said, are being disbanded, and liberal measures
in relation to religion adopted, as fast as possible. The
people—the democrats of the country—are now completely lords of the ascendant. Schools and colleges for
public instruction, are about to be established and supported by the funds of the nation; and Mexico is probably destined, ere long, to become the most brilliant of
American republics.*

14th. A man lately arrived from San Felipe says that
the man calling himself Robidoux,† with whom I came
to Monclova, is an impostor; that he was detected at
that place, as well as at Nacogdoches; and that he was
flogged at Nacogdoches, instead of being robbed, as he
represented. My old friend Davis blamed me for introducing the pretended Robidoux here. I replied that I
had been extremely guarded in doing so, and had repeatedly remarked that I could not give him a responsible mercantile recommendation. Davis denied this, and

* The reforms here spoken of were prevented from taking
effect by a military revolution in a few months afterwards, which
proclaimed Santa Anna dictator, and in its progress dispersed
the Congress; abolished the militia; and perpetuated the standing army; dissolved the State governments; abridged the right
of suffrage; overthrew the freedom of the press, and confirmed
the connexion of Church and State, and the proscription of dis-
senters.—Ed.

† Called Rubideau in chapter IX

we nearly quarrelled about it, but the ill feeling ultimately passed off. If we have all been deceived in this man, who passes for Robidoux, he is surely a most artful fellow.

15th. It is stated by J. McMullin that four or five of the ablest papers in the Mexican capital and elsewhere, are openly demanding a change in the federal constitution, so as to allow free toleration to the protestant religion.   All the papers that advocate the measure, are on the side of the present administration, and most of them are official publications of the government.* If this measure should be adopted, Mexico will be disenthralled from one great obstruction to her progress in improvement.

I saw this evening, Stewart, the person who lately arrived from San Felipe   He says that the man calling himself Robidoux is certainly an impostor, although he may be the person of that name who was once a merchant in St. Louis.

16th. Thinking it cold enough, before sunrise this morning, for a frost, I took a walk around town, to ascertain how the fact stood; but I was met by spring and summer flowers, and no frost.   I stopped at a grocery store, where I found dried grapes, or domestic raisins, such as are produced at various places not far from Monclova. When I first tasted them I did not suspect that they were not the foreign raisins, such as are usually sold in our Atlantic cities. Though abundant in quantity, they are sold at the high price of 25 cents a pound.

Preparations are being made in the principal public squares here, for what is called a grand feast, in which gambling and bull-fights are to be the principal diversions.

---

* Gomez Farias the vice president, then recently acting as president, was favourable to the proposed reform, and continued true to his faith. He has taken a prominent part recently, in the revolution of 1846, for the restoration of the federal constitution in Mexico.

17th I took an excursion this forenoon to a village called Puebla, a little to the north of Monclova. The road thither is a public walk, and affords a most delightful promenade. Cotton-wood trees are planted on either side of the way; and seats are placed at convenient distances, as in the public squares of Philadelphia. In our ramble, we saw some orange trees, and many pomegranate bushes.

The plant called maguey (or American aloe,) from which the liquors called *pulque* and *muscal* are manufactured, was also pointed out to me. This plant, before running to seed, grows to the height of about four or five feet; but the seed stalk rises to that of fifteen or twenty feet. It takes the plant ten years to come to perfection, so as to go to seed, at which period a single one is valued at about ten dollars. When the plant is about seeding, the top and a few of the upper leaves are cut off. The stalk or stump is then hollowed out like a mortar, and the sap flows into the hollow from all parts of the plant, for a period of several days. This sap is taken out daily, and fermented for use. The fermented liquor, called *pulque*, is an excellent beer, though somewhat intoxicating. The *muscal*, or maguey brandy, is distilled from the *pulque*, by a process similar to that of distilling apple whiskey with us; and it has considerable resemblance to that liquor.

I saw, this afternoon, a two horse wagon of the most approved form for a farm wagon, with bows, cover, &c., which was made in the United States. It had been bought in Saltillo, (Mexico,) for three hundred dollars. Such prices show that this country offers fine opportunities for skilful workers in wood.

In the evening of this day, a religious procession paraded from one of the churches round the principal public square of Monclova, the object of the procession being to consecrate the proceedings of the great feast of to-morrow.

18th. I went, at 11 A. M., to see the bull-fight. The preparations consisted of a large and very strong pen, made in the beforementioned public square, with a smaller pen adjoining the large one; the larger being for the hunt, and the smaller for keeping the cattle which were to be hunted. At the commencement of the sport, one of the largest bulls was selected, and in his neck were stuck, so that he could see them, two barbed arrows, eight or ten inches long, with coloured ribands or papers affixed to them. He was then turned loose, into the large pen, and there, three, and sometimes four men, carrying red, and other coloured flags, would run around him, before him, and at him. One of these men was the clown, who was painted black. When the bull was chased to one side of the pen, the spectators would whip him and stick goads into him. By these various means, he was at length stung to madness. Sometimes he would paw and bellow. Then he would run at the men with the flags, who would either dodge him, or throw a flag at him. In the latter case, he would pitch at the flag, and gore it with all his force; or sometimes he would pass it by, and pursue the man who had thrown it, who, in order to escape from his dangerous position, would then jump nimbly on the fence, and turn a summerset over it. After some time spent in this way, seven or eight men on horseback entered the large pen. Each horseman was provided with a *lasso*, or long and strong rope, with a slipping noose at the end. The rest of the cattle were then also turned into the large pen, and the horsemen dashed among them, and threw their *lassos* upon the horns and the hind feet of the bull that had been worried. His furious and desperate efforts to get loose were exhibited for a while; then he was thrown on the ground, the barbed arrows taken from his neck, and he turned loose, to be no longer tortured. The operation with the *lasso*, is probably in imitation of the mode of catching wild cattle with that instrument.

The second bull in size was then brought out to be hunted in a similar manner the rest of the cattle being put into the smaller pen. This bull was younger and higher mettled than the former: his passes were awfully furious, and many a summerset was turned over the fence in order to avoid them. As he strove to get through the fence into the pen, with the other cattle, he was assailed with whips, and pierced by goads, till the blood flowed copiously from his wounds, and he became enraged to the utmost degree. He then turned to chase his antagonists again, and plunged at them with great force: one of them failed in the attempt to elude him: the bull caught him on one horn and threw him to the height of eight or ten feet. As the miserable man fell, the bull rushed upon him and assailed him with feet, head, and horns: then rising from his prostrate foe, he plunged upon him again, and gored him horribly. The attention of the bull was then drawn off, by attacks from other actors in the scene; and while he was chasing one of them, the wounded man was hastily carried off, and shoved through the fence. Thus ended the sports for the forenoon.

At 3 P. M., I went again, and learned that the wounded man was still alive, though dangerously hurt. The sports were resumed—nearly two thousand spectators being now assembled. During a part of the time, in addition to the flags before mentioned, the common blanket was used as a means of annoyance to the bull who was being hunted. The principal fighter or hunter allowed the bull to come very near him; but turned so quickly that he could not reach him with his horns. The hunter then resumed the red flag, and again allowed the animal to pass within a few inches of him, in full chase, shunning him, however, dextrously, as before. At length the brute became wearied, and to some extent timid: so that when the red flag was brandished in his face, he would no longer pursue the man who strove to provoke him. This was deemed a triumph over the bull: and the clown rejoiced wonderfully, with many antic gestures, huzzas, &c.

At evening the weather presented a prospect of rain, which prospect I was in hopes might be realized, for a whole week at least, so as to put a stop to the barbarous amusement.

19th. I went to work to-day. Though the weather was cloudy and damp, yet it did not rain, and the sports, as I was informed, were continued. On my way home from a walk in the evening, I went to see the gamblers. A great throng was present; but it was exceedingly quiet—far more so, I think, than it would be in one of our cities, if so much liquor was displayed. Five or six armed men of the city guard were there; but I judged that their presence was not necessary for the preservation of order, as there were no signs of quarrelling.

My friend Del Valle, condemns the bull-fighting, and wishes that some more rational amusement were adopted in its stead. One of our northern Americans thinks that horse-racing ought to be introduced.

We had this evening good news from the city of Mexico. The repeal of the law of April 26th, 1830, has passed both houses of Congress. The bill still waits the signature of the President, which it will doubtless receive. I now hope to be soon able to accomplish something of the objects of my journey.

20th. I have now learned, to a certainty, that the man calling himself Robidoux, is a villain—and truly he is a most accomplished one.

A large portion of the food consumed here, consists of a kind of cakes called *tortillas*, the process of making which is as follows : A quantity of dry Indian corn is put into an iron pot, and sprinkled over with a little fresh-slaked lime ; then it is covered with water and boiled a very little. It is then permitted to stand for some hours, until cool, when the lime is washed out with cold water, and the corn ground on the metal (of the pot or kettle ?). The cakes are made up immediately from it, with the hands, baked on a hot griddle, and put hot upon the table.

21st. I paid the governor a visit this morning.— He informed me that he expects that the Legislature of Coahuila and Texas, and also the Legislature of several other of the Mexican states, will enact laws the coming winter providing for equal toleration to protestants and other settlers.

22d. The bull fighting still continues. Another dangerous feat was performed to-day. A man riding on an ass, with a pack-saddle, entered the pen and made signals to the bull, who thereupon sprung at him, and catching the ass on his horns, tossed both him and his rider into the air. When they came down to the ground, the biped retreated; but the bull gored the poor quadruped, until he had sated his fury. The man who was wounded in the fight of the first day, is still languishing on the brink of the grave.

In taking a walk towards evening, I noticed that the leaves of the peccan tree were beginning to grow yellow, and to fall off; but I believe there has been no frost here as yet. A plant called Amole, which possesses the properties of soap, grows spontaneously in this vicinity. It is a small species of the maguey. The washerwomen take the root and mash it, and then use it extensively in washing. The clothes must be washed out afterwards, however, with a little soap, as they would otherwise be disagreeable to the skin. I understand that the root of the *lignum-vitæ*, which likewise grows here spontaneously, is also used as a substitute for soap. I may add, in this place, that the indigo plant is among the spontaneous products of these parts.

Nov. 23d. The fig trees are pretty generally shorn of their honours, and the peccan and cotton-wood trees are fast losing theirs. The gardens are neglected, and the Indian corn is beginning to bow before the harvester; but the greater portion of the foliage of the country is still as green as at mid-summer.

I learn that the people here cure pork with red pepper, instead of salt. The seeds of the pepper are ground and mixed with vinegar, and then rubbed upon the meat.

My friend Blackaller showed me, to-day, a great variety of ores of gold, silver, copper, lead and iron, taken from the mountains near this place, and from the mines further south; also a specimen of coal, from the mountains near Santa Rosa. A coal mine is worth more here than a silver one. He had likewise many specimens of Indian workmanship, among which were some of their gods, wrought in clay and burned like common earthenware. Blackaller, who is an English civil engineer, is a very ingenious and scientific man. He came here with the view of establishing mills and manufactories; but having associated himself with an avaricious partner, he has suffered much from ill treatment.

24th. Yesterday was as warm as mid-summer, and this morning at seven it snowed quite fast. This is a specimen of the sudden change of weather in a mountainous country. On the plain and the lowlands, the snow melted nearly as fast as it fell, but the neighbouring mountains, which ascend about two thousand feet above the surrounding region, are still mantled with white. The bull fighting and gambling is over. They had intended to carry on the sport for three or four days more, but the "gray god" of the frozen regions, thought it enough, and with a breath of his indignation he frightened them away.

25th. There is some talk of sending four thousand troops to Texas. Some say that the governor objects to it. Probably he objects to their being sent and employed as other troops have been; but in conversation with me on the subject, he did not express any dislike to their going to protect the inhabitants against the hostile Indians. 26th. I understand that a proposition to permit foreigners to hold land in the Mexican republic, has been made in the general Congress. Such a regulation would be of great importance, if not utility.

27th. There is important news in town this forenoon. It is said that Stephen F. Austin has written from Mexico a letter to the Ayuntimiento of Bexar, recommending resistance to the General Government, and to the State government of Coahuila and Texas, so far as to establish a State government in Texas, without the

authority of either.   It is further rumored, that the governor here is taking measures to apprehend Austin, on
a charge of treason.   The foreigners here express their
astonishment at the generally accredited report of such a
treasonable correspondence.*

28th. This being my landlord's birth day, among the
delicacies at dinner, we had some apple and mince pies,
which were the first I had seen in Mexico. In the
evening, I went, for an hour or two, to a private family
ball, by invitation of Dr. Hewetson. Nearly all the
foreigners in the place were present. The waltz seemed
to be the favourite dance. Some of the company were
not entirely white. Among them were a portion of very
polite people. Some young men, who were very good
dancers, came in their working dresses. It looked strange
to see a person, with the complexion of an Indian, wear-
ing a hat, but no coat nor vest, and dancing with a beautiful white young lady who was dressed in the richest
silk. The ball, however, was but a private one, for the
amusement of the Doctor and his friends ; and perhaps
there would be a more rigid etiquette on a more public
occasion.

29th. I learn, to-day, that S. F. Austin has used very
disrespectful language to the Vice President of the
Mexican United States, and that it is feared that it will
lead to something serious. Austin's recklessness aston-
ishes our friends generally. A letter from a Senator in
Congress, from this State, which has been published,
says that the President is about to send the four thousand troops for the protection of the frontier of Texas,
&c., under Gen. Mejia, who is very popular in Texas,
as I was told when there.

The beautiful sunsets which we have here at present,
are unparalleled by any thing ever seen in the higher
latitudes.   If the air is pure, a vast arch of fiery light of

* S. F. Austin was ultimately arrested and imprisoned at
Mexico, by order of Santa Anna, for near a year and a half, without being brought to trial. In 1835 he was discharged, went
to Texas, took part in the revolution, and became President of
the new republic.

the deepest vermilion colour, rises far above the horizon. Such a flood of effulgence proceeds from the aroff this evening, that shadows are distinctly marked on the opposite houses.

It is said that a few nights ago, at between twelve and one o'clock, there was a strange appearance in the firmament. A streak of fiery light extended across the heavens, from north-east to south-west. After remaining stationary for some time, it seemed to fall asunder in sparkling rays, and was thus entirely dissipated. Blackaller, who is something of a philosopher, as well as an astronomer, thinks it may have been a collection of animalculæ.

December 1st, 1843.—We had a real summer morning, on this first day of the winter. My detention here grows exceedingly irksome : I console myself, however, as far as possible, with the reflection, that. "Rome was not built in a day." I have sold my pistol, &c., for seven dollars. All my disposable property of much value is now gone, and I must hereafter depend on my hands.

December 2d. Texas politics run high here. Some of the colonists find fault with the government for withholding its protection; but they do not wish to be molested when smuggling goods, or introducing slaves.

3d. Accounts from Mexico state that the law of 1830, prohibiting the settlement of Mexican lands by citizens of the United States, is repealed —*the repeal to take effect six months hence.* This delay appears to have been a condition of President Santa Anna's sanction of the law.* I learn from the Mexican papers that two members of the Legislature of Tamaulipas have introduced a proposition to colonize the vacant lands of that State with foreigners, without any restriction in respect to their religious profession. The papers continue their zealous advocacy of such measures.

* Before the six months' delay required by Santa Anna expired, a revolution commenced, in which he bore a prominent part, having for its object the defeat of the liberal measures commended by Lundy.—ED.

5th. The governor has not yet received official information of the repeal of the law of 1830. He states that the President probably considered the delay of six months necessary, in order to fortify the frontiers with troops, before the land to be disposed of should be occupied by foreign settlers. He says that the purport of Austin's treasonable letters was, that the general government being weak and distracted, it was a favourable moment to establish, without its consent, a state government for Texas, separate from that of Coahuila : and he recommended an immediate organization for that purpose. The governor says, further, that the people of Texas have not yet seconded Austin's proposal, and that if they do not, the disgrace and the punishment will fall on him alone. He thinks Austin must be partially insane ; and says that a majority of the Texans do not wish an immediate separation from Coahuila. In this opinion I think him correct. I suppose that Austin presumes a great deal on assistance from the United States, and that in doing so he does not reckon altogether without his host.

7th. I have more applications to-day for work in my shop, at which I am most heartily rejoiced.

8th. The governor sent me, soon after breakfast this morning, a printed copy of the recent act of Congress for the repeal of that of 1830, together with the orders sent him directing its publication. In the evening I called upon him, and he then appointed the afternoon of the 12th instant for me to call upon him, in order to make the necessary arrangements for my grant of land. He states that he is now authorized *to act*, and that he will let me have any of the vacant lands, except those on the frontier and those on the coasts, as a commissioner is coming on to select suitable places for military posts and fortifications in those parts. The Mexican papers state that all articles of merchandize imported for the consumption of the new settlers from abroad, will be free of duties, for the ensuing seven years. These liberal projects of the new administration please our foreigners very much, and they will probably have the effect of counteracting the schemes of Austin, in Texas.

11th. I called upon Del Valle to obtain the form of a petition to the governor for a grant of land. He is unwilling to do any thing in the matter, as he thinks the governor has no right to act, *until the repeal of the law shall have taken effect.* I think, myself, however, that he possesses the same right to act prospectively that the Congress did.

12th. I waited upon the governor this afternoon, and found that upon reflection, he was inclined to Del Valle's opinion. He is not sure, however, that he cannot make grants in the department of Monclova. He will carefully examine the law to-morrow, and give me an answer, if I will call on that day. He says that if he can do nothing more, he will pledge his word that I shall be the first to receive a grant, when the legal obstruction is removed. This, however, will not answer my purpose : I must have something done sooner. 13th. I called at the governor's office, but could not see him, as he was engaged all day.

Dec. 15th. In walking out, at about eleven A. M., I found the weather so hot as to make me glad to take the shady sides of the streets.—16th. I called twice to-day at the governor's, but he was too much engaged to attend to my business. I must meet him at 10 to-morrow morning at the government house.

17th. I saw the governor and Del Valle together. They both agreed that the former could not lawfully treat with me at all, until the act of 1830 is fully abolished. Del Valle told the governor that I wished to introduce coloured people : no objection was made, however on that score.—What shall I do now? I will not yet give over all hopes.

18th. This evening I had some conversation with J. M'Mullin. He told me very frankly, that when Robidoux was first unmasked, he thought me in league with him; and that a trifling dispute which took place between Robidoux and myself, was mere finesse, because even afterwards, I did not speak against Robidoux in respect to business affairs. The fact is, that I spoke precisely as I thought at the time, and this very sincerity was construed into the greatest roguery. I now, for the first time, showed M'Mullin some of my credentials. He remarked that this was unnecessary, as the injurious impressions formerly entertained, had been entirely removed from his mind since our acquaintance.

19th. Preparations are making at Monclova to send a caravan of mules to Metamoras. Forty or more pack-saddles are displayed in front of our house. These Mexicans know nothing at all of wagon-transportation.

20th. I have concluded to let my landlord, J. Back-aller, who is a British subject,* take a grant of land in my stead, with the understanding that I shall colonize it. I can then return home immediately, and bring settlers to this country by the time the prohibition expires. Blackaller now labours under a false charge of having challenged a man, and he must wait a few days for a confirmation by the Fiscal (or Attorney General) of a decision which has been pronounced in his favour by the Alcalde's Court. As the Fiscal arrived to-day from Saltillo, I hope the business will soon be decided.

The city has been illuminated every night lately, in conformity to the customary usage for the seven or eight nights preceding Christmas. Paper lanterns are hung outside the doors, or set within the window casements. Some streets are thus pretty well lighted at present, though in ordinary times the lighting of them is not practised.

Dec. 21. There is more frost this morning, though the weather is not very cold. This month and November are those in which the wheat is generally sown here. —It is reported to-day that eight Mexicans were killed, not long since, by Indians, near the village of San Patricio, in M'Mullin's colony.

* The Mexican law of 1830 was directed against citizens of the United States.

23d. I walked out this morning to the smaller square of the city, and saw some of the preparations for the Christmas feast. The usual observance of a feast in Mexico consists in abstaining from labour, and engageing in some kind of amusement. The principal amusements are gambling and bull-fighting; the latter, however, takes place but once a year. On these occasions, they have the best of cakes and confectionary, and liquors in abundance. The feast days are religiously set apart for holidays. Like our "Sabbath," they are instituted for worship, but spent in amusement. There is, however, this difference, that there is not, on such occasions, a twentieth part of the intoxication among the Mexicans that there is with us.

It is rumoured to-day, that a band of robbers near Saltillo has taken twenty-five mule loads of dry goods from some travelling merchants. A mule load is three hundred pounds.

Dec. 25th. Christmas. Most of the trees are now pretty well stripped of their foliage; but some of the peccan, cottonwood, and willow trees, are still decked with leaves, as green as in mid-summer.

29th. The birds are chirping and flitting about, and we have an abundance of house flies, full of animation and mischief. This afternoon Blackaller attempted to take the altitude of the highest mountain visible from Monclova. Owing to some defect in the apparatus, he could not make a perfect observation; but he concluded that the mountain-top was upwards of fifteen hundred feet above the level of the adjacent plain.

30th. I took a walk to see a wheatfield. The young wheat looks well, though the land is miserably prepared for it.—I have determined to forward the portrait of Washington, by mail, to President Santa Anna, as it is not likely that I shall see him before my return home. I took my intended communication to the President, which is to accompany the portrait, to Thomas Chambers, Esq., to be translated. Chambers, who is a native of Virginia, expresses a strong conviction of the evils and dangers of the slave-system.

Dec. 31st. To-day the cottonwood trees are out in bloom. The mail brings news that Santa Anna has again retired from the helm of State, and gone to his farm. Surely he is a second Cincinnatus.

General Bravo has attempted to get up a revolution in the south of Mexico. He wrote to the President, detailing his plan, and stating that he could command five thousand soldiers for its support, if his excellency would agree to it. He could probably command that number any where, if he had money enough to offer as an inducement. The President put him off, with some expression of indignation, considering it a small concern, as Bravo is a man of much presumption but of little influence.*

1834. *January* 1st. I was to have been at home in July last, according to my calculations. I now do not expect to be there before July next.—This evening a ball was to be given to the members of the Legislature who have recently assembled to hold a session at Monclova. Having received an invitation, I went to look at them for a few minutes. The ball was conducted very much like the other which I attended, except that there were more people of distinction present, including the governor, &c. This is a real jovial night in Monclova and especially characterised by gambling and carousing.

Jan. 2d. To-day has furnished a pretty good specimen of winter in a southern country. In many places the ground and trees were covered with ice half an inch in thickness. Much of the ice that was on the ground melted during the day, but that on the grass, shrubbery, and trees, mostly stuck fast.

---

* A few months after this, Santa Anna openly came into the schemes of Bravo and the other opponents of the reformatory measures of Congress, and advocates of the overthrow of the federal Constitution by military force. The difference of treatment by Santa Anna, of Bravo and of Austin, is very striking, when we consider that the former proposed a military insurrection, and the latter did not.—Ed.

This evening I had some unpleasant words with A.
R. Guild, who took advantage of my deafness, to make
a little fun.   This is exceedingly provoking, and all are
inhumanly thoughtless in regard to it.   Whoever offends
me in this respect, shall be offended.   I will be an
equal in the social circle, or I will have no intercourse
with it.

Jan. 3d. It is reported, to-day, that two men perished
last night on one of the mountains.   This is not surprising, inasmuch as the people here have so little cold
weather that they never prepare for it.   When it comes,
they seldom have sufficient fire for comfort, and they
have no glass windows in their houses.   Of a cold evening they light a candle, place it in one corner of the
room, close the wooden shutters, wrap themselves up in
their blankets, sit down on their skins or cushions, and
while the candle scarcely renders darkness visible, they
exclaim: " *Hay que frio, Valga me Dios!*" (how cold
it is, God bless me !)

Jan. 4th, 1834. This is the forty-fifth anniversary of
my birth day.

> The adage says, " At forty wise,"
> But adages I fear are lies.
> Wise men their business should contrive,
> To have a home at forty-five.
>
> But I have had a work to do,
> That kept me rambling to and fro,
> And conscience doth not chide and strive
> Within my breast at forty-five.
>
> Now let this rhyming begatelle
> Go forth—and, journeying ill or well,
> I pray that all who me survive,
> May fare no worse at forty-five.

The weather feeling cold and looking wintry this
morning, I walked out pretty early, but I could find no
frozen ground, nor even the least trace of ice on standing
water.

The Legislature, to-day, passed an act for admitting
T. Chambers to practice law in this state (Coahuila)

without his having complied with certain formalities of baptism &c., which had heretofore been pre-requisites.

5th. This morning was cloudy, and it again snowed here a little. Towards evening, the clouds, which had enveloped the mountains, dispersed, and disclosed a singular sight. For about one-third of the ascent of the mountains the snow is light: for the next third it is deep: and the upper part is entirely bare! This phenomenon may be thus explained. During the storm and cloudy weather, it was too warm near the foot of the mountains, for the snow to lie any considerable time: in the middle region it was colder, and the snow was shadowed by the clouds, so that it did not melt: but on the upper region, the sun shone above the clouds, and melted the snow on the mountain tops, before they became visible by the dispersion of the clouds.*

6th. I called upon the governor this evening, and showed him my letter to the president, and the portrait of Washington which is to accompany it.

The governor thinks the president will be much pleased with them.

7th. I saw, yesterday, Mr. Egerton from New York, who had just arrived here on his way to one of the new colonies. He is the first person I have met here, with whom I had been previously acquainted. This morning he paid me a visit. He was about to petition for one of the tracts of land that I want, and he intended colonizing on my plan. He says, however, that he will make some arrangement with me.

8th. I learn that S. F. Austin has been apprehended at Saltillo, by order of the General Government, and taken back to Mexico.† Egerton says that when Austin

---

*May it not have been the fact that no snow fell on the mountain tops, owing to the clouds not rising above them ?—Ed.

†Austin was kept in prison for nearly two years, without trial. He was ultimately released, and upon his discharge took a prominent part in the Texan revolution, but he died ere it had been long in progress. He was son of the original proprietor of "Austin's Colony" in Texas.—Ed

presented the proposed new Constitution for Texas, to
the general Congress, he requested that settlers should
be allowed to hold slaves: but to this the Congress
would by no means agree. He will probably now be
punished for his treasonable communication to the
Texans.

The feasting in the Plazuela (or small square,) which
began on Christmas day, two weeks since, is now over.
The gamblers are gone; and the owners of the booths
are taking them down.

I have had another visit from Egerton, who came accompanied by his partner, or contemplated partner, a
Mr. Soto, who does not speak English. Egerton proposes that he and Soto shall obtain a grant of land, then
sell out to me, and let me have the entire management;
but they are to be allowed to introduce three hundred
families on the tract, and they require me to secure the
payment to them of half a cent an acre for the land which
shall be occupied by the five hundred families that are
proposed to be introduced by me. I cannot listen to
this proposal if I can do better. Egerton's avowed object is, to make all the money he can ; and beyond that,
he cares nothing about the business. He is busy in en-
deavoring to induce the Legislature to modify the coloni-
zation-law.

10th. I had applied to J. Davis to take up, in his
name, a grant of land for me. To-day he informs me
that he declines acting in the matter.—Egerton has
applied to the governor, and has obtained, as he says,
one of the tracts which I expected to take. He now
wishes to sell it to me, but his demand is too exorbitant.
I rejected it, and then made him a proposition, but we
did not come to any definite conclusion. He knew the
purpose for which I had come here: he knew that, for
the present, the law of 1830 stood in my way : he was
told that I had obtained the promise of having the grant
as soon as I could legally treat with the government in
an official manner :—yet he has stepped between the
government and myself, apparently with the sole view

of extorting money from me, and from those who may interest themselves in my enterprise before I can lawfully act myself.

In the evening I received a note from Egerton, in which he proposes that I shall contract to furnish him with four hundred settlers, to pay him, or make the settlers pay, eight or nine thousand dollars for the privilege, and to receive, for myself, one fourth of the premium lands as a compensation for my trouble.* It is very provoking to be thus tormented by heartless speculators. Egerton and Soto have tried, before, to engage me in their schemes: but they failed, as they will now. I will agree to nothing but what is honest and straight-forward.

12th. The Curate here is a true descendant of the inquisitorial times. Being displeased with a person in his employ, he ordered him to be sewed up in a sack, and kept there for some hours. The man, however, contrived to get out, and went to the Alcalde and entered a complaint. But the Alcalde, being a bigoted tool, decided in favour of the priest. The man then applied to the Legislature, and that body immediately deprived the Alcalde of his office, and imposed on the priest a fine of twenty-four dollars.†

13th. This morning I received a visit from Egerton, who being about to depart from the city, came to take leave of me. He said a good deal about philanthropy, and regretted that it would not suit me to embrace his propositions, as we might have done much together, to promote the cause in which I am engaged. I doubt not his willingness to promote it, provided he can make his own fortune by doing so.

I have made arrangements for a trip to Metamoras,

* The premium lands were those which, by the custom of Spain and Mexico, a grantee of land was entitled to keep himself, without price, in consideration of his labours in introducing settlers upon the remainder of the grant.—ED.

† In a few months after this occurrence, the State Legislatures were abolished altogether, by a revolution effected by the religious bigots, centralists, &c.—ED.

in company with J. Davis. I expect to start in a week, and to return here at the end of one or two months.

Many of the natives, in these parts, closely resemble our aborigines ; but they have an outlandish mode of' dressing, particularly the men.

I learn, this evening, that the robbers who have so long infested the country about Saltillo, have become so bold, and so terrifying to the inhabitants, that some of the citizens have been induced, through fear, to take sides with them, in resisting the lawful authorities. The Legislature has just passed a decree giving to the governor extraordinary powers for the purpose of reducing them to submission, and it is believed that something effective will now be done with them. Troops are to be sent hence to Saltillo, immediately, in order to convoy, from that place to this, a sum of money belonging to the government.

15th. Egerton does not leave town yet. It is thought he will have difficulty in procuring the repeal of the last colonization law ; and even if he succeeds, it is probable that some provision will be made in the new law, to check the inordinate speculation that is going on in the Texas grants.

16th. I called to-day to see the deputy Lombrano, but he was not within. A coloured woman, who is his god-daughter, accompanied me as interpreter. She was cordially embraced by Lombrano's wife. Such treatment of a colored person, by the wife of a member of a Legislature, was strange to my eyes.

17th. Some Indians of the Lepan tribe are in town. They seem to be as much a novelty to the Mexicans, as savages are to us.

18th. In company with J. Blackailer, who went as interpreter, I called again to-day upon the deputy Lombrano. I informed him of my errand to this country, and explained my plan of colonizing, which he highly approved. He manifested a decided hostility to the introduction of slaves into this part of the country. I informed him of the plans of some of the colonists, and their practice under the old law, of bringing in slaves, bound, by indentures, to service for ninety-nine years. I asked his attention to the new law, now before the state Congress, and suggested the influence that a prohibition of such indentures would have in attracting the right kind of settlers. He replied that the present Congress of Coahuila and Texas was disposed to be liberal towards colonists; but that it would never listen to any measure tending to increase the present amount of slavery in the country.*

Lombrano is said to be quite an active and influential member of the Congress. He thinks that the regulation restricting colonists in matters of religion, will very soon be abolished.

M'Mullin says that *slavery*, as he calls it, is worse in Mexico than in the United States!

It is necessary here, if one wishes to rise, to oppose slavery, but there is many a wolf in Mexico, from our country, in the guise of a sheep.

Jan. 19th. It is real summer weather to-day, and many fresh flowers may be seen. The temperature, at evening, is as agreeable as the imagination can conceive.

At this moment, around the houses of my friends in the United States, the shrill blast, charged with stinging frost, is whistling; the domestic animals are looking, morning and evening, to the hand of man, for the food which is to prevent them from perishing; the poor man is shivering in his thin and tattered mantle, while his wife and children hover over a few embers to preserve the vital fluid from congealing. But *here*, how strong the contrast! The animals feast on the green grass, or repose on the lawn; the rich man and his family promenade the streets, or lounge in their piazzas; and the poor sit at their doors, and enjoy the innocent mirth of their half-clad children, who gambol in the yard, or in the street, near their humble habitations.

20th. I called and took leave of the governor this morning. He re-assured me that he would accommo-

---

* Texas had been excepted from the operation of the decree for the immediate abolition of slavery in Mexico, but the offspring of the Texan slaves were to be free.—Ed.

date me, as soon as possible, with a tract of land to colonize. I told him of the speculations of Egerton & Co. He expressed his regret that I had not found some confidential person to obtain the grant for me, before Egerton applied. I told him that some of the grants, now in the hands of speculators, would probably be forfeited; and that in such case, I should be ready to take them. He understood me, and assented to the project.

21st. I went to visit the chamber of the Legislature, that body not being in session to-day. Lombrano showed me the portrait of the late President [Guerrero?], which is placed over the speaker's chair. He was the intimate friend of Santa Anna, and his memory is deservedly held in high estimation among the Mexicans.*

CHAPTER XIII.

Narrative of Lundy's journey from Monclova by way of Loredo, to San Patricio, on the Nueces river, and thence to Aransas Bay, in Texas.

Jan. 23d, 1834. Having this morning concluded a written agreement with J. Blackaller, to obtain for me two grants of land, I left Monclova in the afternoon, in company with J. Davis and two Mexican servants. Davis is going to Texas to purchase goods, which he expects to obtain at or near La Bahia (Goliad.) He takes with him nine mules and two horses, in addition to those we ride, and three thousand dollars in specie. It is my present intention to accompany him to San Patricio, on the Nueces, there to part from his company, and proceed, myself, to Metamoras.

I saw a wolf on the road two or three miles from Monclova.—We proceeded on our route till dusk, when we encamped near the upper part of the Salado river, where we found grass in plenty, though somewhat dry. We had found none on the previous portion of our afternoon's journey.

* It was Guerrero who, in 1829, proclaimed immediate liberty to the slaves.—Ed.

Jan. 24th. This morning I examined the grass and found the stalks to be all green, while most of the leaves were dry. The horses can eat it very well. Proceeding on our way, we saw several wolves. About midday we passed a small village, nearly all of which belongs to a wealthy man named Sanchez, who owns immense quantities of land about here, as well as several lots and houses in Monclova. This village, which is called El Tapato, is provided with a neat church. We have come thus far on the main wagon road to Santa Rosa. Not long after leaving the village of El Tapato, we came to a spring famous for the heat of its waters. It is enclosed within a large stone wall. This spring throws out a stream of water large enough to turn a small grist mill. At the distance of some rods from its source, I could not hold my hand long in the stream, by reason of its great heat. For some distance along this stream, the leaves of the *mesquite* were green, the warmth of the water having prevented the frost from killing them. We stopped, for the night, at a cluster of cabins, on the land of the before mentioned Sanchez.

25th. As we set off in the morning, we saw, turned out and driven to pasture, one hundred and fifty asses and mules, and perhaps two hundred sheep and goats. Sanchez has a sugar establishment on his hacienda,* provided with good stone buildings. The position is at the edge of the mountains, and the land such as I have described about Monclova, exceedingly fertile when irrigated, but when not, quite unproductive. After leaving this hacienda, we turned off from the Santa Rosa cart road, passed between lofty mountain peaks, and entered upon the vast plain of the Rio Bravo del Norte, otherwise called the Rio Grande.*

Here we found immense quantities of flowers and green foliage, among the plants and shrubbery. In some places whole acres were as thickly covered and as beautiful as any flower bed I ever saw. We saw, to-day, a

* Estate.

† Lundy usually calls by the name of the Rio Bravo, the river now more usually known in the United States as the Rio Grande.

large brown Mexican tiger, also many quails and other birds.   During the afternoon, there were in sight, in one direction, the mountain peaks of Candela, in another, the mountains near Santa Rosa; and in a third, those not far from La Punta, in New Leon.   We came to the Salado river again, crossed it, and encamped, at evening, near a hacienda, where there were the largest palm trees that I have yet seen.

26th.   The morning being cloudy and drizzling, we prepared to lay by a while, by covering our packages, saddles, &c.   Our landlord, however, came and offered us the use of a fine building, occupied as a granary, which we gladly accepted.   He has a large stock farm here, and makes excellent cheese of which he gave us some.   There appeared to be considerable timber in the neighbourhood, where the land had been irrigated. Tigers, leopards, leopard-cats, wolves, beavers, otters, rabbits, and ground rats are found in these parts.   The weather continuing rainy, we remained two days and three nights with our host, who is called Don Jose Maria Miguel Vidaurri.   He appears to be about fifty-five years of age, but is really seventy-five.   He is uncle to the governor of the State, and is a good deal of a politician, being, like most people in these parts, favourable to Santa Anna.   His dwelling house was built in 1740, with mud walls and a flat roof.   It has stood well, for ninety-four years.

28th.   The rain having ceased, though the weather was still cloudy, we resumed our journey, accompanied by a guide.   Re-crossing the Salado, we passed, for eight or ten miles, through a poor looking country, rolling and rocky.   Then we came to a large tract of good land, with plenty of grass, plants and weeds, but very little water.   There was no timber, except a little mesquite and small shrubbery, in occasional spots. We saw, on either hand, deer and rabbits, skipping about in great numbers.   There was no road, except the paths of the mustang, or wild horse, which were very numerous, crossing each other in every direction. We saw hundreds of these animals, during the day, some, at a distance, feeding on the luxuriant pasturage, others running before us, as we travelled. One fine drove of about forty, some of which were sleek and noble, passed so near, before us and across our way, that our loose horses seemed much inclined to join them. Headed by a large white or gray steed, they galloped off finely, their long flowing manes and tails giving an elegant appearance to their movements. We started another drove of sixteen or eighteen, in the afternoon, and gave them a little chase; but they were soon far enough away from us. At near sunset, we encamped for the night in the open plain.

29th. We saw a large herd of fine fat cattle, which were nearly as wild as the horses. Before noon we came again to the river Salado, which here forms the boundary between Coahuila and New Leon.* We crossed it by a ferry about seventy yards wide, in a very large canoe, dug out of a huge cypress tree, with three steps to descend into the bow. Our horses were taken over at a ford, some distance below The whole river bank here, to a considerable depth, is composed of earth or loam, and small lime-pebble-stone, intermixed and consolidated, so as to form a novel species of rock. We found at the ferry a man who had been chasing wild horses, one of which he caught with the lasso; but the horse which he rode, not being accustomed to the business, threw him, and both horses ran off together, taking along the man's saddle, gun, &c. At a *ranche*, near the ferry, we got some good new cheese for three cents a pound.

Davis tells me to-day, that Egerton expressed doubts to him, at Monclova, as to whether I was really the person that I represented myself to be. This was insincere in him; for he knew me, and acknowledged the fact to some persons in Monclova.

At evening, we encamped again in the open plain.

30th. This morning a part of our horses were

---

* New Leon is the State of which Monterey, lately become famous for the battle there, is the capital.—ED.

missing, but about ten o'clock the man brought them in again. We proceeded along our wild path, till about four, P. M., when we struck the wagon road from La Punto, in New Leon, to Laredo, on the Rio Bravo. In this road, we found some fresh travelling tracks of a man, a horse, and a narrow-wheeled wagon, which brought back to our minds the idea of a settled country. Most of our journey to-day was within the limits of the State of Tamaulipas, into which we had passed from that of New Leon. As we approach the Rio Bravo, the land improves in quality. Instead of the thick bushes of dwarf mesquite, the thorn of twenty different species, the prickly pear in profusion every where, and twenty other kinds of prickly plants, heretofore seen, we now find only a scattered shrubbery, but little of the prickly pear, and a great deal of grass of a very fine quality. In occasional spots, upon the low grounds, the mesquite grows to a large size, yet there is a great deficiency of water. On the elevations, everywhere, one may see my favourite little *mouse-ear-bush*. It is said to denote the presence of lime-stone. I am glad to find that it is evergreen, or rather *ever-mouse-coloured*. The first garden that I make, near the places of its growth, shall be adorned with it.

January 31. Last night was the coldest that has occurred since we have been out.—It is one year to-day since my eldest daughter was married, and ten months since I have heard a word from her.

In many parts of the plain here, which extends on both sides of the Salado river, there is an indigenous plant, whose appearance much resembles that of our common white turnip, when small.

Shortly after mid-day, we met a gentleman from Laredo, with five or six attendants, and a large drove of horses and stock-cattle. He told us that we were yet seven leagues from Laredo. At the middle of the afternoon we encamped for the night, having found that horses and mules cannot end urehard travelling, when they are fed on grass only. During the day we had seen no wild animals, except one large and saucy wolf,

and a few rabbits. The rabbits here are larger, and
have whiter ears than those of the north.

February 1st, 1834. The land which we pass to-day
is beautifully rolling, and, in most parts, very rich.
Standing water is found in some places, where streams
run in wet weather. At length we came in sight of
Laredo, and at noon we reached the ferry, over the Rio
Bravo, opposite the town. There are at this place an
island and a bar in the river, and a ledge of rocks, extending across it. We forded the stream, which had in
its bed as much water as is found, at dry seasons, in the
Ohio, below Wheeling. The falls here, present a serious
impediment to navigation ; but I suppose that keel-boats,
carrying thirty or forty tons, might now be taken through,
with perfect safety. Laredo is a poor looking place.
It contains about 2,200 inhabitants. The people look
like mulattoes. They are friendly and clever; but not
one of them can speak English. Laredo is the first
settlement that I have seen in Tamaulipas, it being on
the outskirts of that state.

In the afternoon a revenue officer came and demanded
of Davis two per cent on the amount of money which
he brought with him. Davis believing the demand
illegal, refused to pay it : they went together into town,
to consult an acquaintance of Davis, who decided against
the officer, and the claim was abandoned. This was
one of many instances of attempts to impose on strangers,
which have been made by persons who take advantage
of the change of government, and the subsequent unsettled state of affairs, to aggrandize themselves.

Feb. 2d. We left Laredo, to strike across the plain
in the direction of San Patricio, in company with some persons, going that way, with several mule loads of sugar
which they had bought at Monterey, in New Leon, at
about three cents a pound. It is good brown sugar, put
up in rolls, being better than the inferior qualities produced in the West Indies and Louisiana. Four men
and a boy, with fifteen loaded mules, went on before
us. We shall be obliged to travel slowly, as each mule
carries a load of three hundred pounds.

Much Indian Corn is raised on the river bottoms, in these parts, but not on the high, or ridge land.

Coming early in the afternoon to a good place for water and grass, our muleteers encamped there for the night.

3d. Ever since I left Bexar (San Antonio,) I have seen, in almost all parts of the country, the dwarf *lignum-vitæ*, and a bush called " Como," both of which are evergreens. The latter bears a fine berry or fruit, which is said to be very delicious. The weather being cloudy, with a slight rain, we lay by for the whole day, as it would not do to let the packages of sugar get wet. The men set themselves at work, in making ropes out of " *iste*," a kind of stuff much used in this country, for ropes and bagging. It consists of the fibres of a plant, called " *letchugia*." The finer kinds are used for shoe thread, &c., but it is too brittle. The root of the plant, is said to be an antidote to the bite of a serpent.

In the afternoon, I conversed with Davis, on the subject of slavery, and found, that in spite of his bitter prejudices against the blacks, he will be willing to employ them as hired labourers, when he finds that Texas must be a free state.

During the evening, the horses were heard running, and our people became alarmed, fearing that Indians or robbers were in the neighborhood. The guns were quickly examined, and preparations made for a fight. Scouts were sent out, with swords and pistols, to reconnoitre the enemy, but none was found. We retired, late, to rest, and I slept soundly; but I cannot answer for the rest of the company.

4th. In travelling this forenoon, we came to a large tract of land, as well adapted to farming and grazing as any that I ever saw. The *mesquite* growing on it, gave it the appearance of a peach-orchard, in New Jersey. On viewing this delightful place, I could scarcely avoid exclaiming :—" O that my brethren, now groaning in the house of bondage, might reach this blissful Canaan, and enjoy the sweets of liberty, which a wise govern-

ment would guarantee to them." Pursuing this train of
thought, I fell into a reverie, concerning the future condition of the descendants of Africa, in connexion with
this land, and forgot, for the time, the part assigned me,
as a humble, unworthy instrument, in pioneering them
hither.

5th. It being a little rainy this morning, we lay by,
at the place where we encamped last evening. I am
glad that it rains here in the good old-fashioned manner—coming down in drops. At Monclova there was
no rain ; all was " Scotch mist." At sunrise to-day,
there were some very red clouds in the east, which cast
a distant rainbow, although the sun was totally obscured.
This was a phenomenon, such as I had never seen before.

While detained by the rain, I employed myself in
making button moulds, from the hedge-thorn. I could
whittle them out very well with my knife, while standing in the rain ; but I could not write so well in that
situation. It is said that a Yankee can make a wooden
clock with his pen-knife.

The weather having changed, we resumed our route,
about noon, and travelled through a most delightful
country, containing as fine farming land as the sun ever
shone upon. We are told that some of the reservoirs
of water, in these parts, dry up occasionally ; but, even
when most of them are dry, water may be obtained in
many places, by digging to the depth of a few feet.

We are now about half a degree farther north than
Monclova, and the vegetation here is not quite so forward as in the plains near that place; but there is nevertheless an abundance of young grass, and plants on every
hand. Some of the grass has evidently been green all
winter.

6th. After travelling several miles to-day, we ascended a high ridge, about three hundred feet above the
plain that we had left. This ridge is the highest land
between the *Rio Bravo del Norte*, and the *Rio de las
Nueces*. From its summit, one may see, in a clear day,
to a distance of near one hundred and twenty miles.

From the whole appearance of the ridge, I am satisfied
that it was once the margin of the *Rio Bravo,* which
must have been a wide river then.   The ridge stretches
a long way, in nearly the same direction with the course
of the Bravo.

On the summit of this ridge, the ground rats are both
numerous and industrious, as in the sandy lands of Texas.
They dig up large quantities of the reddest sand and
earth that I have ever seen.

In the wet season, the wild horses frequent these parts
in great numbers; but the water is now dried up, and
none of them are to be seen.   Since ascending this
ridge, or mountain, I have discovered a novel species
of laurel, the leaves of which resemble those of the live-
oak.   Yesterday and to-day we have met with a new
species of thorn; it is of a deep green foliage, and grows
in the very best manner that can be imagined for the
purpose of making live fence.   Another bush, entirely
new to me, was discovered to-day.   Its leaves are of a
singular shape, and of a beautiful deep green tinge.   It
is now exuberantly decked out in splendid yellow blossoms.

After leaving the mountain, by a gradual descent of
ten or twelve miles, we entered a fine rich valley of land,
similar to that we passed yesterday, before mounting the
ridge.   Here we passed a handsome copse of live-oak,
being the first I have seen during the present journey;
and then we came again to reservoirs of water, and
abundance of thick grass, which had been pastured somewhat closely by wild horses.

We were considerably annoyed by musquitoes in
our journey to-day, especially on the high lands—a vexa-
tion which a northern man would hardly have anticipated on the sixth of February.

7th.   We were detained again, till near mid-day, by
the misty weather, which deterred our company from
setting out with their sugar.   We have come but two
hundred and forty Mexican miles, in the two weeks that
have elapsed since we left Monclova.   After starting

to-day, we passed through a country as delightfully rolling as I have ever seen. In most parts the wild horses
have eaten the grass as close as it is ever found in any
pasture field at the north. We saw but one of these
animals—most of them having gone, as it is thought, to
a milder region, during the cool weather. The whole
country, to an immense distance, affords some of the
best pasturage in the world. We learn that some persons from Alcantro, have recently pastured vast flocks
of sheep here. One man had six or seven thousand.

8th. The landscape, to-day, presented a greener appearance than heretofore, occasioned, I suppose, by the
circumstance, that although we have advanced a little
in north latitude, we have also descended into a region
lower and nearer the sea than that we have left. The
various strata, in the region on this side of the mountain
ridge which I have mentioned, may be thus described :
viz. 1. The surface of the highest elevations is composed of a reddish, or pale sand, with a portion of loam.
2. The middle heights are of limestone, with brown
loam. 3. The lowest parts are more or less alluvial,
exhibiting a very dark loam, with occasionally a small
portion of sand.

Immense numbers of wild horses were seen, at a distance, to-day. The paths of these animals, as we approached their watering places, were as well beaten as
the most public road. We passed one of the pens used
for taking them, where, doubtless, many of them have
been captured, and numbers killed. Their bones are
very numerous, near by ; they are also scattered, in vast
numbers, over the adjacent plain.

We killed, to-day, a rattle snake, having several rat-
tles, each rattle indicating, as the reader is probably
aware, a year in the age of the animal.

9th. Just before daylight, this morning, we had a
smart thunder shower, in which I got a little wet and
rheumatic. I had lain out in the open air, for several
nights past, although Davis had a tent, a part of which I

might have occupied. I rejoice to find that this delightful country is within the region of rain.*

The business of drying our clothes, &c., prevented us
from starting, till near noon. On our journey, one of our
company shot a duck, of the largest species. Wild
turkies, as well as ducks, are numerous in these parts.

This afternoon (Feb. 9th) was so warm that we had
to shade our faces with our handkerchiefs, to prevent
the sun from burning them. We travelled several miles
on the borders of a stream, not running at present, which
falls into the Nueces, below San Patricio. Its bed is of
limestone; and though it does not flow all the time, there
are constant pools of standing water in it. Its borders
are well supplied with timber, of various kinds; but on
the uplands, at a little distance, scarce a bush is to be
found. The country is rich and beautiful, abounding
in excellent grass. We saw large herds of fine domestic
cattle; also many wild horses, deer, rabbits, geese,
ducks and quails. At evening, we encamped on the
banks of the stream above mentioned.

10th. This morning we breakfasted on an excellent
Mexican dish. One of its ingredients is corn, ground,
sweetened, and dried, the other is milk. The corn is
ground, when green, on the "*metal*," in the same manner, I believe, as for making tortillas; it is sweetened,
dried, pulverised, and preserved for use. When the dish
is to be prepared, the milk is boiled, and, while boiling,
the sweet meal is stirred into it, until it is about of the
same consistence as "mush." It is eaten warm and is
very palatable and nutritious. It is called "*atolede
leche*," or, to spell it in English, *attolayday laycha.* We
obtained the milk, for making it, of the keepers of the
cattle, mentioned yesterday.

It is said that we are now fifteen Mexican miles from

*The country between the Bravo or Rio Grande, and the
Nueces, has been generally supposed to be of a poor quality.
The part described by Lundy, as very good, is presumably
farther in the interior, and to the northwest of that which is so
inferior.—Ed.

San Patricio, (or St. Patrick.)   A Mexican mile is about eight per cent. shorter than an English one.

The elm trees along the creek here are literally covered with long Spanish moss, being the first that I have seen on this journey.

Having resumed our route, we came to another creek, now not running, called *Dulce Agua,* or sweet water. This, like the last mentioned, falls into the Nueces. After crossing the bed and valley of this stream, we found the land more rolling again.   There was no timber upon it, but it was evident that trees would soon grow up, in the lower places, if the fires were kept down.   It is wonderful to think of the vast quantity of extremely rich land which has been presented to our view, during the last few days.   An enchanting prospect to a northern man, for the tenth of February was exhibited to-day, in the great number of flowers that overspread the country.

We did not reach San Patricio this evening, owing to the dilatoriness of our company in starting this forenoon.   A foreigner, not long since, remarked, that a Mexican has no idea of the value of time.   This opinion, so far as regards our muleteers, might seem well founded.

11th. Soon after leaving our encampment we crossed a strip of land, about forty rods in width, which reminded me of the " *swales*" of Michigan.   A |thick even grass covered the whole, and the water stood, in all parts, from three to twelve inches in depth.   The land here, with much of that we saw yesterday, would probably produce good rice.

At length we reached the river Nueces, which we struck at some distance above San Patricio.   The timber in the valley of the river is far more abundant than I had anticipated.   Many beautiful groves chequer the landscape.   From the elm and white ash trees, on the margin of the rivers, immense quantities of the best Spanish or Mexican moss hung dangling, while the towering and umbrageous evergreen liveoaks gave an interesting aspect to the whole scenery.

Having come to the ford, opposite San Patricio, we ferried over our baggage, and entered the town. Davis wished to stop at the house of an acquaintance, but not finding him at home, we rode through town, and encamped a quarter of a mile to the North.

San Patricio, or St. Patrick, is beautifully situated on a high and dry plain, on the East side of the Nueces, about a mile distant from the river. I have rarely seen a prettier location. The place contains about thirty families, nearly all of whom are Irish. All the houses but one are composed of pickets, thatched with bulrushes. There are, in the place, a few mechanics' shops, and three or four small stores.

I learn that Dr. Beales has brought to Aransas Bay, Texas, some thirty families, of various nations, and gone with them up the country, to occupy the land of which he has a grant. My informant thinks they will all leave him. In that case he will probably forfeit his grant, unless the government favours him, as Americans are still debarred from taking land as settlers.

I called to-day on an old gentleman, at San Patricio, by the name of O'Brien, who came out with me from New Orleans to Brazoria in the schooner Wild-cat. He and his youngest daughter were all who reached this place, out of ten persons that I left at Brazoria, intending to come on. Of the rest, five died of the cholera, one became insane, and the other two went back to New Orleans, or elsewhere.

This evening I saw, near our encampment, a flock of about four hundred fine fat sheep. They have very large tails, and some of them have four horns, two rising and two falling.

At the request of my friend O'Brien, I concluded to lodge with him to-night. His daughter made us a dish of tea, which was the first I had seen for a long time. The rheumatic pain in my back, resulting from exposure in our encampments, was so great that I could not sleep in a bed, but was obliged to rest in a chair.

12th. Instead of proceeding to Metamoras at present, I concluded to go on with Davis to Aransas Bay, which is fifty or sixty miles to the North North East, from this place. A French gentleman from *La Bahia* (or Goliad) joined us, and we went on, ahead of the muleteers. We were now in Texas. The land, for most of the day, was level. We found very large plains, covered with nothing but grass; but near the streams there was a good deal of liveoak. At near sunset we encamped out, as usual.

13th. Having crossed the Aransas river, and passed over a tract of land, which, in some places, was very sandy, we reached the river of the Missions, and soon after came in view of the church, near which we encamped. This is an old Spanish mission, but at present there is no religious establishment kept up. There are here half a dozen Irish families, most of whom are recently from Philadelphia.

16th. Having laid by yesterday and the day before, I concluded to go on to Aransas-Landing with Davis, who expects to purchase goods from two vessels, from New Orleans, which are lying there.

We find our French companion a clever and intelligent man, and possessed of an intimate knowledge of this part of the country. He is an excellent hand at making encampments comfortable. He formerly resided in Philadelphia, afterwards at La Bahia, Texas, and is now about to settle in the village of Buenaventura, near Monclova.

The collector of revenue for the port of La Bahia came to-day, with his wife and attendants, and passed some time with us. He made a seizure of a portion of the clothing brought by a settler from Illinois, named Peter Hynes, who came here with his family—the quantity being greater than the law, as construed by the Collector, allows. Hynes made great complaint of this treatment.

After mid-day we set off, and travelled several miles to the " *Copano*," or Aransas Landing. The soil, on our way, was dark and rich, but much of it too level and too wet to be desirable. The Aransas is a very beautiful bay, abounding with oysters of a fine flavour.

CHAPTER XIV.

Passage from Aransas Bay, Texas, to New Orleans, and thence to Cincinnati and Nashville, including visit to Lane Seminary, near Cincinnati.

Finding that the two vessels before mentioned, were going soon to New Orleans, I concluded to take passage thither in one of them, viz. the Philadelphia, Capt. Lambert, and to return thence, either to this place or to Metamoras. There being some unanticipated delays, I was obliged to remain at the "*Copano*," or Aransas Landing, for twelve days, viz. till February 27th.

I saw there some emigrants, mostly Irish, going to the colonies in the interior. There were also about twenty Indians, men, women and children, of the Karaunkaway tribe. On one occasion, these Indians brought in a fine deer, and sold it to a merchant, for two bottles of whiskey, a pound and a half of poor tobacco and three or four hard buscuit. They seemed pleased with their bargain, and were very friendly. On the 20th, Capt. Holden, of the schooner Dart, shot a pelican, which measured seven and a half feet between the tips of the wings. On the 22d, J. Davis set out, with the goods he had purchased, to return to Monclova.

27th. We hoisted sail, on board the Philadelphia, at 3 p. m., and got under way. We had much difficulty in finding the channel, as there are bars of sea shells, on either hand. It took us three days, or till March 2d, to reach the bar, at the mouth of the bay. There we lay eleven days more, or till March 13th, on account of stormy weather and unfavorable winds, which prevented our going through the inlet and proceeding to sea.

While thus detained the hands gathered a quantity of black sea-wax, which is said to be a volcanic production. It was in pretty large cakes, five inches thick, and had the appearance of anthracite coal, and the smell of bituminous. It burns like pitch, and is said to be better than that substance for use in ship-building. It is often met with at sea, where it floats on the waters, like oil. When first taken up, it is of a dirty yellow colour, but it becomes of a shining black, when hardened on shore.

Our vessel, the Philadelphia, is owned by an old seaman, who still works as a common sailor on board of her. By industry and economy he acquired the means of purchasing her, but not having an education to qualify him to command, he employs a captain and mate, contenting himself with a subordinate post.

One of our passengers is a Louisiana creole, a planter, named Cucullo. He is quite a reasonable and pleasant man. He says, " give us proofs of the practicability and advantages of free-labour, in the culture of sugar, and we will soon listen to them." He states that the sugar planters calculate on making one hundred and fifty dollars a year, by each slave ; but that they do not often clear so much as that.

While we were lying in the bay, the schooner Wild-Cat came in from New Orleans. I went on board of her, and found some newspapers from New York and New Orleans, which contained the first intelligence from home that I had received for several months. I had some talk with the captain, and found him to be one of Austin's roarers.*

March 15th. At 8 A. M., we weighed anchor, and sailed out of the bay, through a very serpentine channel. It was not more than a hundred yards from the land on our right, to the breakers on our left. Having got out at sea, we passed, in the afternoon, a great deal of driftwood, brought from the mouth of the Mississippi by the easterly wind. We also saw a fine large turtle, swimming on the surface of the sea. His back was covered with moss, interspersed with shells. Three hands went

* The advocates of a State government for Texas, separate from Coahuila.

out after him with a harpoon, but they did not succeed in taking him.

17th. We were boarded, to-day, by a United States revenue cutter. 18th. On taking our longitudes and latitudes at noon, we found that we were not quite half way on our passage to New Orleans. We still meet a great deal of drift wood, some of it very small, and a portion consisting of fresh chips. Doubtless the Ohio has recently overflowed, and these are the effects. The captain says, that the Gulf Stream now sets west from the mouth of the Mississippi, which arises, it is presumed, from the great amount of water discharged at present, by that river. 19th. We move on with a light wind and at a snail's pace.

20th. We had, this morning, a fog-storm, or in other words, a high wind with thick driving fog. This was succeeded by a violent gale, and the roughest sailing that I ever witnessed. We had a most restless night. The place of my bed was thrown down, by the violent rocking of the vessel, and I was precipitated several feet. I thought we were all tumbling to chaos.

21st. The gale continuing with unabated fury, we lay too till twelve o'clock. At 4 P. M. the sea still continued high. "Old Ocean" is not to be appeased in a moment after a thirty hours contest with "rude Boreas." During their strife, neither had much mercy upon us. Sometimes they would toss us aloft, towards the sky ; then they would pitch us down headlong, towards the coral caves. Now they would rush furiously over our deck, prostrating every thing in their way; then they would thump our poor vessel in the head and sides, when she crossed their path, as did the battering rams of old the walls of a besieged city.

22d. This morning the clouds had dispersed, but there was still much ocean spray. Towards noon, the increased paleness of the water gave a sure indication of our approach to land, it being caused by the discharge of the Mississippi, which whitens the blue Mexican gulf for a long way from the mouth of that river. In the afternoon, the sea was less rough than in the morning, but the white-capped billows continued to chase each other in the wildest confusion.

23d. We cannot ascertain our exact position, the sun being obscured by clouds at noon, so as to prevent an observation.   24th. The mate is displeased at my frequent examination of the compass, and at my taking notes.   He and the owner showed a disposition to treat me rudely ; but they soon found that it would not be tolerated.   The sordid owner had before expressed dissatisfaction at my consuming his ink by writing so much.

25th. We found ourselves, before day-break, in the turbid waters of the Mississippi.   A fog coming on soon after, we were obliged to lay to a good portion of the day; and when it cleared up, the wind was so light, that instead of advancing, we were driven back by the current of the river.

26th. The fog being thoroughly dispersed this morning, by a smart breeze, we discovered the land in a north-east direction, and fifteen vessels lying at anchor. Immense masses of drift-wood were floating about the mouth of the Mississippi.   Many vessels went out to sea, to-day, among them the Dart, which had been at Aransas-bay at the same time with us, and had made a passage of but six days to New Orleans, while we had been so long on the way.   In the afternoon, a pilot coming on board, we weighed anchor and proceeded up the river, to a place where several vessels were waiting to be towed up by steam.   There were, this morning, probably thirty-five or forty sail of vessels in sight, from this place.

27th. This morning we shot two alligators, in the south-west pass. In the afternoon the wind having fallen, we dropped anchor near the shore, where we were visited, and greatly tormented, by multitudes of gnats and musquitoes.   They kept me awake at night, till a late hour.

28th. We passed fort St. Philip on the west, and Fort Jackson on the east.   They are splendid establish-

ments. The first person that I saw about Fort St. Philip
was a poor negro,—a slave, no doubt, and an emblem
of the kind of liberty which obtains here.

29th. We passed numerous plantations devoted to the
cultivation of rice, which is the principal product of the
lands along the banks of the river, in this vicinity. We
saw also some orange trees. The water, in the river,
is now higher than the adjacent lands, and would inun-
date them, but for the protection of the embankments.
Before noon we overtook a tow-boat, which had passed
us in the morning, with three other vessels in its train.
We now lashed our vessel to it, and went on with the
rest. One of the vessels proved to be the brig Bourne,
of Baltimore, having on board a cargo of slaves. She carried aloft the United States flag, which none of the other
vessels displayed. The name of this brig, is, most in-
appropriately, that of an eminent Virginia philanthropist.* In the afternoon we saw many orange and fig
trees, and also passed some sugar plantations, on one of
which near two hundred slaves were engaged in hoeing.

March 30th.—At about five miles below New Orleans,
we passed the battle ground, celebrated for the conflict of
January 8th, 1815 ;—we also passed many splendid es-
tablishments for the cultivation of sugar, &c., as well as a
very large and rich flower garden, which contained an
immense number of roses in full bloom.

In the afternoon we arrived at the city of New Orleans, after a tedious voyage of about a thousand miles ;
the distance, in a direct line, being but about six
hundred.

As I was destitute of funds, and not likely to obtain
them here, I induced the captain of the Philadelphia to
consent to wait for my passage money, until I could obtain it elsewhere

March 31st, 1834.—Having concluded to proceed to
Cincinnati, I went on board the steamboat Champion,
and engaged a deck passage for that place, upon con-

*The Rev. George Bourne, a zealous abolitionist.

dition of payment on my arrival. We started at one o'clock, P. M., and proceeded up the Mississippi.

April, 1st, 1834.—The Mississippi, as we pass along, is still higher than the adjacent fields. 2d. In conversation with the captain of the Champion, I found him very friendly. He has seen the Genius of Universal Emancipation, and approves of its doctrines.

3d. A man died on board the boat to-day, of a disorder supposed to be the cholera. We stopped in the night, and buried the corpse, at a place where we took in wood.

5th. We passed, this afternoon, the village of Providence, Louisiana. The place was nearly inundated, there being a crevasse or breach of some fifty rods in width, through the embankment below the town, another of considerable magnitude above it, and several smaller ones in other places, where the water was running, like creeks, from the river upon the land,—thus reversing the order of nature.

8th. Another man appears to have an attack of the cholera ; and yet another has had symptoms of the disease. The first case is a very bad one. In the other, the symptoms yielded promptly to the application of camphor and laudanum.

April 9th, 1834.—We have heard, to-day, glorious news from the Island of Antigua. The local Legislature has resolved on the immediate abolition of slavery, in preference to the system of gradual emancipation prescribed by the British Parliament. The days of American slavery are numbered—glory be to God!

10th. We arrived, this afternoon, at the mouth of the Ohio, and passed from the Mississippi into that river.

April 11th.—The cotton-wood trees of the country through which we are now passing, are in bloom, as they were at Monclova, fourteen weeks since, on the first of January.

There is a man on board our boat who has with him, as slaves, a woman and three children. The woman is a kind of wife. The man declares himself an opponent of slavery!

14th. We arrived at Louisville, where I applied to a resident of the place for a small loan, but met with a refusal. Several coloured persons on board the boat then lent me as much as was necessary to supply my immediate wants. The coloured people are every where my best friends.

15th. We arrived in the morning at Madison, Indiana, where the Champion stopped for the present; and I left her and went on board the Mount Vernon, for Cincinnati.

16th. I have found, in the Mount Vernon, several coloured persons who wish to migrate to Texas. One of the coloured stewards loaned me a file of the "Emancipator," published at New York.

In the afternoon we arrived at Cincinnati, where I received the melancholy intelligence of the decease of my friend Evan Lewis, at Philadelphia *

In the evening, I attended some lectures at the African Methodist meeting-house, in Cincinnati, which were delivered by students belonging to Lane Seminary.† They appointed a meeting, for me to lecture, to be held at the same place on the evening of the 18th.

18th. We had a large meeting at my lecture this evening. Among the audience were twelve or fifteen of the Lane Seminary students.

21st. I visited the Seminary, and found there some

---

*Evan Lewis was a zealous and well known friend of Emancipation, in whose care and editorship Lundy left the "Genius of Universal Emancipation" during his travels.

†Lane Seminary is a well known literary and theological institution, established near Cincinnati, at which discussions were instituted, on the subject of slavery, not long before the time here referred to. Their results were very important, in the conversion to abolitionism of students, both from the North and the South, who proved able and efficient labourers in the cause of freedom.—ED.

warm friends. I had previously met, in private company, some of the professors and students.

22d. The editor of the Cincinnati Gazette, C. Hammond, published in his paper of to-day, a communication of mine, on the affairs of Mexico.

23d. I wrote to-day, to my friends S. H. Saunders, Lyman A. Spaulding, Dr. Parrish, Samuel Webb, James Mott, Dr. Preston, Abm. L. Pennock, Thos. Shipley, &c., respecting my present situation, views and prospects.

25th. I left Cincinnati, and went by steamboat to Louisville, on my way to Nashville. At Louisville, I was detained a week, by the canal round the falls being closed by mud, so that steamboats could not pass through.

May 2d, 1834.—The boat Fame in which I have taken passage, got through the canal to-day. 3d. This evening we arrived at, and entered the mouth of the Cumberland river, at its junction with the Ohio. It is one year, to-day, since I left Philadelphia, on my Mexican mission.—The coloured people on board the Fame, have found out who I am, and have offered me any assistance that I might want. I have taken a deck passage, and shall try hard to support myself, though my funds are quite exhausted. I have yet left, however, a little coarse provision.

6th. We arrived at the shoals of the Cumberland river, where the Fame was moored, and we all went on board the Eclipse, which came along very opportunely. As we proceeded, the water became more shallow, and the passengers got out and walked, while the boat was warped over the shoals. Late in the night we arrived at Nashville.

7th. I make my home, at Nashville, with my friend Thos. Hoge, Jr. I am here informed, that since the death of Evan Lewis, the Genius of Universal Emancipation is edited by Dr. E. A. Atlee, of Philadelphia.

8th. This evening I went and conferred with sundry coloured people of Nashville, and its vicinity, at the house of A. M. Sumner. 13th. I have applied for a loan of two hundred dollars, to H. R. W. Hill, an extensive slave-holder of this place. He is a Methodist, an avowed friend of emancipation, and a man in good esteem with the coloured people. My friend Wm. Bryant, of this vicinity, has offered to endorse my note for the amount.

14th. Hill will accomodate me if I will put a note in bank, which I prefer not to do. The coloured friends of the cause propose to raise me one hundred dollars.

CHAPTER XV.

Third journey to Texas and part of Mexico; or journal of passage from Nashville to New Orleans, and thence by way of Red River, Nacogdoches, San Felipe, San Antonio de Bexar, and Rio Grande, to Monclova.

Having completed my arrangements, I left Nashville and proceeded to Smithland, at the junction of the Cumberland with the Ohio river, where I arrived on the 25th of May, 1834. There, after four days waiting for the opportunity, I took passage in the steamboat Pacific, for New Orleans. We passed from the Ohio into the Mississippi, on the 30th, the boat lying by, at night, on account of her heavy freight of cotton and the low state of the water, which rendered her passage dangerous.

June 1st, 1834. Our boat ran aground, on a bar in the Mississippi, where she remained several days. 3d. I had a conversation with a passenger, the Rev. —— Quinn, of Nashville. He stoutly maintained that the *empresarios*, or Tennessee speculators in Texas lands, are entitled to all the surplus lands in their grants, after they have accommodated the number of settlers that they agreed to introduce, as the condition of receiving the grants.

7th. The Pacific not having yet got off the bar, I left her, and went on board a flat-boat belonging to Daniel Bedell, a respectable farmer who resides near Vincennes, Indiana, and is a genuine advocate of universal eman-

cipation. His boat is loaded principally with the products of his own farm. He takes an interest in my arrangements relative to Texas, and wishes to know more
of them when they are completed.

10th. A sudden rise in the river having enabled the
Pacific to get off the bar, she overtook us, and I went
on board of her again. Late in the night of the 14th,
we arrived at New Orleans.

19th. While waiting at New Orleans for a passage to
Matamoras, I became more particularly acquainted with a
coloured gentleman named M. B. Evans, a hair dresser,
who was introduced to me some time since by Joseph
Cassey of Philadelphia. I also had an interview with
Madame Lafitte Brocard, who informed me that her
brother, Nicholas Dronette a dark mulatto, recently an
officer of the Mexican army, had received a grant of land
from the Mexican government, for the purpose of colonizing it with coloured settlers from Louisiana. A letter of introduction to him was given me by James
Richardson, son-in-law of Madame Brocard.

22d. This evening I visited the dismantled dwelling
of Madame Lalaurie, which was a short time since almost totally destroyed by the citizens of all classes, on
account of her cruelty to her slaves.* The mayor was
present on the occasion, and actively engaged with the
rest.

26th. The papers of to-day contain the account of
the discovery of another fiend, in the person of a Mrs.
Pardos, who resides in the lower part of the city. In
addition to other manifest cruelties, it is said that she
caused several teeth to be extracted from her little slave-
girl, merely to gratify her fury. The Mayor has promptly
issued his warrant, and the little victim has been brought
before him.

27th. A murder was committed during the night of
the 25th inst., on the levee, near where the boat lay, in
which I had engaged passage for the Red river. So
little notice was taken of the matter, that many persons

* The woman here spoken of escaped from New Orleans,
and never returned to that place.—Ed.

residing near the place, had heard nothing of it up to this morning. Every day people may be seen dead drunk in the streets here. In other respects, if we except the treatment of the people of colour, New Orleans is not more disorderly than our large cities at the North. And even as to the slaves, the inhabitants in general discountenance cruelty towards them ; and free persons of colour are quite as much respected here as in any other part of the country. The present mayor of the city has a coloured family, and no other, and is very friendly to the coloured people.

In the afternoon, the steamboat Lady Washington, in which I had taken passage, started for Natchitoches on the Red river, that being the route I have taken, to return through Texas to Mexico 29th. We left the Mississippi and entered the Red river to-day. There we found the alligators very plenty and very daring. In the afternoon of the 30th, we reached Alexandria, where I found Capt. Walker, with whom I descended the Red river and ascended the Mississippi, in 1832. Leaving Alexandria, we went over the falls, with four and a half feet water in the shallowest part of the channel. This is the most difficult place of navigation on our passage.

July 1st.—We arrived at Natchitoches in the afternoon, making the time of our passage from New Orleans four days. Here I must wait three days for the starting of some wagons with which I am to proceed to Nacogdoches.

There was a man, much reduced by the ague, put on board the Lady Washington, a short distance below this place, as we were ascending the river. When we arrived here, he was so weak that he could not walk. He lay on board the boat, until she was about to depart on the morning of the 3d. Then he was thrown ashore, at the water's edge, and left lying in the sun. The poor man was not noticed by the crowd of people standing on the bank, thirty or forty feet above him. As they were dispersing, I came down to the place, saw him lying on the beach, and immediately went down to him. He was almost heart-broken. Having given him some consoling assurance, I went for my umbrella to protect him from the sun. I then made an appeal on his behalf to some persons in the streets, one of whom promised to attend to him. I did not leave him until a cart was brought, and he taken into it, to be carried to lodgings. Several applications, made for his reception, were unsuccessful : but at length the editor of the "Frontier Reporter, B. P. Despalier took him in.

July 4th.—I started from Natchitoches to go to Nacogdoches in Texas, in a company of three wagons, each drawn by four yoke of oxen. Having put my baggage on board one of the wagons, I walked myself, carrying my gun.

July 8th.—Having reached the Sabine river, we crossed it by a ferry, and entered the Texan territory. We have progressed, so far, only at the rate of 13 miles a day. I do not, this time, travel *incognito*, as I thought it necessary to do, in my former journeys in this region. 9th. A small party of Indians, Chickasaws, I believe, came up with us this morning, on their way to Nacogdoches. I gave them some fine biscuit, for which they appeared quite thankful.

12th. In the country which we are now traversing, the beautiful groves of Mexican china trees, near the houses, together with the thrifty fields of corn, cotton, &c., contrast finely with the sandy deserts of Louisiana that we have left behind. The land here, however, is not so rich as in many other parts of Texas. There has been, within the last two years, a considerable improvement made in this part of the country. Much excitement prevails in it, at present, in reference to the New York speculators in Texan land scrip. One of their agents is here, offering the scrip for sale. The old settlers are highly exasperated against him: and they threaten the speculators with their heaviest vengeance.

I arrived on the 13th, at Nacogdoches, where I found Williams, the man who shot the slave of Vann, the Indian chief as mentioned in my former journal. I happened to make a remark, for which Williams appeared quite desirous of quarreling with me.

14th. I went about four miles into the country, to the house of Wm. Goyens, a very respectable coloured man, with whom I became acquainted here in 1832. He still takes a deep interest in my enterprise. He has a white wife, a native of Georgia. They appear to live happily together, are quite wealthy, and are considered as very respectable, by the people generally. Goyens has undertaken to procure me a horse, and I am arranging my baggage so as to pursue my journey on horseback.

17th. To-day a deserter from the United States' fort, beyond the Sabine, having been convicted of stealing a pair of silver sleeve buttons, in Nacogdoches, was publicly whipped twenty five lashes, and then drummed out of town, with bells and tin kettles, bearing on his back a large label, inscribed with the word "thief."

18th. I became acquainted with a white man, named David Town, who originally resided in Georgia. Thence he removed to Louisiana, taking with him a black female slave, who was in fact his wife. She was a very capable woman, and had several very likely children. Eight years ago, Town removed from Louisiana to Nacogdoches, where he emancipated his wife and children, who, up to that period, had been slaves, in the eye of the law. They all live together here in harmony, are quite industrious, and make a very respectable appearance. The daughters are as fine looking young women as can be seen almost any where, and are free, in their whole demeanour, from the degrading restraint, so observable among coloured people in our country. The Mexican ladies of Nacogdoches are very sociable with them.

19th. A ball was given to-night by some of the Mexican residents of Nacogdoches. Among the earliest dancers, was Wm. Goyens, the coloured man before mentioned. Afterwards some of our Northern Americans joined in the dance. The ladies were all Mexicans.

22d. Two brothers of the wife of Wm. Goyens, who,

like their sister, are white, have been here about a week, having come to visit her, from Louisiana, where they reside. They appeared well satisfied with their coloured brother-in-law, whom they had not seen before : and they took a very friendly leave of the family to-day.

" Amalgamation," even by marriage, is not at all dreaded here. Parties of white and coloured persons not unfrequently come over from Louisiana, procure a Catholic Priest to solemnize the marriage contract for them, and then return. A white man lately made a proposal of marriage to one of the mulatto daughters of David Town, before referred to; but he was refused, on account, I believe, of his not being strictly temperate.

29th. Having procured a Cherokee pony, through the aid of friend Goyens, I left Nacogdoches on horseback this forenoon, to proceed on my journey. My baggage is so considerable, that I am obliged to walk much of my way. At evening I passed a house which was fastened up, the tenants being absent. I therefore crossed the Angelina creek, which is a branch of the Neches, and encamped near it, in the open air. Before I could boil my coffee and pitch my tent, a violent storm arose, in which I got so wet that I passed a most uncomfortable night under my linen canopy. 30th. I lost my way in the bushes for some time to-day. I nevertheless travelled eighteen miles, to the house of a man named Bradshaw, where I spent the night. 31st. Having crossed the Neches, and gone twenty miles, I lodged at the house of Young Masters.

August 1st, 1834. On a part of my route to-day, there was but one house for a distance of eleven miles. At the place where I put up at night, two men came a distance of five miles, to grind a scythe: grind-stones must be scarce in these parts.

2d. I reached the Trinity river, and having crossed it, I put up at the house of Nathaniel Robbins, who has on his farm a number of coloured people that are claimed as slaves, by a person in Louisiana, named Mays. Mays is at present in Nacogdoches, where he made up a party

of nine men, a few days since, and came here to take
the coloured people, *vi et armis.* Instead of succeeding,
however, he and his whole band were taken prisoners.
The before mentioned slave-shooter, Williams, was
among the number ; and it is said that he was the most
easily captured of them all.

I will here insert a sketch of that portion of Texas
which I have now crossed.   The section from the Sabine river to Nacogdoches, was described in my journal
of 1832, and the description was published soon afterwards in the Genius of Universal Emancipation.   The
two branches of the Nandey creek, which unite a little
below Nacogdoches, and border the town on the east
and west, are handsome mill streams, with good land
on their margins.   From there to the Angelina, there
are a number of beautiful small streams, and numerous
springs.   The surface is undulating, approaching to
hilly.   On some elevations there is a good deal of sand,
in others red gravel and loam, full of iron ore.   The
soil of the bottom lands is a darker loam.   The growth
between Nacogdoches and the Angelina, consists, on
the uplands, of Oak of four kinds, viz . the white, the
post, the black, and the red oak ; of pine, black-jack,
hickory, and persimmon trees : on the lowlands it is of
walnut, peccan, maple, sugar-tree, sycamore, linn, elm,
ash, hackberry, water-oak and plum, together with honey-
suckle, reed-cane, and a thick coat of luxuriant grass
underneath.   Grapes are exceedingly numerous and of
large size.   As we approach the Angelina, we find some
fine prairies, but not large ones.

The Angelina is a considerable stream, with a deep
channel and a moderate current.   Some rock is found
in the beds of the streams, and in the hills, but there is
little on the surface of the country in general.

From the Angelina to the Neches, the growth is similar to that mentioned before.   The land is much diversified, a part being sandy, a part gravelly and timbered,
and a part prairie—the prairies increasing in size as we

proceed westward. In this section there are many small streams of water.

The Neches is a beautiful and swiftly running stream, capable of sustaining an immense number of mills. It is said to be navigable a part of the year, nearly as far up as the road where I crossed it. Its bottoms or alluvions, are wide and rich.

From the Neches to the Trinity, the land is more level and of a somewhat better quality than that previously passed over. One of the prairies on the route is three miles wide, very large and beautiful, and equal to any that I have seen within the limits of Texas. Another large prairie, near the Trinity river, which is overflowed in the wet season, is composed of the richest black loam. If protected from inundation, by embankments, it would afford the very finest kind of soil for tillage. The timber on and near the river, is very large and fine, and of the same kinds before mentioned, except that the pine has disappeared, and the peccan become more abundant.

The Trinity is a fine stream, from thirty to a hundred yards in width between the tops of its banks. After rains, its waters are very turbid, much resembling those of the Mississippi. In the dry season, the river may be forded at several places. It overflows its bottoms, at high water, to such an extent that they cannot be cultivated without embanking; yet they afford an immense range for the feeding of cattle and other animals.

In nearly all parts of the foregoing described country, corn, cotton, and peaches, and every species of vegetation adapted to the climate, thrive well. Spanish moss is plenty. Large herds of horses and fat cattle, range this vast common. Game of every kind is very scarce. Fish are abundant in the streams, and alligators are numerous.

As we approach the Trinity, the mesquite and prickly pear first begin to appear. There is also a plant growing near lakes and ponds, which bears a nut that resembles an acorn in size and shape, and a chestnut in taste.

I never saw it any where else, but it is said to grow also near the Red river.

3d. Leaving the Trinity and proceeding westward, I came directly to extensive prairies clothed with a beautiful coat of grass, the soil being of a dark loam and evidently fertile, the surface handsomely rolling, and the country apparently healthy. As I passed on, the scenery became charmingly diversified by the alternation of prairies and timbered land, the soil of the latter being in some places sandy, and generally less fertile than the prairies. The timber consisted principally of post-oak. I crossed numerous wet weather streams, where the water, which had stopped running, was standing in pools.

4th. The land which I have passed to-day is more level, and the prairies not so rich as near the Trinity. The timber, in the low lands, is larger, and covered with immense quantities of Spanish moss. There is plenty of water standing in the beds of the creeks, but I have not seen a single running stream this side the Trinity. Near evening, having travelled 20 miles, I found a deserted cabin, which I made my quarters for the night.

5th. The fore part of this day's journey was over a country more level and less fertile than before. The grass on the prairies was thin and short. Water is scarce, and the country unhealthy.

In the latter part of the day the land was more rolling and of somewhat better quality; and among the timber there was some very fine cedar, being the first I have seen in Texas. I also came across two running streams.— Having travelled 23 miles, I encamped in the edge of a beautiful prairie, sixteen miles distant from the Brazos river.

6th. Directly after quitting my encampment, I came to a fork in the road, one branch leading to San Felipe, and the other to La Bahia. I took the latter. As I approached the Brazos, the soil improved in quality. The timber on the uplands, is principally post-oak; on the bottoms it consists of cedar, ash, elm, hackberry, water-

oak, peccan, &c.   The water-oak is a species intermediate between the live-oak and the other kinds.   There
is some rock in the edges of the streams and the brows
of the hills, of which a portion is limestone.   I now
crossed a fine mill stream, then came to the Navisoto
river and followed it two miles to its junction with the
Brazos, where I crossed the latter river in a canoe, at
the ferry, my horse swimming as I held his bridle.   The
keeper of the ferry, John W. Hall, has laid off a town,
or the site for one, on the west side of the Brazos, opposite the mouth of the Navisoto, which town he calls
"Washington."   I here received information of Indian
depredations further west, which induced me to leave
the road for La Bahia, and take that for San Felipe.   I
proceeded five miles beyond the Brazos, over a very
rich country, alternated with prairies and timber, and
then put up for the night.

7th.   Soon after starting this morning, I was overtaken
by another traveller bound to San Felipe, and we proceeded together.   The country, to-day, is as fine a one
as I ever saw, rich and beautifully rolling.   Many of
the people are sick, however.   Having crossed several
fine running streams, with wide, black, timbered bottoms, and travelled 28 miles, we came to the house of a
man named Edwards, a brother of the famous Texan
revolutionist, where we put up for the night.   Our host,
whom we found very intelligent, showed us several late
Brazoria newspapers.

8th.   Having started early, we arrived at San Felipe
in the forenoon, where I found Col. Almonte,* who was
there as commissioner from the Mexican Government.
I presented to him a letter of introduction, quite flattering to myself, which I had received from Adolphus
Sterne.   It was kindly received.   As Col. Almonte ex-

---

* The same who was subsequently minister to the United
States, and recently conspicuous in Mexican affairs, in connexion with Santa Anna.   He was at the time here referred to, on
a mission from Santa Anna, to ascertain the state of affairs in
Texas.—ED.

pects to leave San Felipe in three or four days, for Monclova, by way of Bexar, I have concluded to wait and
accompany him.

August 9th, 1834.   We have accounts of a new revolution in Mexico.   It seems that President Santa Anna
and the Congress have disagreed.   Almonte tells me
that the president wished to pursue a moderate course,
in reforming the abuses of the church, but that Congress
was desirous of prostrating the priesthood at once.   The
president did not dissolve the Chambers, as it has been
reported, but he declared some of their proceedings un-
constitutional.   The people are generally on the side of
the president, and it is hoped that no great difficulty will
ensue.*

There was some excitement in town to-day, respecting
the object of my present mission.   I was called before
the Alcalde, (though not officially, as they since informed
me,) and required to explain my purposes.   Several
persons, among whom the most conspicuous were R. M.
Williamson, the Alcalde, and Dr. Peebles, talked quite
stoutly : but when they found that my plans were not
exactly what had been represented, all ended cleverly.

Previous to this interview, I was told that a proposition had been made by some one to buy a barrel of *tar*
for me.   Something was said in my favour, by the only
two persons in San Felipe who knew me ; and this probably saved me some trouble.   I gave them all to understand, however, that I was not to be easily intimidated.

11th.   I left San Felipe this morning, it being arranged
that I am to join Almonte hereafter.   In the afternoon I
took a wrong road, the ways being so blind here that
one cannot always see them.   At near sunset I encamped,
20 miles beyond San Felipe.   Soon afterwards a Mexi-

---

*In Lundy's diary of June 25, he mentions a report, the truth of
which he doubted, received at N. Orleans, by letters from Tampico, that "Santa Anna, whose patriotism has been considered of
the most undoubted character, recently pronounced in favour of
the church and army, and is declared an outlaw by the Congress."

can mail carrier arrived, and joined me in my encampment.

12th. After travelling several miles, I reached and crossed Cummings' creek, which is a fine stream. I then went on to the Colorado, at Dewees' ferry, where I crossed it with my baggage, in a canoe, swimming my horse as before. Thence I proceeded two and a half miles down the Colorado, to the ferry of Beeson, and put up with him. Being unwell, I remained at Beeson's ferry, waiting for Col. Almonte. 14th. In the evening I learned that Almonte had crossed the Colorado at Dewees' ferry, where I did, and that he will proceed from there to-morrow.

Aug. 15th. I left Beeson's ferry early, and at about eleven I overtook Almonte. Three Northern Americans form part of our company; one of them is S. H. Jack. Almonte has a companion, and three or four servants. In the afternoon the weather became so hot that we all encamped under some shady live-oaks, near a small fish pond.

16th. On this day, which was cool and rainy, I had an unlucky accident with my horse. He stumbled and fell, with his own head and my leg under his body. After some little time, we were fortunately extricated, without any essential injury to either. In the morning we crossed the river Navidad; and about noon we arrived, quite wet, at the Labaca.* There we put up, to stay till to-morrow, at the house of ——— Daniels. I found myself more unwell at evening.

17th. The weather continued cold and rainy. I discovered, in the morning, that I had all the symptoms of cholera, and resorted immediately to my camphor and laudanum. The disorder was checked; but I continued so unwell as to be confined the whole day. At noon the rest of the company left me, and proceeded on their route. 18th. I was confined the whole of this day, a fever having taken the place of the cholera.

*Or Lavacca, as usually written in English at present.—Ed.

19th. I set out in the morning and having travelled seven miles, stopped to feed my horse. I then became too unwell to go further to-day. The people where I stopped, had just fled from Gonzales, expecting the cholera at that place. They did not invite me into their cabin : so I pitched my tent at a short distance, and did as well as I could. At night, however, they made me a little coffee.

20th. Being nearly recovered, I went on eighteen miles to Gonzales, where I again overtook Almonte and his company.

21st. Being too unwell to proceed, the company left me, and I remained ill at Gonzales for six days.

27th. I started in company with a Mexican, who arrived at Gonzales, from Bexar, yesterday, and who returns to-day. Between Gonzales and San Antonio de Bexar, I passed over the same ground as in my journey of last year. I was quite ill, but made out to travel, so that we reached Bexar, at noon on the 29th.

Bexar had truly the appearance of a " deserted village," most of the inhabitants having fled some time before, on account of the cholera. They had now begun to return however, the pestilence having abated.

I found Col. Almonte at Bexar, and paid him a visit in the afternoon.

30th. I met to-day, Dr. Amos Pollard, lately of New York, but now of Columbia, Texas, near San Felipe. He is a decided friend of our cause.

We had news to-day, that some difficulties which arose a while since, between Monclova and Saltillo, as to which place should be the seat of Government, and which difficulties it was feared would end in bloodshed, are now amicably settled, and things will go on precisely as before.

I remained at Bexar six days, during which time I was ill, more or less, with symptoms of cholera.

September 4th, 1834. Almonte and his companions left Bexar before me, this morning, I having been disappointed by a man who had promised to procure me another horse, in exchange for my pony which was somewhat fatigued. After waiting in vain, for an hour and a half, I took the pony and went ahead. At noon I passed Almonte and his servants, while they were stopped at a small stream to take refreshment: I however joined the rest of his company, and went on with them.

At near sunset we reached the Madina river, crossed it, and encamped on the west side. The Madina is a beautiful stream, with clear water, a rapid current, a hard pebbly bed, and moderately high banks. The land in the vicinity, is a rich dark loam, in some parts gravelly and pebbly, in others entirely clear of stone, and plentifully timbered with trees of a variety of kinds. This is a delightful section of country, and an advantageous one for settlers.

5th. Before starting this morning, we killed a fine deer and a turkey, near our camp. When Almonte and his servants came up, we all went on together. The country through which we passed in the afternoon, was quite destitute of water.

6th. We travelled this morning from 7 till 11 o'clock, before finding water. We then came to a reservoir or small lake, where we stopped to refresh. After sun-set, we reached the Rio Frio, * (cold river,) and encamped near it.

7th. We travelled to-day about 21 miles, and came to the Rio Leonidas, where we encamped. This river is not designated on the maps.

8th. We went on 24 miles, at the end of which we reached and crossed the river Nueces, and encamped on the western side. This river, which is a beautiful stream, was so full that our horses could hardly cross without swimming.

9th. After travelling during the day, we encamped at night on the same beautiful plain near which I encamped last year. 10th. We proceeded over the im-

*Lundy states in his journal, that this river is the same which he had called the San Miguel in his corrected notes of the preceding summer.

mense plain, upon which there is no water to be found, and having passed it, reached the river Bravo, opposite the village of Rio Grande.* On crossing the river, I found my friend, the deputy Lombrano, in the village, and took coffee with him.

11th. We left Rio Grande for Monclova, taking what is called the middle road, which runs more to the south-east than that which I travelled last year, and does not go through Santa Rosa. Our *soi-disant* friends, Gray-son and Jack, now left us, and took the eastern road to Monclova, which is the shortest, but is very little in-habited, and very barren of water. These men are bit-ter enemies of the Mexicans.†

In the afternoon, having passed through the village of Gigedo, we came to a large hacienda, owned by Don Francisco Madero a Mexican gentlemen of well known hospitality, where we put up for the night.

12th. Our company, having found such comfortable quarters and generous entertainers, concluded to rest till to morrow. We spent the day very agreeably. Our host, Madero, owns several thousand sheep and goats. He sold last year, sugar produced on his estate, to the amount of one thousand dollars.

I should have mentioned before, that the name of Col. Almonte's particular companion, is Edward Grit-ten. He is an Englishman by birth, but has long re-sided in Mexico. His manners are urbane, and he is ap-parently of an amiable disposition.

13th. This forenoon we ascended a considerable moun-tain, on the top of which we found water, and stopped there to rest a while. We then descended into a plain, and encamped at night in the middle of it, having travel-led 24 miles during the day, and found no water since we left the mountain.

---

*Called, on the maps, the "Presidio del Rio Grande."

†Some of the Texans alleged that Almonte was a spy; and it was supposed that Grayson and Jack escorted him to the Rio Grande, for the purpose of watching or restraining his move-ments.—Ed.

14th. After travelling fourteen miles, we came to the river Sabinas, a beautiful stream, three or four rods wide, with a very rapid current, and so deep now as nearly to float a horse in crossing. Here we stopped some time, for rest, refreshment, and bathing. Then proceeding until our day's journey amounted to thirty miles, we encamped for the night at a *ranche*, where we could get nothing but goats' milk. Of this they gave us as much as we wished, and would accept no pay for it.

15th. Our journey to-day was 25 miles, resting at noon and encamping at night by small reservoirs of water. 16th. At noon to-day we took our rest at the *hacienda*, upon which is the warm spring mentioned in my former journal. At evening, having gone 30 miles, we encamped on the border of the Salado river, at the upper part of it, almost in sight of Monclova. 17th. Our company separated this morning, Almonte and companion going on early, and others being detained by the straying of their horses. I went on by myself, the heat being so excessive, that my horse almost gave out, and I found it necessary to rest from 11 till 4 o'clock, at a ranche. It was not till dusk that I arrived at Monclova.

CHAPTER XVI.

Lundy's stay at Monclova on his second visit, and his journey thence to Matamoras, by way of Alcantro, Comargo and Reinòso.

September 18th, 1834. My first step on the morning after my arrival at Monclova, was to call on my old friend Blackaller, in order to ascertain what he had done in pursuance of our agreement that he should apply for two grants of land, on my behalf. I learned from him, to my great surprise and extreme mortification, that he had failed in his efforts to obtain the land. He stated that he had presented a petition to the governor, who was about to issue the grants, when he received advices from the Legislature, that they were about enacting a new law prohibiting the further granting of lands in any part of the state, and requiring him forthwith to cease from issuing any such grants.

Thus, after all my hardships and perils, I am completely baffled in my attempts to establish colonies in Texas. But my labour will not, I hope, be wholly in vain. If I do not profit much myself, others who are grieved, persecuted, wounded and sore, may obtain the opportunity to do so, through my exertions, and this will afford me a fund of consolation, fully equivalent to wealth.

In the afternnon I called upon Santiago del Valle, and received, through him, a letter from President Santa Anna,* acknowledging the receipt of the portrait of Washington, which I sent him last winter.

20th. It appears from the accounts we have, that the political atmosphere in this part of the country, is very unsettled. The governor of Coahuila and Texas has resigned his office, and another has been temporarily appointed. The elections for a new Legislature are going on, however, throughout the State; and some persons hope for a better state of things on the assembling of that body.

In the evening I had a long conversation with Col. Almonte. He tells me that all is now quiet in the interior. The "plan of Cuërnavacca," being the same which Santa Anna recently adopted, and which has been called

---

*The following is a translation of the letter here referred to:

MANGA DE CLAVO, February 20th, 1834.

Senor Don Benjamin Lundy:

Dear Sir,—Your very polite letter of the 8th of January last, informs me to my great satisfaction, that you have had the goodness to deposit in the mail the portrait of the celebrated republican, Senor Geo. Washington, with the intention of its coming to me as a relic. I have received it with the greatest satisfaction, and I return you my best thanks for so distinguished a favour, which I shall know how to appreciate, as fully as the illustrious personage that it represents deserves, and whose exalted virtues I would that it were possible for me to imitate ! This opportune occasion affords me the honour of submitting myself to your orders, as a most attentive friend, S. S. L. B. S. M.

ANTONIO LOPEZ SANTA ANNA.

a *middle course*, appears to be very generally agreed to.* By this *"plan,"* the reforms in the church establishment will not go on quite so fast as some desire, and the severity of the punishment intended for refractory priests, is, in some degree, mitigated. In short, the work of reform is to proceed, as fast as the increasing intelligence of the mass of the people will prepare them for it.

The colonel also assures me, that the Mexican government will cause its laws in regard to slavery to be respected. The *"insurgents"*† in the colonies will be curbed, and will find out, as soon as the government is fairly settled, a little more of what Mexican power really is ; and then the laws which they now trample upon will be enforced. Among these laws, Mexico has one similar to that of England, relative to fugitives from slavery. No person from a foreign country will be permitted to touch a slave who escapes and takes refuge in Mexico.

It appears that the general government has not yet done with Austin. A report prevailed here a few days since, that he had escaped, but it is not confirmed nor credited now, as he was still in confinement at the latest dates from the city of Mexico. In the mean time, our late fellow travellers, Grayson and Jack, are going on to Mexico, to present a remonstrance from a little knot

---

* I have been unable to find "the plan of Cuernavacca," in the newspapers, or in any of the works on Mexico, though it is referred to in them. Reference to it may be found in the National Intelligencer of August 26th, and September 6th, 1834, and in Niles' Register of July, 1835, (vol. 48, p. 342.) This plan was the work of a body of insurgents, who met at Cuernavacca, and undertook to change the constitution and laws, in defiance of the authority of Congress. It was the commencement of a series of revolutions, extending down to 1834, sanctioned by Santa Anna, and which, instead of the reforms that Almonte spoke of, resulted in the destruction, step by step, of popular liberty, and in the restoration of the dominion of religious intolerance. Santa Anna has recently, (1846) in a public address, acknowledged that these measures were erroneous, and in defiance of the popular will.—Ed.

† The Texans.—Ed.

of politicians at San Felipe and Brazoria, against Austin's imprisonment.

22d. Taking a walk down town, this morning, I accidentally saw the Texan delegate, Oliver H. Jones, and also the noted Bowie.* They seemed to know something of my public labours; but nothing very particular was said in our conversation.

A hint was given me to-day, that a party is forming here to discourage my undertaking. The present acting government is said to be against me. I do not credit these rumours, further than to think that two or three Northern American slaveites, now here, may compose such a " party."

23d. I had some further interesting conversation with Col. Almonte, in which we agreed to correspond together, and he gave me his address. He tells me that I can obtain land in Tamaulipas, without going to Victoria, the capital of that State. I hope, therefore, to arrange the business at Matamoras, unless I may conclude to do something further than to apply for land for myself in Tamaulipas. Everything relative to that matter is now involved in uncertainty, and depends on circumstances.

In the evening, I saw my old friend Padilla, at his office. He offered to give me any assistance that I may want while here, in the way of information, &c. 24th. I employed myself in examining papers, and in making a list of interrogatories to Padilla, with a view to obtain some important information.

25th. I had another long conversation with Col. Almonte, in which he assured me that if I should apply to the State of Tamaulipas, for a grant of land, he would lend his influence in support of the application.

I found some difficulty to-day in getting a little money from J. Blackaller, on account of a sum which he had engaged to furnish me, he having security by property

---

* Col. Bowie was one of the men who, with Travers, Crockett, &c., perished in 1836, at the celebrated defence of the Alamo, at San Antonio de Bexar. The bowie knife takes its name from him.—ED.

of mine in his hands.   I fear that he is a traitor, not only to myself, but also to the cause in which I am engaged, and to which he professed friendship.

Sept. 26th. The weather here is very warm and dry, there having been no rain for a long time, except a light shower on one evening. The farmers and gardeners are obliged to depend entirely on irrigation.

In company with my friend Padilla, I had this morning a long parting interview with Col. Almonte, who starts in the afternoon for Monterey. We had much friendly conversation together, a portion of which related to public affairs. Padilla is a liberal man, but if the Texan rebels expect to find him a traitor to his country, they will discover their mistake, in due season.

28th. It has been quite rainy, yesterday afternoon, last night and to-day.   As there was not a single person in town who speaks the English language, that I could call a friend or cared to associate with, I remained nearly all day within my lodgings. Just before night, however, I walked out in order to dissipate *ennui*, and recreate my sinews.   On my way, I came to a good looking house, near which an intelligent looking elderly man was standing.   I halted, paid my respects to him, and made some remark respecting his establishment.   He could not understand English, but he invited me in, and after some conversation by signs, showed me the interior of the premises.   There was a store attached to the dwelling house, and in the rear there were spacious yards and gardens.   He had also, in adjacent buildings, an establishment for bolting flour, a large bakery, and a manufactory of soap and pot-ash.   In every department, all things were clean, and snugly and neatly placed.   He had, moreover, a very intelligent looking family about him.   How communicative would this man have been if we could have understood each other.   This little accidental interview, and the occupation of narrating it, have relieved me from the pains of *ennui*, for more than an hour!

30th. I changed my manner of boarding to-day, so as hereafter to cook for myself altogether.

Oct. 1st, 1834. I have an irksome time, with nothing to do. I cannot even see the Secretary of State, to get from him some information that I want, as he is very much engaged. To relieve myself from *ennui,* I went a fishing, in the forenoon, but it being too late in the morning, and the weather too warm, I only got one "glorious nibble."

In the afternoon we received news of the result of the elections in Texas, for three members of the approaching Legislature of Coahuila and Texas. The district of Nacogdoches sends a genuine Mexican, named Grande; the middle district, or Austin's colony, &c., has chosen Stephen F. Austin, now a prisoner at Mexico on a charge of treason; and the District of Bexar has chosen a Mexican, whose name I do not recollect. The "*foreigners*" here, express astonishment at this result. They say that the "foreigners" in Texas have no representation at all!

Oct. 3d. Blackaller being about to start for Santa Rosa, to remain some days, we settled our small accounts. I wished him to procure for me the petition that he had laid before the governor, for the two grants of land; but he said that there would be no likelihood of his obtaining it, if he should make the attempt. I was determined, however, to have something, to vouch for the fact that the application had been made; and I therefore drew up a paper, setting forth the fact of the application, and the causes of its failure, which he signed. In respect to our other business, it is due to him to say, that up to this time he has acted fairly.

I learn that a gentleman named Viesca, a resident of Parras, with whom I had a slight acquaintance last winter, is elected governor of Coahuila and Texas. He is a worthy and influential man.

4th. I paid my respects again to Padilla and Del Valle, accompanied by Blackaller as interpreter, and had much conversation with both of them. Padilla gave me information and explanations, concerning the laws and regulations of the colonies, that I consider highly important.

5th. A north-easterly storm of wind and rain commenced here on the evening of the 3d, and continued
with violence till this morning, and with more moderation through the day.   Such a storm, is very rare in these
parts, and the people are quite unprepared when one
occurs.   It has made great havoc with many of the
mud-walls and mud-roofs.

In the afternoon there was great rejoicing in town,
accompanied by the ringing of bells and the firing of
guns, on account of the election of Governor Viesca,
and of news from Saltillo, that that place had relinquished
its contest with Monclova for the seat of government.
In doing this, Saltillo made a merit of necessity, as all
the rest of the towns in the State had decided against
her pretensions.

7th. My funds having run out, and my friend A. R.
Guild to whom I looked for assistance, not having returned from Saltillo as soon as he was expected, I applied this morning to Blackaller, who was to leave for
Santa Rosa in the afternoon, for some aid, but he did not
hold out the least idea that I could have any more money,
though he has considerable property of mine in his possession, even though I should starve!   Late at night,
after I had spent my last cent for provisions, and was
reading the letters of Junius, to beguile my thoughts
when unable to sleep, I was delighted to see my friend
Guild enter the room.   He had just arrived in town,
most opportunely for me.   Before retiring, he gave me
assurance of help, and I then felt more disposed to sleep.

8th. My friend Guild wishes me to do a job of harness-
work for him, and though I am extremely anxious to
proceed to Matamoras, my present circumstances induce
me to remain here a few days longer.

I had a conversation to-day with R. M Williamson,
of Texas, about purchasing a league of land in Milam's
grant, for which he is the agent.   He says the cost
of a league cannot exceed ninety dollars, and that I can
obtain the land if I wish.

10th. I sold my watch to-day to Guild, and from the

price obtained, repaid to the wife of Blackaller a loan of eight dollars which I had obtained from him. 11th. Guild went to-day to St. Buenaventura, fifteen miles west of Monclova, leaving his store in my charge. I have now my hands full of entrusted business; Blackaller's dwelling house and domestic animals being in my care, while his wife attends his store, in another part of the town. 13th. Guild having returned to the city last evening, I am now quite busy upon his work.

I should have mentioned before, that apples, peaches and quinces, of very good quality, have of late been quite plenty in Monclova. They are sold in the streets and along the side walks, nearly as cheap as in the United States.

15th. Guild informs me that owing to difficulty in procuring trimmings, he can give me but half the work he promised. I shall therefore be badly off for funds to take me to Monclova, yet I am resolved to move in some direction shortly, even if I must, as a last resort, fast, beg or starve.

18th. A. R. Guild left for Saltillo again this morning. As he could not give me all the work he had promised, and he knew the exhausted state of my purse, he tendered me, in a feeling and liberal manner, a present of five dollars, in addition to payment for my work. I accepted it, merely as a loan. As Blackaller has returned from Santa Rosa to-day, I shall now be released from the care of his property.

21st. I left Monclova to-day for Matamoras, mounted on my Cherokee poney, which I had kept, during my stay, at pasture out of town, with a man named Borrero. The price of pasturing is 25 cents per week. The soreness of the poney's feet is not entirely cured, and I know not how I shall get along with him on a rough route.

My road from Monclova was first to the east, and then a little more southwardly. The landscape was highly diversified. On either hand were to be seen enormous mountains, consisting partly of ridges and partly of isolated peaks, and extensive vallies, containing numerous

ranchos.* The road itself, was generally level and
good. In some parts the grass was abundant, in others
extremely scarce. At night I encamped in the open
plain, under a mesquite bush, which sheltered me very
well.

22d. A part of my road to-day was good, and a part
very rocky. I passed through the mountains south-west
of Candela, where the country was awfully rugged, the
water very scarce, and no grass to be found. Three
deer came so near me, and were so tame, that I could
have shot them with a pistol. Towards evening I came
to a very large spring which issued from the foot of a
high mountain, but the water was quite lukewarm. I
then passed on, in hopes to find grass and more water,
before night, but none was to be seen. I had to pass
over a high mountain, at a gap, of which I reached the
summit at dusk, and found there scarcely any grass,
and no water for myself or horse. Indeed there had
been rarely a blade of grass to be seen for the last fifteen
miles. Here we were obliged to encamp, in a place
tremendously wild for sleeping in alone; yet, though I
had a poor supper, and my horse a still poorer, I slept
soundly and pleasantly.

23d. My tent was so wet with dew this morning
that I was not in a great hurry about starting Upon
setting out I proceeded through the mountain, where I
saw some more very tame deer, then over a plain, destitute, like the mountain, of water, till I reached the village of Tlaxcala, at about 11 A. M. I was now in
New Leon, and had crossed the great road leading from
Candela to Monterey. In the afternoon I went on a few
miles further, to the village of *Boca Leones*, which is a
snug place, and quite a considerable town. Passing a
little beyond the village, to a place where grass and corn
fodder was to be had for my poney, I encamped there.

24th. After journeying for some miles eastwardly,
through the plain, I entered what is called the " Gap,"

* Farms.

which is a wide serpentine chasm, between enormously high mountains, the most grand and magnificent perhaps that the new world can produce. The bottom of the "gap" or passage, which is in some places a mile or two wide, is literally covered with small stones. It is a horrible place for horses with bare feet. My pony suffered dreadfully. A smart little river winds through the bottom of the passage, by a gradual descent. Having gotten through the gap before night, I encamped near the little river above mentioned, my horse faring badly, for the night, owing to the scarcity of grass.

25th. In travelling a few miles eastward, I got clear of all the mountains, and passed a large hacienda, where there is a fine church. The land is level and rich, but deficient in grass, and produces little of any thing, without the aid of irrigation. Towards night I came where the grass was abundant and excellent. My road lay near the course of the river, and I once crossed it. There were many ranchos along its borders, as well as vast numbers of horses and cattle. I saw there, a large hollow cypress tree, which must have been some forty feet in circumference, at the distance of one foot above the ground, as it took fourteen lengths of my cane to measure round it. The Mexican palm grows to a larger size here than I have seen any where else. Having travelled about 25 miles, I encamped at evening in a plain, among scattered bushes, where the situation and prospect were most beautiful.

26th. In travelling several miles this morning, I could find no water to make some coffee; but towards 9 o'clock I came across two men, with some stock horses, who had just encamped for breakfast. They resided, as I learned, at one of the distant ranchos, and had been out after their animals. As they had with them a little water, I got some coffee, and joined them in the breakfast encampment. We made about half a pint of coffee answer our purpose, in the scarcity of water. They had some very good cake and cheese, of which I partook at their invitation. They were very sociable and friendly, though we could understand but few *words* that each other said, the deficiency being partly made up by signs. After leaving these hospitable Mexicans, I soon came to a rancho, where I bought a gourd, to supply the place of one of my water bottles which I had accidentally broken; and in going two miles further, I came to a stream, where I put my horse to grass, and made for myself a more abundant quantity of coffee that what had, of neces-sity, sufficed for three persons in the morning. After resting some hours here, I filled my gourd and bottle from the river, and went on till near dark, then encamped. The weather was rainy, but I was well protected by my little tent, except when I went out to attend to my horse, in doing which I got wet, so that the night was uncom-fortable and somewhat sleepless.

27th. The rain continuing till 10 A. M., I did not set out before that hour. Soon after starting, I came to the bed of a considerable stream, flowing from the south-west, the water of which was all taken out to the neigh-bouring ranchos. In going a few miles further, I came to and crossed another stream which was of considera-ble size. I judged it to be one of those before seen, or all of them united. After proceeding thence till near sunset, I took shelter for the night at a rancho.

28th. I set out in the morning, in company with a Mexican and his wife, the woman riding while the man walked. We were soon overtaken by two other Mexi-cans who joined our company, and we all kept along together. About 4 P. M., we suddenly came in sight of a smart looking town, which to my surprise, I was in-formed was *Alcantro*, instead of Camargo, towards which I had supposed myself to be travelling. Since I left Monclova, I had not seen a person who could speak any English, except the word "yes," and this convenient monosyllable had generally been returned, whenever I in-quired if I was in the right road. It now appeared that the river along which I had come from the mountains, was Alcantro creek, and the lesser streams which I had crossed, were its tributaries. On the west side of this

river or creek stands the town of Alcantro, in a pleasant situation, three miles distant from the Rio Bravo
(or Rio Grande.). Its population is about two thousand.
Many of its buildings are quite elegant—in fact the most
so of any that I have seen in Mexico. We stopped at
the town, intending to stay only a short time, but my
company dallied so that we did not get away that night.
As my funds were again becoming low, and I was obliged frequently to buy corn and fodder for my horse, I
encamped in the edge of the town, instead of stopping
at a public house. I could not find, in the place, any
person able to speak the English language.

29th. We, that is to say the four Mexicans and myself,
set out early, on our way to Camargo, and having proceeded some miles to a rancho on the border of the Rio
Bravo, we stopped there to feed our horses. At this
place one of our company staid upon business, and the
others dallied so long that I rode on and left them. I
found the ranchos quite numerous along the river, but
the immense herds of cattle and horses keep the pasture
down, so that grass is exceedingly scarce. Towards
evening, coming to a place where the grass was better
than common, I encamped there for the night.

30th. Having left my horse untied during last night,
to give him a better chance for feeding, I found this morning that he had wandered to a considerable distance.
In hunting him, among the woods, I lost myself: but
soon afterwards I found the horse. At that moment the
sun made a dim appearance through a dense fog, so that
I could know the points of the compass. I immediately
bent my course eastwardly, thinking that I should thus
strike the road, and that when there I could find my encampment. It so happened, perhaps providentially,*
that the course I took brought me directly to the camp
itself, instead of to the road at a distance from it.

I then resumed my journey, and passed several ranchos,

*Lundy's manuscript places the word providentially in a pa-
renthesis, with a note of interrogation, thus: (providentially?)

all on the bank of the Rio Bravo. At one of them I saw Col. Soto, the partner of Egerton, before referred to. He had stopped a moment, last night, at my camp, but we did not then know each other.

About noon I arrived at the San Juan, a fine large stream, and crossed it by a good ferry, to the town of Camargo, which stands on its eastern or lower side.

I went up into the town, and stopped with Don Nicholas Garcia. Camargo is more handsomely situated than Alcantro, but is not so neat a village. Its population, as I judge, is about two thosand.

I left Camargo a little before sunset, and proceeded three miles on my way. I had brought with me a little corn for my horse, and that was all the food he got during the night.

31st. Having set out at day-break, I rode several miles, before I could find any grass. At length, on coming across a little, I put my pony to it for a while, then went on a little distance to a ranch,* where I got him some corn. In the afternoon I found some spots where grass was a little more plenty, and encamped at one of them, feeding my horse during the night, partly with some corn that I had taken care to bring along with me.

November 1st, 1834. As I went forward to-day, the appearance of the country changed very much, and the grass became more abundant. It was evident that there had been more rain than in the country through which I had before passed. The road diverged considerably from the Rio Bravo, and passed over a high stony region. Before sun-set it came again to the river, at the town of Reinosa,† which is handsomely seated on a bank, near the Bravo. Reinosa is about the same size as Camargo. I put up, in the town, with a South Carolinian,

---

*This word is spelled by Lundy, sometimes ranch, sometimes rancho, and sometimes ranche.

†Spelled "Rhinoso," in the manuscript.—ED.

named Johnson, who is married to a Mexican lady, and carries on the business of a carpenter.

2d. As my horse was much fatigued, and I had found two intelligent persons in Reinosa who could speak English, I determined to remain over to-day, and make inquiries concerning the country, &c.

There are rumors here, that the Mexican authorities have seized, or captured at sea, two United States vessels : that three thousand United States troops have marched into Texas : and that troops are enlisting at Monterey to fight against Santa Anna : but all these rumors want confirmation.

In reference to this part of the country, I will here remark, that in passing from the mountainous region of this state, (New Leon,) towards the Rio Bravo and the sea coast, the land becomes much better timbered, and is in many parts quite level. The soil is generally rich, but in some places it is slightly mixed with sand. Where the land is rolling, the eminences are full of limestone, some of which is visible, and some is loose and broken into small pieces or pebbles. In fact, a large portion of the country may be denominated an immense bed of limestone.

The wood is generally of mesquite, which, as we proceed southwardly, towards the sea coast, grows large and is very plenty. There are various species of thorn, all over the country. There is also, in the upper parts of the country, a bush which in the lower region grows to the size of a tree, and which is called by the Mexicans, ebony, or rather " *ebano*." It is a deep coloured, and thickly leaved evergreen, and makes a very striking appearance. Its wood becomes black by the effects of age.

Water is scarce in this region, as it is in all level countries, but much Indian corn is nevertheless raised on the bottoms of the Rio Bravo, without the aid of irrigation. The water is carried out of the creeks, in order to fertilize the soil, wherever it can be done conveniently.

Immense numbers of cattle, horses, sheep and goats, are raised in the valley of the Bravo, upon the western side of the river. From Alcantro downwards, the bottoms or alluvions are wide, and the islands numerous. Some views that I had of the river, reminded me of the appearance of the Mississippi above its confluence with the Ohio.

The bottoms, on the Bravo, are in general, either pastured or cultivated with Indian corn. The uplands are altogether devoted to pasturage, except where they can be irrigated. The land generally is exceedingly fertile, and produces largely, when it can have the benefit of water.

About Reinosa, and a little way above it, the rains are more plentiful than further in the interior : and I learn that lower down they are still more abundant than here.

I have become acquainted at Reinosa with Dr. Gilliams of Matamoras, formerly of Philadelphia. He talks of engaging in colonizing within this state, (Tamaulipas,) and intimates that he would like to have my assistance. I may see him again on this subject.

Some gentlemen here, finding that I had a letter from president Santa Anna, have evinced much anxiety to understand what I was doing *with* him, or *for* him. The people are much divided in opinion respecting his policy. Many think, or affect to think, that he aims at monarchy. I yet hope however that they will prove to be mistaken.

Oct. 3d. I left Reinosa in the forenoon, and proceeded toward Matamoras. On the route there was much water standing in ponds, or lagoons. The land is good, and grass is more abundant than further north. At the end of twenty six miles, I encamped for the night.

4th. On my journey to-day, as also during the last two or three days, I have passed a number of shops, where cakes, segars, and muscal or maguey brandy, are kept for sale. I saw also on the road many carts going to Matamoras loaded with lime, and some returning thence, with boards for building. The land is generally level and rich, and the grass, as I progress, becomes more

abundant.   Towards night I came to an immense open
prairie, of which a great portion was without a bush, and
covered with a luxuriant coat of fine long grass, upon
which countless numbers of cattle, horses, &c., were
feeding, as were also vast numbers of wild geese, nearly
as tame as the domestic.   For a long time in the afternoon, I had travelled without finding a single house, the
weather being rainy and the road very slippery.   As the
rain was like to continue, so that if 1 encamped out I
could not kindle a fire with the wet materials that I must
use, I kept on, across the prairie and a few miles beyond
it, until I came, after dark, to a village, where I got a
shed to sleep under, and learned that I was within six
miles of Matamoras. Consequently I had travelled forty
miles, being my greatest day's journey since leaving
Monclova.

5th. After passing over a thinly wooded district of
country, and seeing some prairies to the right hand, I arrived at Matamoras, at 10 o'clock in the forenoon.

* * *

CHAPTER XVII.

Stay at Matamoras and its vicinity.

November 5th, 1834.   On my arrival at Matamoras,
I found Mathew Thomas, who referred me to George
Francisco, and from him I learned that Nicholas Drouet,
the mulatto man spoken of in my journal of June 19th,*
resided one mile out of town.   Accompanied by Francisco, I proceeded thither, and presented to Drouet my
letter from his nephew James Richardson. He gave me
an invitation to make my home with him for a while,
which I accepted.

6th. Two young mulatto men, formerly of New Orleans, called at the house of Drouet to-day. One of
them is an engineer on board a steamboat which runs

*See page 113.

from Matamoras to the mouth of the Rio Bravo, the other is a cabinet maker, who carries on his business in Matamoras. They both expressed great aversion to returning to the United States. One of them is about purchasing a large quantity of bricks of Drouet, who has recently burned a fine kiln. Coloured people prosper here in pecuniary matters.

7th. In company with Drouet, I paid a visit to-day, to the General commanding the Mexican forces here. He expressed his warm approbation of my plan of colonization, and encouraged Drouet to introduce his coloured brethren into this country. After this interview, I went to see the steamboat which plies from here to the mouth of the river, and found it to be a snug boat, with three boilers. The river at Matamoras is no wider than at many places higher up. The current is rapid, and the water of a pale reddish hue.

Nov. 9th. The weather is soft and damp, it being now the " rainy season " of this region. Drouet is busy in gardening, which seems singular in the month of November. He has many fine cabbage plants and young radishes, the latter of which he is setting out. They average six inches long and three quarters of an inch thick, though it is but three weeks since the seed was sown. Frost is not looked for here before the last of December, if it comes at all.

In the afternoon we had a respectable meeting of coloured people, at Drouet's house. They warmly approved of my plans for colonizing, and assured me that pecuniary assistance should be given if found necessary.

Dr. Gilliams has promised me a copy of the colonization law of this state, (Tamaulipas,) which I have not yet seen. I am resolved not to leave the country, if I can help it, until something to the purpose is accomplished.

10th. After an ineffectual search of several days, I this day engaged a house to work in, at harness making. I soon found, however, that it was in such bad condition that I must look for another. Dr. Gilliams has given me a job at repairing harness. He had some time ago prevailed on a man from New York, who professed to know something of the saddler's trade, to open a shop here: but he soon found that he was no workman. I called to see this man, who spoke very discouragingly, yet he did not shake my resolution to make a trial of the business. A wholesale merchant named John Stryker, who came from New Jersey, has interested himself in procuring me a suitable situation.

11th. I cannot get a house at as low a rent as I wish. None is to be had for less than from eight to ten dollars per month.

12th. I succeeded at last this morning in obtaining a suitable house, at nine dollars per month, in a part of the town which is said to be the best for mechanical business. I have already nearly a month's work engaged, in fitting up saddles, harness and carriages.

From the Vermont Chronicle of Oct. 4th, which I saw this morning, I find that the coloured school of Prudence Crandall, at Canterbury, Connecticut, has been broken up by a mob! This in the boasted "land of steady habits!" Is it the steady habit of New England to war against weak and defenceless, though pious and philanthropic woman?

I was cured to-day of an attack of dysentery, by taking camphor and laudanum, which remedies I believe are without parallel for the cure of this and similar complaints.

13th. Having got my bench made, I went to work to-day in right good earnest. I had another application to do work. Thus I am in hopes to *live*, here, till I am ready to remove elsewhere. Dr. Gilliams has advanced me three dollars, and I have commenced boarding myself in my own hired house.

15th. There are rumours here that a large Mexican force is on the way to Texas. I am too busy to listen much to the town talk.

16th. Another meeting of the coloured people was held at N. Drouet's house to-day. They adopted resolutions favourable to the emigration to Mexico, of their brethren in the United States.

I have made some acquaintance with Henry White, a respectable and very intelligent coloured gentleman from Philadelphia, who now resides at Brazos Santiago, a port near the mouth of the Rio Bravo.

17th. I obtained to-day a translation of the colonization law of Tamaulipas. It is far more favourable to my enterprise than I expected.

A ta ball here a few evenings since, some young black men were present, as well as some white clerks to our northern merchants. One of these clerks called the black men " d—d niggers," and said that they ought not to be admitted. He was promptly taken to task for his insolence, by one of the black men, and a fight ensued, in which the clerk was knocked down and considerably hurt, by falling, as it is supposed, on the sword of a cane which he had in his hand. Both parties were taken into custody by the city authorities, and put in prison, where they still remain.

22d. For some days past I have been busy in my shop, with nothing of importance to record. To-day I saw one of the colonists of Dr. Beale's grant, who with two others, had left the settlement and come down the Rio Bravo in a flat boat. They had to lift the boat over some shoals in the river, but the circumstance of their getting along at all is important in reference to the value of the river as a channel of intercommunication.

30th. This forenoon I called upon the Consul of the United States at Matamoras, and showed him my credentials. He seemed disposed to be friendly with me.

In the afternoon I called by invitation at the house of Henry Powell, a very intelligent and respectable coloured man, who migrated hither from Louisiana. He takes a deep interest in my enterprise, and will join as a settler, immediately, when I commence a colony.

Dec. 1st, 1834. The flowers, the green leaves, and the soft spring-like weather, seem to challenge the veracity of the almanac, which proclaims this to be the first

day of winter. Winter—and I am still here at Matamoras, feeling like a fish out of water. I have no heart
to work in my shop; for I am conscious that I ought to be
doing something else. I must submit, however, to *cir-
cumstantial* fate, and cherish the virtues of patience and
perseverance.

2d. It was rumored yesterday, that Texas had declared war against Mexico, and to-day, as an offset, it
is reported, that Gen. Bustamente is marching against
Texas, at the head of 4000 troops.

4th. I called upon George Fisher, now a resident
here. His demeanor was extremely forbidding. He
informed me that he would attend to any thing of a business nature, if the object were expressed on paper, but
that he had no time for conversation! I suppose the
aristocrat wanted a letter of introduction, but he will
get none from me. It is no wonder that he made himself unpopular in Texas.

I do not find one foreign white man here, except a
cooper named Morris, that is as friendly as he ought to
be to the Mexicans. The sole object of the foreigners
in general, who come to this place, is to make money;
and they indulge in all the unholy prejudices against people of colour, which they brought with them, or have
contracted from their associates here.

5th. I changed my residence to-day, and took board
with Henry Powell, the respectable coloured man before spoken of. He kindly furnishes me, upon his own
offer, with the use of a very neat and convenient room,
free of rent. I am to pay, for board, sixty-two and a
half cents per day, or $4.37½ per week, which is more
than it cost me to board myself; but my total expen-
diture, which I found too burdensome, will be diminished.

7th. I have formed some acquaintance with a native
of Vermont, who resides here, named Gilman Smith.
He appears to be a decided anti-slavite, in principle and
in practice. Upon learning who I was, he made me a
small present in money. He also loaned me files of the
Vermont Chronicle and New York Observer, from which

I learned a little more of the proceedings of our friends and their opponents, in the United States, and how the noble work goes bravely on.

In the afternoon my friend Powell insisted on my going with him to a circus, which a company has opened here. There were, as I judged, over two thousand persons present. Some of the performances were good; and everything was very much in the Mexican style.

9th. G. Smith has furnished me with a late number of the New York Observer, which contains James G. Birney's letter to the Presbyterian Church, on the subject of slavery. Birney has embraced genuine anti-slavery principles. The seed sown in Kentucky has germinated and grown, and it will soon produce fruit.

10th. I called to-day upon a translator, a native of New York, who seems quite friendly to my enterprise, and engaged him to translate for me a communication to the governor, and also to prepare a formal petition for a grant of land.

12th. This is a great holiday among the Mexicans, being the anniversary of the birth of a Mexican girl, a long time ago, who dreamed that she saw a ghost, or something of the sort, and was consequently *sainted.* As I did not go out, I saw nothing of the parading.

13th. The last four or five days have been cold, cloudy and uncomfortable, with the wind at the North, the weather being of that description which seamen would call a real "*norther.*" But this morning it became moderate, and in the afternoon fair and pleasant.

14th. I went for half an hour to see the proceedings at an election for the office of Alcalde, which took place to-day. The voting was done *viva voce;* and every thing was very regular and orderly.

In the evening I went to see a *fandango.* Several hundred persons, mostly of the lower classes, but many of them well dressed, had met in a spacious yard, and were dancing by moonlight. It was very much like the Haytian fandangos.

Dec. 15th. The weather is such as belongs to what,

in New Jersey, we would call a most delightful May-day.

It is rumoured that the governor of this State (Tamaulipas) is about to come on a visit to Matamoras. If he should do so, it would save me the expense of a journey to Victoria, the seat of government, for the purpose of presenting to him my application for land. I have therefore concluded to wait here awhile.

16th. The soft and delightful spring-like weather still continues. All industrious people, and especially the carpenters, bricklayers and plasterers, are as busy as bees.

It is reported to-day, that a great change is about to be made in the holders of civil office, and that a general sweep will be made of those under the governor's appointment. Some of them here are a little fractious. It is also reported that Gen. Mexia has placed himself at the head of the Texan revolutionists, and intends hostile measures against the Mexican government.

18th. The mail of last night brought intelligence that the governor will not come on here himself, but will send some troops to compel the refractory to obedience. I must therefore now prepare to visit Victoria.

21st. The persons composing the municipal authorities of Matamoras, have been sent off prisoners to Victoria, to take their trial, for refusing to act with the new political chief, recently appointed by the governor.

Friend Powell gives me this evening, strong hopes of obtaining a small loan, to enable me speedily to visit the governor at Victoria.

22d. A young coloured man named Smith, formerly of Hatborough, Pennsylvania, called on me this evening, and presented me with five dollars. I shall not forget him.

Dec. 23d. Vegetation in this vicinity continues to go on finely. In the gardens one may see very pretty lettuce, cabbages and onions, and in the lots beautiful looking corn, waist high. There has been, as yet, nothing like frost here.

24th. My coloured friends have agreed to furnish me

a loan of twenty dollars, to enable me to proceed immediately to Victoria. I intend going, as soon as some
work that I have promised is finished.

25th. This being Christmas day, the shops and stores
are shut. The *administradore* (collector of the revenue)
called on me and offered me a good job of work that
will occupy three days. When that is done, I hope to
go south, to Victoria, immediately.

27th. I fear that Nicholas Drouet will not do much
in the way of colonization, and such is the impression of
his coloured friends, as he appears to have been unfortunate in his speculations. Hence I shall not wait for
his co-operation.

29th. Last evening, two genteel young black men
stopped at one of the most dashing hotels in the city,
which is kept by an Irishman, and called for something
to drink. The bar-keeper informed them, that although
they kept a public house, they did not keep it for negroes. To-day, the young men complained to the Alcalde,
and although that officer is suspected of being deeply
bribed by the foreigners residing here, yet he fined the
landlord ten dollars, for the insolence of his bar keeper.

31st. A paper was loaned me to-day, by my friend
Gilman Smith, which contains the manifesto of James
G. Birney, issued on his secession from the Colonization Society. It is a noble document. O, how the
leaven is working!

January 1st, 1835. New Years day, and I am still
here! I had a hard ride to-day, on an unsuccessful
search for my horse, which was left with Drouet, and by
him suffered to escape, together with one of his own.
This, however, will not prevent me from prosecuting my
journey to Victoria.

2d. Drouet desires me to wait, for him to accompany
me to Victoria, after he has arranged his difficulties, but
I shall go on soon, whether alone or not. 3d. It is again
rumoured that the governor is coming here. A day or
two will test the truth of the rumour.

4th. This is the forty-sixth anniversary of my birth.

I could scarcely believe it, were it not a matter of incontrovertible record, as I feel so young, and the time I have lived seems so short.

6th. The report of the intended visit of the governor to this place appears to be confirmed to-day.

8th. Drouet paid me a visit, and showed me some papers to-day. He appears so selfish, that I fear I can do nothing with him.

This day commences another week, and I have as yet effected nothing here. How swiftly does time pass away, and how slowly do I improve it!

Jan. 11th. The weather continues moist and spring-like. As yet, there has not been a semblance of frost, except in a few particular places, and there it was very light. The gardens exhibit an abundance of green vegetables, where they have been attended to; and, in the fields, young cane, Indian corn, and flowering plants are growing beautifully.

This forenoon I took a walk a mile out of town, in company with my friend G. Smith, to see a gentleman from Vermont, named Richard Pearce, who has been in this country several years, and who, a few days since, invited me to a visit, and an acquaintance with him. I found him a warm advocate of universal emancipation, and disposed to join me cordially, in the plan of making experiments to show the value of free labour. He has been a planter himself, and has full confidence in the success of my plan. We spent the day with him and his family, and had a great deal of interesting conversation.

12th. I had the satisfaction, this morning, of seeing my horse again. After several weeks absence, he had been found and brought in, by a Mexican. He has fattened surprisingly. Although it was almost mid-winter, yet he stood in no need of hay or grain.

The weather to-day is delightful for all kinds of outdoor work, and there are fine roasting-ears of Indian corn, in the market.

14th. There were fresh reports to-day of the governor's near approach, which I hope may prove correct.

In the evening I saw Richard Pearce again. He is decidedly in favour of an experiment with the labour of free people of colour, on a sugar plantation, as soon as possible.

17th. I have been of late just as busy with work as a man can possibly be, so much so that I have hardly time to say it. As I worked during the whole of last night, I feel somewhat stupid to-day.

18th. This afternoon, G. Smith and myself paid another visit to our friend Richard Pearce, who translated for me, into Spanish, my certificate from the Acting Committee of the American Convention for the abolition of slavery. He was very communicative, and gave me much valuable information, on the subject of my enterprise. It appears that he is quite a literary and scientific man, as well as a man of business. He graduated in an Eastern College, and was afterwards the principal of an Academy. Since his residence here, he received, in 1832, from the President of the United States, the appointment of Consul for this port. This appointment was afterwards revoked, on account of his party-politics, as it is supposed.

I find that my friends Pearce and Smith are quite exempt from a general vice of the emigrants from the United States who reside here, namely that of profane swearing. This vice is so habitual, with most of them, that it is common for the Mexicans to designate a Northern American, by applying to him an epithet consisting of the noted oath, peculiar to a portion of the Anglo-Saxon race.

We staid at supper with friend Pearce, when his amiable lady placed before us some excellent fried bacon, butter, and choice pumpkin-pie, all the production of their own farm.

19th. It appears from a Victoria newspaper that a certain Dutchman, a Baron Rakinitz, has applied for, and probably obtained a grant of the land lying all along the river Nueces, and extending thirty miles into the interior. This is the best part of the very tract that I was about to apply for. Thus, while I am compelled by unfortunate adventitious circumstanses to wait here, one European after another steps in, and takes up the land that I want. I will see the governor shortly, if he is to be found in the republic.

21st. It is a year to-day since I left Monclova for the United States, to obtain funds. When, alas! shall I be able to return thither?

23d. I saw to-day the amphibious animal called the armadillo. It is about the size of a muskrat, with a shell and skin resembling in texture those of the alligator, and having wreaths or seams, like those of the rhinoceros, around its body, from the head to the end of the tail. It is a pretty creature, and wonderfully expert at burrowing. It appears that the people of Reinoso have driven off some government soldiers that were stationed at that place. There are many conjectures as to the probable consequence of this step. The troops are now here; and some think they were sent down this way at the instigation of the governor of this state.

Drouet wishes me to postpone awhile my journey to Victoria, lest *another* revolution may be at hand. I tell him, however, that revolution or no revolution, I will not wait a day after I get ready to start. He fears that we may be apprehended for Spaniards: but I am prepared to obviate that, so far as relates to myself. My purse, however, is so meagre, that I may on that account be compelled to wait a few days longer.

24th. We hear nothing, as yet, of the arrival of the governor. I now find there will be some difficulty in procuring the small amount of funds necessary, in addition to what I have, to enable me to proceed to Victoria. But I am strongly urged to do a job of work which will probably place a sufficient sum in my hands. Moreover, by waiting a few days, I can have the company of a good interpreter, on my journey. Hence I have no alternative, but to submit as patiently as possible to this wearisome detention.

26th. A horrible event occurred this evening. In the

course of the day a journeyman in the employ of a French tailor, took, without leave, a pitcher full of water from the shop of a Spanish barber, a near neighbour to the Frenchman. Though this was but a common sort of occurrence here, the Spaniard was highly incensed, and angry words passed between him and the Frenchman, in which the life of the latter was threatened. After dark the Spaniard followed up his threat, by attacking the Frenchman on the pavement, in front of his shop, with a bludgeon and some sharp instrument; and before the people could interfere, he had inflicted upon him several mortal wounds. The wounded man survived but a short time. The murderer was arrested and sent to prison.

27th. There was a good deal of stir to-day, on account of last night's murder, but it did not prevent the commission of a similar offence. This afternoon two Mexicans having quarrelled, one of them threw a brickbat at the other, upon which the latter immediately ran up to him and stabbed him through the heart. I saw the corpse carried in a blanket, along the street.

29th. It is rumored that another murder was committed to-day, but I have not learned the particulars, having been hard at work all day, though somewhat unwell. I have now as much business on hand as I can possibly do, before the time when I *must* set out for Victoria. It has now become almost certain that the governor will not be here soon.

January 30th. Last night was the coldest we have had this winter. There was a pretty smart frost, which is said by some to be the first of the present season. I had seen none before, in more than twelve months. There was also, this morning, a little ice on the small puddles round about. But this weather has left many green plants, shrubs and trees, in all the pride and beauty of bloom and foliage. Perhaps even the milk of the young corn-ears has not been curdled by it.

February 2d, 1835.—Having worked all last night, I felt somewhat stupid to-day. In the evening I had the great satisfaction of learning that the governor had just arrived in town. I now hope that, after all, my journey to Victoria may be dispensed with.

4th. The report of the governor's arrival has proved to be unfounded. It is confidently asserted, however, by those in official stations, that he will be here soon. If I do not learn by the mail, which will come in a day or two, of his being on the way, I shall quickly be on the move myself.

Yesterday was the coldest day, and last night the coldest night we have had here this winter. The ice formed as thick as a dollar, on the still waters of some small puddles. But as the wind kept up during the night, there was little or no hoar frost to injure even the most tender vegetables.

5th. It is rumoured to-day that another *revolution* has been set on foot in the south. In this age of revolutions, rumours, &c., there is no knowing what to believe on the first reception of a report of this kind.

It is now fine weather, and beautiful cabbages, lettuce, green corn, &c., are in the markets, and sold along the streets.

7th. To-day I presented my passport to the "political chief," and had it endorsed by him, and completed my other arrangements, in order to set out for Victoria to-morrow.

CHAPTER XVIII.

Journey from Matamoras, by way of San Fernando and Padilla, to Victoria the capital of Tamaulipas, and stay at the latter place.

Feb. 8th, 1835. This morning I paid my friend Richard Pearce a visit, and obtained from him a letter of introduction and recommendation to the government printer at Victoria, whose name is Samuel Bangs. He is a native of Boston, but has resided long in this country, and is said to enjoy, in a high degree, the confidence of the Mexicans.

I also got a handsome letter of introduction to the governor, from the "political chief" at Matamoras. This was obtained through the intercession of the landlord of Powell and myself, a Mexican of good standing, who went unasked, and solicited it.

At 9 A. M. I set out from Matamoras and proceeded to the house of Nicholas Drouet, who concluded to accompany me to Victoria. At 11 we left his house, being escorted, for a few miles, by Henry Powell and another coloured man, named Jeff Hamlin.

The land over which we passed to-day was mostly level, and much of it prairie. What wood there is, is mostly mesquite, but there is considerable thorn, and some prickly pear and Mexican palm. The soil was a dark rich loam, clothed in some parts with an abundance of large coarse grass, in others of a finer kind, affording a luxuriant pasturage, upon which large herds of the finest cattle, together with many horses, were seen feeding.

Many quails, some other fowl, and a few wolves were seen on the route, but game, in general, appeared to be scarce.

After travelling 15 miles, we came to a considerable stream, on the borders of which there were several ranchos in view. The water of the stream was all turned out of its channels for irrigation, &c., except what stood in numerous pools or reservoirs. In some low places we saw large numbers of skeletons of fish, mostly of the gar species. They had run out of the channel during freshets, when those places were inundated, and had perished when the waters subsided.

Having crossed the above mentioned stream, we proceeded two miles beyond it, and there encamped for the night.

Feb. 9th. We started at sunrise, and travelled over a country considerably diversified, and much of it consisting of prairies. There was no wood, except mesquite, thorn and other shrubbery. Grass was plentiful, and immense herds of cattle and horses were feeding upon it. Many of the horses were more than half wild. Much of the grass and shrubbery was quite green, and there were, in spots, many flowers of a variety of kinds.

After passing in view of several ranchos, we came, towards night, to one situated on the bank of what had been a running stream, though the water was now all turned out. At this rancho we got some water for ourselves, but could obtain none for our horses, which had not drank since ten in the morning, though we had passed in sight of a number of small lakes at a distance from the road.

After going three miles further we encamped, having travelled 33 miles during the day.

10th. We went on to-day without finding water for our horses, until the middle of the afternoon, when we were also disappointed of obtaining any. The animals were nearly famished, and as it was 12 or 15 miles further to water on the road, we stopped at the ranch to rest and feed awhile; but they could eat scarcely anything. A cow fell into the well at this ranch, and they cut her to pieces to get her out!

We saw to-day a number of deer, of a species that was quite new to me. They have short horns, little or no tail, and a curious white spot of considerable size on the extreme of the rump. They were very tame, and ran after us a little way. I suppose them to be the animal called the "*gazelle*." We also saw a large number of fine cattle and horses, but not so many as yesterday. The animals have to go several miles from the road for water. The length of our journey to-day was 30 miles.

11th. This morning we found the country on our way first rolling and then hilly. Some small mountains were visible to the south.

At about 10 A. M. we arrived at San Fernando, a poor place, with perhaps 2,000 inhabitants. It is seated on the north side of the San Fernando river, upon a high bluff, at least 150 or 200 feet above low water mark. The front doors of the houses were nearly all closed, and every thing was as still as a Sabbath in Boston, or as any other day of the week in Burlington, N. J. We concluded to spend the day and night at this place. Among the inhabitants we found a Louisiana creole, but though he was engaged in merchandizing, he could give us little or no information of any value.

12th. Having got ready to start from San Fernando at 8 o'clock this morning, as Drouet speaks the Spanish language, I left it to him to ascertain which was the right road. When about starting, I asked him if we were to cross the river at a place where we had previously been to water our horses. He carelessly replied, "yes." I then rode on before, for some half a mile to the place referred to, and there filled my gourd with water from the river, for use on the journey. I then looked back, but could see nothing of Drouet, he having stopped for something on the way. I rode back to see what detained him, but could not find him. Returning to the river I went up and down its bank, but could see him nowhere; and there were several roads diverging in various directions, so that I could not be sure which was the right one.

Having before had some words with Drouet about his remissness in giving me information that I asked for, and having found him possessed of a high idea of his own consequence, and too supercilious to pay the proper attention to others, I now lost all patience with him, and went forthwith and hired a man to go on with me, for one day, as a guide.

I got under way with the guide, between nine and ten o'clock, when I soon found that the road was not the right one which I had supposed to be so, from Drouet's answer to my enquiry. After we had crossed the river, and rode a short distance, we met with Drouet, who had been a mile or two further, and then returned, to look for me. When we met, we came near to having a sharp quarrel. He wished me to let the guide go

back at once. I told him that he should not return a
step, yet a while, for I was determined to have with
me some one that I could depend upon, to show me
the road, the watering places, &c. So I kept the guide
along with us, until Drouet got in a humor to be friendly
again, and then permitted him to return.

The San Fernando river, which we left in the morning, contained not more water than would be sufficient,
in the United States, to give it the name of a large mill-
stream; but it was evident that a great deal flowed in
its channel at times. Its bed is rocky and pebbly, and
abounds in shoals and bars. The water is clear and
pure. The land, for some distance on each side of the
river, is very rolling, and considerably stony and rocky,
much of the rock being limestone. There is no wood
except the mesquite, ebony and thorn, and various kinds
of shrubs, among which the palm-tree and frickly pear,
especially that kind which has a straight stem and is
leafless, are plenty and of large size. In the vallies, the
soil is fertile ; on the hills it is good for nothing, except
for the stone.

During this day's ride, we passed over some rich val-
ies and plains, finding no water until at twenty-five
miles distance from the San Fernando, where we came
to a considerable creek, the water of which was brackish
and had stopped running. After going five miles beyond
this creek, and passing near mountains of considerable
size on our left, and seeing others at a distance, we encamped.

Feb. 13th. A Mexican traveller, who stopped with
us at our encampment last night, went on in our company to-day. The weather was quite warm, as it had
been previously, for the last two or three days. When
we had proceeded twelve miles, we stopped at a large
rancho, where there were two springs beside each other,
the waters of one being fresh, and those of the other
quite brackish ! These waters soon unite, and form a
considerable pool, from which there flows a fine little
stream, bordered with trees of a goodly size.

As we proceeded, the country became hilly. The soil was mostly of a dark rich loam; the mesquite bush was seen everywhere; the ebony was plenty and large, and there was some lignum vitæ, together with a small kind of tree, resembling the *compeche* of the West Indies.

Late in the afternoon we came to the village of *Santander*, or *Ximenes*, as it is now called, which contains a population of about a thousand inhabitants, and has one of the neatest churches that I have seen in Mexico. At the distance of a mile or so, east of Ximenes, there is a large *hacienda*, called "Santa Anna," with elegant buildings upon it, as well as a fine large stream of water, which is conveyed over the hacienda, and into the town of Ximenes, by the aid of a dam, constructed of elegant rough-cast masonry. We went on two leagues beyond Ximenes, making our day's journey thirty-six miles, and then encamped.

The country which we passed to-day, grew more uneven, and was in some parts very stony. The road for a few miles of the distance, was the most stony and rocky that I had ever seen.

Towards noon, we came to a large rancho or hacienda,* situated on the bank of a fine stream called the San Antonio. The bed of this creek is deep, yet it sometimes overflows its banks. On its bottoms or alluvions, in addition to the kinds of wood used in these parts, there is a great deal of large cypress, and some ash and cotton-wood.

After going a few miles beyond the San Antonio, we arrived, in the afternoon, at a decayed village of considerable size, called *Padilla*, which now contains some three or four hundred inhabitants. It is seated on the south-west bank of a considerable river, which is called

---

*The word rancho seems to be employed to designate sometimes a farm and sometimes a farm house or hut: and hacienda to designate sometimes an estate or plantation, and sometimes the mansion house upon an estate.

La Purification, or *Santander*, and is the largest stream that we have seen since leaving Matamoras. Its banks are low, and its waters pure and pebbly. At a few miles beyond Padilla, we encamped, having travelled twenty-seven miles to-day, and reached within one day's journey of Victoria.

15th. Soon after starting this morning, we were over-taken by a Mexican, who was going to a sugar planta-tion at some distance off our road, on the right-hand. Drouet had before told me that we should pass by this plantation, but he did not mention that it was off of the direct road. When we came to where the roads forked, I asked him how far the sugar plantation would be out of our way. He either could not, or would not tell me, but said he would go that way, "any how." I bade him do as pleased, and instantly turned my own horse the other way, while he went on to the plantation. After passing two ranchos, I reached and crossed another smart river, called the Carona, or *Rio de Carona*. On its mar-gin there were an abundance of large cypress trees, to-gether with cottonwood, ash, &c.

Shortly afterwards, I came to another poor village, with a fine church, and about two hundred inhabitants.

The land to-day, was much like that passed over yes-terday, but less stony. On the lower parts there was a great deal of grass, and many fine cattle, horses and sheep. For the last two or three days, we have found the air perfumed by a most aromatic fragrance, emitted from the numerous flowers. We have also noticed a great deal of misletoe, on the trees.

As we approached within a few miles of Victoria, the road became level, or slightly descending, the soil of the richest kind, and the country considerably settled, al-though little else but "stock." (cattle, &c.,) was seen on the way.

The city of Victoria, the capital of Tamaulipas, stands near the foot of the main ridge of those stupendous moun-tains, whose upper parts form the famous table-land of

Mexico. At this city, I arrived before sunset, and there took lodgings with a grocer.

16th. Having last night tied my horse, in a yard destitute of gate or bars, back of the house where I put up, he either broke his rope or some one cut it, and he escaped. This morning I spent two or three hours in a fruitless search for him. I then gave a boy 25 cents to look for him, but he could not find him. I therefore offered a dollar for his recovery, and he was, in consequence, brought back by a young man, in the afternoon.

I am not sure that he was not taken away for the purpose of obtaining a reward for his return. My landlord was of the opinion that some one took him out.

During this afternoon, I called on Samuel Bangs, the Bostonian, who is the government printer at Victoria, and presented to him my letter from Richard Pearce. I found him polite and disposed, in every way, to befriend me. I next waited on the governor, showed him my passport and credentials, and with the aid of an interpreter, named Ambrosio de Apuricio, a native of Cuba, and now a director in a college here, I informed him of the nature of my business with him. He approved highly of my design, and after reading my application, observed that he must consult the Council of State, and would see me again, to-morrow at 4 P. M. I then returned to S. Bangs, and inquired where I could obtain a room, to occupy during my stay in town. He thereupon kindly offered me the use of a comfortable apartment in his printing office, which I accordingly took. He also sent my horse, by one of his boys, into the country, to be taken care of. In the course of conversation, I learned from him that he is a relative of the editor of the Christian Advocate and Journal, a well known periodical of the Methodist Episcopal faith, published in New York.

17th. The city of Victoria, in its position at the base of the high mountains, very much resembles that of Santa Rosa, as described in my former journal. Its inhabitants are nearly all Mexicans. Some of the buildings are neat and commodious, and among them is a college recently established for teaching the various languages. A pretty smart river, which runs by, furnishes water to the city, as well as to numerous ranchos in the vicinity. The orange trees here are larger and more numerous than I have seen in any other place, and are loaded with golden fruit. The summits of the neighboring mountains are mostly adorned with large fine timber.

The latitude of Victoria is 22 deg. 50 min. North. This place was formerly call *Aguallo*, and it is but recently that its name has been changed to Victoria. In the time of Spanish misrule, that despotic spirit which in ancient days erected pyramids and mausoleums] by the labor of an oppressed people, displayed its pride here, by putting up large and spacious walls of hewn stone, for various purposes. Many of these walls are now going to decay, and the materials of some of them are taken for other purposes.

Drouet having reached the city yesterday, called upon the governor this morning, and made his proposals for land, which he says were kindly listened to. He neglected, however, to provide himself, before leaving home, with papers, as well as with everything else that was needful ; and how soon he will accomplish his business no one can well conjecture.

In the afternoon I went myself to pay the governor a second visit, agreeably to his appointment, but he was either too much engaged, or could not get the business arranged with the Council of State. He therefore appointed nine o'clock to-morrow morning for another interview.

18th. This morning I called again upon the governor, according to appointment. He had not yet been able to assemble the members of the Council of State, as one of them had been sick. I had a good deal of conversation with him, in reference to the location of my colony. He appeared still as friendly as at first, to my enterprise. There were with him some other Mexicans of distinction, who having understood the nature of my errand, appeared decidedly favourable to it.

An extra session of the State Legislature of Tamaulipas has been convoked, and the members met here to-day, and organized. I understand that the business for which they are convened, is of a very important and urgent nature; but it is not supposed that they will remain in session many days.

19th. The governor met the legislature to-day, and delivered his message or speech, in person.* Of course, nothing will be done at present, in my business.

The day passing heavily, I walked out of town, and took a view of the surrounding scenery. Of the multitude of orange trees in the vicinity, many are now in full bloom: others have fruit in all its stages of growth. Ripe oranges are sold at twelve and a half cents a dozen. Fig trees are very numerous, and the noble bread-fruit tree is abundant.

20th. It is stated to-day that Santa Anna has again resigned his office of President of the Mexican republic, by reason of the impaired state of his health. The general Congress, which is in session, has refused to accept his resignation, but has permitted him to retire to his estate, for the present. The Vice President Gomez Farias, has been removed, and another person appointed to act in his stead until the period of a new election by the people.† A proposition was before the national Congress, at the last accounts, to separate Texas from Coahuila, and erect it, not into a state, but a territory. How this will take with the political rowdies of Texas, I do not know.

The governor is still too much engaged to attend to my business.

---

*The session was probably held in secret, as Lundy says nothing of the nature of its business. The whole country was then in a ferment, and the time was near at hand when Santa Anna came out openly for the destruction of the State Legislatures.—Ed.

†Gomez Farias, the Vice President, thus removed, was opposed to the schemes of Santa Anna, and favourable to the federal system, and the abridgment of the power and prerogatives of the established clergy.—Ed.

Feb. 21st.   I am still waiting with anxiety upon the governor.   This afternoon I walked out, and found the weather as warm as that of June in New Jersey.   I noticed willow, sycamore, peccan and lime trees, the latter having fruit on them.

22d.   I spent most of this day in the company of my friend Bangs, and his interesting little family.   His wife is a native of lower Virginia, and is a very pleasant and agreeable woman.

23d.   There is nothing done yet in relation to my business.   Friend Bangs is inclined to do something in the way of colonizing, and wishes me to assist him.   It is probable that we shall agree upon terms in relation to it.

24th.   Nothing done in my affairs to-day.   It appears that Drouet put in his petition, in a clumsy way, asking the privilege of introducing only fifty families of settlers. As this request did not require the approval of the Council of State, the governor, as I understand, has had the papers made out, comfortably to the prayer of the petition.   But Drouet now says that there is a mistake in the petition, and that he will try to have it rectified, so as to increase the number of families to two hundred and fifty.

25th.   To-day I handed the governor a note, describing the boundaries of the grant of land, asked for in my petition.   This note was translated without charge, by Apuricio, the interpreter and college director, before mentioned.   Drouet says, this evening, that the governor has signed some colonization papers, which he supposes to be mine ; but I am fearful that he is in error.

26th.   Bangs says that he has presented his petition for permission to colonize two hundred and fifty families, and that the governor agreed at once to grant it. I expect to introduce the families on his behalf, upon this grant.   Drouet has got his papers, without alteration, so that he is authorized to introduce fifty families only.* My application required the sanction of the council, as already stated ; this sanction is said to have been given, and I am told that the papers are nearly ready for me.

Feb. 27th. Yesterday was as warm here as a hot June day north of the Potomac. To-day the wind is northerly. It is cloudy, with signs of snow, and quite cold. As we should think nothing of such weather, at the North, it is quite amusing to see the Mexicans, not only cloaked, blanketed and shivering, but also with their ears tied up, to keep them warm, as they are walking the streets. They have so little cold weather here, that they know hardly any thing about it.

At noon the clouds had dispersed, so that the mountains were visible. Their summits, perhaps 1500 to 2000 feet high, exhibited a sprinkling of snow, which extended a little way down their northern sides. This was the first semblance of good old winter's habiliments, that I had seen for thirteen or fourteen months. The air felt quite chilly in walking the streets, but I could not perceive that the tenderest young leaf, nor even an orange blossom, was injured in the town.

At evening it was more moderate, but I supposed it had been too cold, for people in office to do any business. Perhaps the blood was somewhat congealed in their fingers.

28th. I prepared, to-day, a draught of an agreement between Bangs and myself, relative to my colonizing his grant of land. We are told that both his papers and mine are ready for the governor's signature, but it is still so *cold* that nothing is doing in the offices.

March 1st, 1835. It was cloudy and quite cold this

---

*It was the usage of the Spanish and Mexican governments, to give to the person who should introduce settlers, of the Catholic religion, a quantity of land, for his own emolument, in addition to what was to be occupied by the settlers ; the grant of a certain quantity to be valid, if the specified number of settlers were introduced upon a portion of it, within a limited time.— Ed.

morning, the month of March having somewhat of the *lion-aspect*, in its infancy. Doubtless it will become more lamb-like, as it grows older. In the afternoon, the weather having become clear and pleasant, I walked out with friend Bangs. Some of the peach trees are still in blossom, though they generally commenced blooming early in February. The young leaves of the peccan trees, look, at the present time, much like those of our northern hickory in June. Those of the willow, the sycamore and cottonwood, which is a species of poplar, have attained about half their full size.

Many inquiries have been made respecting the object of my visit here, and most of the Mexicans of distinction, now in Victoria, have ascertained it. They all appear decidedly friendly to my enterprise.

There is, too, more apparent liberality, among the inhabitants of this state, (Tamaulipas,) in regard to religion, than in any other of those parts of Mexico which are settled principally by the natives. Here, they all, with very few exceptions, look to perfectly free toleration in religious matters, almost immediately : and the most intelligent calculate upon the total severance of church and state, at no very distant period.

2d. My funds having again become exhausted, and my friend Bangs having offered some days since, without solicitation, to accommodate me in case of need, I took from him to-day a loan of eight dollars. He went with me to the governor's secretary, by whom I was informed that my papers were in the hands of the governor, who would no doubt despatch them to-day. I called myself, on his excellency, afterwards, but he had so much other business on hand, that he put me off till to-morrow morning, at which time he desired me to call.

In the afternoon, I went on the top of one of the highest houses in town, to view the surrounding prospects, which I found to be very fine. Ranchos and sugar plantations lay in every direction. The cane-fields have at present a very beautiful appearance.

3d. I called on the governor at eight o'clock this

morning, and had a long conversation with him. I find that he and his legal advisers interpret the colonization law in a manner widely different from that of most foreigners and some Mexicans, with whom I have conversed. Conformably to the governor's interpretation, the Council of State consented to let me have a grant of thirty leagues and thirty *labones* of land, on condition that I settle, *on the same land,* two hundred and fifty families : the land to be mine, and I to make such terms as I please with the settlers, either as purchasers, donees, or tenants. But the government will not give to these settlers any other lands, although, to those who come *at their own expense,* and ask for land, it will give what the law specifies. The terms thus extended to me, are the same as those of the recent grant to the Baron Rakinitz, before mentioned. They are so different from what I expected, that I requested time to consider them, and proposed to call again to-morrow, to which the governor assented.

4th. Upon my calling on the governor to-day, he was so busy with the Legislature, that he put me off again till "to-morrow."

5th. This forenoon I went again to the governor, but it was too " frio " (cold) to attend to business. I proposed an intervew at 4 P. M., which was acceded to. I accordingly went at that hour, but it was still too " frio."

6th. Accompanied by S. Bangs, who went as interpreter, I had considerable conversation with the governor to-day. He offered me a grant on the same terms with that of the Baron Rakinitz ; and at my request, gave me a copy of their treaty, to take to my lodgings and examine in detail.

7th. I saw the governor again this forenoon, and proposed to take the land on the terms granted to Baron Rakinitz, with the exception of two articles, one of which stipulated that the government should furnish the settlers with some farming stock on a credit, and the other that the *empresario* (undertaker or contractor) should give satisfactory security for the payment of the price of the said stock, as well as for the performance of the whole contract. The governor assented to the omission of these two articles, and assured me that my business should have prompt despatch.

Drouet has not yet obtained any alteration in the terms of his grant, which specifies no time for the doing of any thing. He wishes me to fulfil his contract for him, but I have informed him that it will not suit me, at which he is very angry, and talks like a man partially insane.

9th. I went this morning to see the governor, but was informed by his secretary that he was unwell. Going again at 11 A. M., I found him in his office. He gave the papers relative to my business, to a messenger, to take to the secretary for completion, and requested me to accompany the messenger. I did so, but the secretary was not at his office, I went again, however, at 3 o'clock, and found him in, but he told me that he could not arrange the business till to-morrow forenoon. So I must pass another sleepless night.

10th. On going to the secretary, I was required to purchase four sheets of stamped paper, on which to copy my contract, and to pay for them the sum of six dollars. I was thus placed under the necessity of borrowing more from friend Bangs, who now furnished me with nine dollars. In the afternoon the papers were signed by the governor and myself, and handed over to me, together with three dollars of what I had paid for the stamped paper, the secretary having over estimated the quantity that would be requisite.

After the business was completed, I showed Drouet my papers. He talked like a fool, or a madman. Bangs, who was present, was more out of patience with him than I was myself.

CHAPTER XIX.

Journey from Victoria (formerly called Aguallo,) to Matamoras; and passage thence to New Orleans.

March 11th, 1835. I took leave, this morning of the governor. As he was busied with the members of the Legislature, which body had just adjourned, I informed him that when he was more at leisure, my friend Bangs would call upon him for instructions as to the mode of procedure in commencing my colony. I then went and took leave also of S. Bangs and his hospitable lady. She insisted on my taking with me a fine roast fowl, some bread and cheese, &c. My gratitude to this worthy family cannot be expressed, much less, I fear, can their hospitality ever be reciprocated. The traveller seldom meets with strangers half so kind.

I started from Victoria for Matamoras, at about 11 A. M. Drouet was in the house from which I set out, until a few minutes before my departure. He then walked out, to avoid bidding me farewell. Poor fellow!

My road was the same on which I had come from Matamoras, until I reached the first village from Victoria. Then I unfortunately took a wrong track, and kept it, passing some fine fields, until I came to a rancho, when I discovered my mistake, got some supper, and some corn for my horse, and then turned back. Before reaching the village again, I encamped for the night.

12th. Having returned to the before named village, I came on thence to Padilla, and some miles this side of it, before encamping. On the way, I saw a fine flock of very wild turkeys, and some geese.

13th. This morning I passed over the very stony piece of road before described, walking myself all the way. Then I took a by-road, in order to pass a large rancho and obtain water for my horse. The cattle on this rancho are watered from a well. Thence I proceeded to Ximenes, and came on ten miles this side of it, to a large rancho called Tinieblo, owned by a Louisiana creole named John Lecture. Here I found that I had again taken a wrong road, and come several miles out of the way. It being late, I spent the night there, but could get but little feed for my horse. There is a fine spring at this rancho, and many more in its vicinity. These springs rise from the foot of a high ridge, along which many ranchos are scattered.

14th. The owner of the rancho kindly sent a man with me five or six miles, to put me in the right road. The land was very rich and beautiful, and immense numbers of horses were grazing on it, but the grass was short. During the day I overtook two foreigners on foot, one of them an Englishman; the other, who was apparently an Irishman, said he was acquainted in New York and Philadelphia. He had sore feet and legs, was out of money, and wished to get to Matamoras to find employment. I told the Englishman that I would give the poor fellow half a dollar to help him along. He replied that he was short of money himself, but he thought he had sufficient to take his comrade through. This nobleness of soul only determined me to give the trifle mentioned, although as I told the Englishman, I had very little " *dinero*," (cash.) The poor Irishman appeared quite thankful for the pittance.

Coming, before sunset, to some fine grass, I encamped, in order to recruit my poney upon it, as he had fared badly last night and to-day.

15th. Starting early this morning, I met at day-light, some travellers, one of whom delivered me a letter from my friend Richard Pearce, at whose house, near Matamoras, I had previously seen the bearer of the letter.

Soon afterwards I passed some muleteers, who had just taken breakfast at the road side. They kindly offered me some bread and roasted meat, which I accepted, as also some water, of which article I was then destitute. The Mexicans are generally kind and hospitable; but they have, like other people, some villains among them. Yesterday, at one of the ranchos where I stopped, all my sugar and part of my cheese was stolen, while I was out of sight of my baggage for a few moments.

At night I reached San Fernando, and put up at the same house as when there before, the inmates all appearing glad to see me.

16th. Just before day I was roused by a light rain, my bed having been made, for the night, down in the yard, back of the house. The wind in the morning was southerly, and brought along with it the ocean spray. Having walked around the town of San Fernando, and found nothing worthy of note, I set off at noon. In the afternoon I was joined at a rancho, by a Mexican traveller, mounted on a large and elegant mule. I kept along with him some distance, but finding that he would ride too fast for my poney, I soon suffered him to go ahead. Before sunset I stopped for the night at a luxuriant piece of grass, in order to give my horse a feast, as he had fared badly, on account of the scarcity of feed, since leaving Victoria.

17th. While I was travelling this forenoon, there came a genuine old fashioned rain, in which I got a thorough soaking. At noon I stopped at the rancho where Drouet and myself had our first quarrel. I now found that when we were there, Drouet had been abominably careless about getting water for our horses, as there was, at the place, a fine well, with a good bucket and trough, where we might have given the poor animals as much as they wanted.

The rain coming on again, while I was at the rancho, and proving to be a real " norther," I concluded to spend the night there. Some course cut grass was furnished my horse, but no corn could be had for him. The Ranchero, [owner, or inhabitant of the rancho] keeps a small store here. Like every Mexican with whom I have conversed, ne approves highly of my project of colonizing a portion of the African race in this country.

18th. Having taken my coffee, and the weather being clear and pleasant, I set out at 7 A. M., and went on to the rancho beside the little lake before described. Here the water was all dried up, except some in a well. Of this, I got some for myself and horse, for which I paid 6¼ cents, and gave the same price for a bowl of soup, with a little boiled beef and a tortilla. In the afternoon, my horse being wearied, I rode on leisurely, and before sunset, encamped, in company with a Mexican traveller, at twenty-five miles distance from Matamoras.

19th. I rode on early with the Mexican six miles to a rancho, where I got for my breakfast some milk and fresh meat, for which I paid nine cents, being the last money that I had. Proceeding thence, as I approached Matamoras the ranchos or small farms* became more numerous. The people were busy in ploughing and planting, as they had been at many places that I passed during the previous days. I said they were *ploughing*; but that was a mistake, for there is little or no ploughing done in this country.† They merely *scratch* and *mangle* the soil in a miserably sorry manner.

At 3 P. M. I arrived at Matamoras, and put up at my old quarters with friend Powell.

20th. I visited Richard Pearce to day, and induced him to undertake the translation of my contract with the government of Tamaulipas.

21st. I received from friend Pearce the translation of the contract; and also got a letter from S. Bangs, containing the governor's answer to the questions I had left. From these answers it appears that I cannot locate my grant of land until I bring on a part of the settlers! This information, which I had not anticipated, will render it necessary for me to hurry home and expedite the migration as fast as possible.

*The reader will here learn the sense in which Lundy used the terms "rancho."—ED.

†The plough still used in Mexico is said to be the same kind which the Romans used two thousand years ago.

24th. To-day I agreed with Powell to keep my horse for the use of him, until my return from the United States.

25th. I proposed to J. Stryker to loan me $70, to be paid at New York on my arrival there. He answered that he had no use for money there, at present, but would try to negotiate the business with some one else in Matamoras. I did a little more work for him today, and engaged some of two other persons.

26th. I learn that three men who lately brought a drove of hogs to this place, from near Gonzales, in Texas, were killed on their way home, by some Indians, between the St. Antonio and Gaudaloupe rivers. One of them, named Kimball, was known to me in Texas, as a worthy man.

27th. Stryker has failed in negotiating my loan, but will make further effort, if I cannot obtain it otherwise.

29th. I was to have had a meeting of the colored people of Matamoras to day, but it did not take place, they being little used here to such things.

30th. After further unsuccessful attempts to negotiate my loan, I went to Richard Pearce, who came to town with me, and we called on J. Butterworth, a merchant from New York. He offered to give ten dollars in aid of my object; and R. Pearce, and a gentleman from the Shetland Islands named Ogilby, undertook to collect some additional sums by way of donation. I then called again on Stryker, who agreed to let me have 35 dollars, upon condition of my paying 50 for him at New York. He promised to furnish me the money *day after to-morrow,* which will be better than to-morrow, for " *to-morrow*" never comes.

31st. J. C. Woods loaned me 30 dollars at 2½ per cent. per month, and Butterworth, who appears to me like a very clever man, gave me the $10 before promised. Ogilby engaged a passage for me to New Orleans, with Capt. Kemp of the schooner Augustin, now lying at the mouth of the Rio Bravo, (Rio Grande,) upon condition of paying " whenever I can." So I am now in hopes of getting off soon.

April 2d, 1835. I took to-day from Stryker the $30, for my bill on Mr. Haydock of New York for $50, as I could do no better, and must have means to travel after I reach New Orleans.

The colored people here, at length, held a meeting this afternoon, and passed some good resolutions, approbatory of my proposed colony.

3d. To-day a priest here has prosecuted two northern Americans, for omitting to kneel when he was passing them with the " host."*

4th. Having procured a passport, and taken leave of my friends at Matamoras, I set out before noon on horseback, for the "*Boca del Rio*" (mouth of the river.) The land that I passed, resembles that above Matamoras, and there are many ranchos on the road. Towards night I came to open prairies, where there were large ponds of very shallow water, but no marshes, the ground being quite firm. During the day, I saw immense numbers of rabbits and water fowl. I encamped about sunset, in a prairie near the river, eighteen miles below Matamoras.

5th. I went on early, and before 9 A. M. reached the mouth of the river, where I found that the captain had arrived before me, and was preparing to get under weigh. Leaving my horse to be returned to Matamo-

---

*Niles' Register of July 4, 1835, vol. 48, page 314, contains the following reference to the above mentioned, or a similar transaction, viz. " Great excitement is said to prevail at Matamoras among the foreigners in consequence of the imprisonment of Messrs. Boyd and Lee, American merchants, and the subsequent harsh treatment they received. The Mercurio of Matamoras, says that a few days before, the parish priest, while conveying the sacraments in the usual cortege, to the house of a sick person, was met by the above named gentlemen, who did not pay to the procession those marks of reverence which are customary. The priest, irritated, appealed to the spectators, ordering them to seize Messrs. Boyd and Lee, and throw them into dungeon, which was done, without the least hesitation on the part of the people, or interference on the part of the magistrates."

ras, I went on board. The steamboat took us in tow;
but the water on the bar, at the river's mouth, was so
shallow that we stuck fast. After some hours' exertion,
we were hauled over the bar, by windlass and anchor,
into deep water ; we then set sail, and were out of sight
of land before night.

9th. For the last three days we have had a strong
head wind, and I have been almost constantly sea-sick.
To-day the wind died away, and left us completely becalmed. An observation was taken, which showed
that we were nearly in the latitude of Tampico, and were
blown far off the coast, so that New Orleans was more
distant, than when we first set sail.

11th. We have had the wind fair, and moderately
strong, for the last two days ; but at noon to-day, we
found, from an observation, that we had not yet got as
far north as the mouth of the Bravo, whence we started;
we were in fact, about midway between that place and
the north-eastern shore of Yucatan.

At dinner to-day, I met with a little curiosity. On
cutting the flesh from the upper joint of a leg of fowl, to
which I had been helped, I found that the bone had
been broken quite off, the ends slipped half an inch past
each other, and that thus lapped, the two pieces had
grown together again, like two pieces of iron, welded
without hammering down. I should not have expected
any bones in the range of animated nature to grow together in that manner.

14th. For the last three days, we have had the wind
mostly fair, but much of the time light and flagging. To-
day it rose, at nine o'clock A. M., dead ahead, and increased to a gale, at 11. At 3, the sea had become
very rough, and broke over the deck frequently : the
vessel rolled and plunged furiously : and the white
foam flew, blearing most awfully the face of old ocean. At
half past three, we found it necessary to tack and steer
to the south-east, instead of on our right course. Before
doing this, the water had become light coloured, indicating our approach to the Louisiana shore ; but we

could find no bottom by soundings. During the afternoon, we saw some drift wood, from the Mississippi
presumably, and many birds. The gale continued a
considerable part of the night.

15th. At sunrise I find the sky clear, the wind changed
to the south-west, and the course of the vessel to the
north east; and the water of light green, or rather drab
colour, but no signs of land yet. At 7 A. M., a great
number of pelicans were flying about us, and land was
discovered, supposed to be the light house àt the south-
west pass of the mouth of the Mississippi. This was truly
a cheering sight! On a nearer approach, the light house
proved to be that on the south point of the pass.
We then changed our course, and entered the river-
water of the Mississippi, which was nearly as white as
the river itself.

At nine A. M., there was a total calm. The birds were
playing around in flocks, both in the air and the water.
The wind was blowing, at a little distance, so near us
that we saw thousands of white-caps foaming and wrang-
ling on the waves, yet not a zephyr kissed our cheeks!
The light-house, above mentioned, was plainly discerni-
ble from the deck; but there we lay, *wabbling* about,
in the most irksome and vexatious manner.

At near 11 A. M., the wind having risen again, we
went on our way, and were soon after boarded by a boat
with three pilots, one of whom staid with us, and the
others left, to board other vessels that were in sight. As
we proceeded we saw a cluster of houses, and, at noon,
the light house on the north-west point of the south-
west pass. At the middle of the afternoon, we doubled
the south point of the pass, the breakers rolling on the
bar most majestically. Soon afterwards, having got
fairly into the Mississippi, and into a safe harbor, and the
weather having become so foggy that we could not see
the light house, our sails were taken down, and our vessel moored at anchor.

April 16th. This morning was the coldest that I have
witnessed for fourteen months past, the wind being high

and northerly, the sky cloudy, and nothing left of the dense fog of yesterday. A number of vessels were lying in the pass, among which were three steam tow-boats. One of these, the "Natchez," came along side at 11, A. M., and took us in tow, in addition to three other vessels which she had in her train already, of which one was a Mexican from Campeachy. We soon after overtook another large schooner under the Mexican flag, and added her to our little fleet.

One of the vessels in our train is from Vera Cruz, and is commanded by a captain that I saw at Aransas-bay, last spring. He informs me that Stephen S. Austin has been released from imprisonment; but being sick, he has not yet left the Mexican capital.

17th. At 9 A. M., we passed Johnson's old sugar plantation, which is the first of note as we ascend the river.

18th. We are now at New Orleans, where we arrived early this morning. Being somewhat short of means to pursue my journey, and finding no one at New Orleans able or willing to assist me, the captain having received half my passage money at Matamoras, has kindly consented to wait for the balance of $18, until I can find means to remit it to New Orleans for him.

Finding, to-day, a steamboat which is to leave for Nashville in some two or three days, I engaged a passage in her, and put my baggage on board.

21st. Early this afternoon, I was informed that my old friend, George Carey, of Cincinnati, was now in this city. As our boat was to leave in the evening, I immediately hunted him up, and we had a short, but very agreeable interview. He was rejoiced to see me, the more so as my friends, according to his account, had come to the conclusion that even if I had not lost my life, it was at any rate all over with my enterprise. This I expected would have been the case, for I was aware that they had not heard a word from me for about ten months.

CHAPTER XX.

April 21st, 1835   Having taken leave of friend Carey, I went on board the steamboat, and at dusk we started from New Orleans to proceed up the Mississippi.

22d. As our boat goes prosperously on her course, I find a number of the deck passengers afflicted with symptoms of cholera. I have taken four of them in hand, and hopes are entertained that they will soon be well. I make no charge for my services, for, not being an authorized practitioner, I am unwilling to suffer the imputation of being a quack.

23d. From the steward of this boat, I have received the melancholy news of the death of my dear friend Thomas Hoge, Esq., of Nashville. Many years since we mutually engaged that, whichever of us survived the other, should publish a biographical notice of him that was first taken hence. This sad duty now devolves on me, quite unexpectedly, as he was much younger than myself. Being unable, at present, to learn the particulars of his disease, I can only mourn the loss of an intimate, valuable, and warmly cherished friend. He took a lively interest in my Mexican scheme, and I expected him to be one of my most efficient coadjutors in promoting it. But alas! "*sic transit gloria mundi,*" may be inscribed on the tomb of every man of enterprise, in all ages of the world ; and the highest hopes are soonest blasted in all the workings of human effort.

30th. For the last week, we have proceeded up the Mississippi, stopping at Natchez, Vicksburg, Montgomery, Memphis, and Randolph, with some detention in discharging freight, &c., and nothing remarkable to narrate. I find that there have been recently many cases of cholera on the river. My patients have all been relieved, except one, whose complaint is dysentery.

An occurrence took place to-day, which I think worthy of notice. One of the deck passengers stole a pencil from another. When detected, the culprit undertook to buy a sort of reprieve, by giving the owner $2, as hush money. The story came, however, to the ears of the captain's mate, who would not suffer the affair to to be hushed so easily. The offender was called out, and a regular trial and conviction took place. He was sentenced' to be put ashore, at some convenient place, and in the mean time was locked up in a complete prison. It is well for commanders of steamboats to be rigid on such occasions, as the property necessarily exposed in them, is so considerable, that villains would throng them, if they could escape with impunity.

May 1st, 1835. At about 2 P. M. we came in sight of the mouth of the Ohio river.

> And now we can see,
> The land of the free.

How beautiful the green shores of Illinois seem to the mind, when contrasted with those of Kentucky and Missouri, from which they are separated by the waters of the majestic Ohio and Mississippi; the realm of liberty on the one hand, and that of slavery on the other.

Proceeding up the Ohio we reached Smithland about midnight, and entered the mouth of the Cumberland river.

2d. We reached Eddysville, fifty miles up the Cumberland, early this morning, and stopped to land freight. There, my funds and provisions being both exhausted, I borrowed a little money of one of my fellow passengers, called Capt. Carter, who resides near Nashville. He is acquainted with Wm. Bryant, and is very friendly to the cause of emancipation. He says he has one slave, who may go free whenever he wishes to leave him; but that he will never sell him at any price. There is also travelling in company with Capt. Carter, a young man who is likewise zealously opposed to slavery, and who is very friendly with me.

3d. We stopped half of this day at Clarksville to land freight. Since the 29th ult. I have been afflicted with the severest cold that I recollect ever having experienced. A cough and affection of the lungs succeeded, which has continued to grow worse ; and to-day I have been confined most of the time to my birth.

4th. NASHVILLE.—We reached Nashville early this morning. The weather was very rainy, and my health no better; but I made out to walk up to town, where I soon met with my friend R. P. Graham. All were glad to see me, as they had received no intelligence from me for a long time, and had concluded that I was not among the living. I took lodgings with friend Graham, and saw Dr. Nye, who kindly got me a physician.

5th. William Bryant visited me to day. The interview was truly affecting. He had given up all hopes of ever seeing me again, thinking that I had certainly lost my life.

G. V. H. Forbes heard that I had arrived, and immediately called to see me. He gave me the first intimation of the bequest made to me by my good old friend Wm. Turpin.* Forbes takes much interest in my situation, and is exceedingly friendly.

6th, 7th and 8th. My disorder now prevents all conversation on my part, and I have a serious time of it. I am frequently visited, however, by my physician, Dr. Jennings, and every possible comfort is administered by friend Graham, and his kind and amiable lady.

9th. I was taken to-day in a carriage by friend Forbes to the banking-house of Yeatman & Woods, to negotiate a draft for $300, on Turpin's executer at New York. 10th. I keep close house, but am somewhat better. Wm. Bryant has spent some hours with me to-day. He informed me that he received about $130 for me since I left Nashville last summer, and paid off with it a part of what I had borrowed ; also that fifty or sixty

* A legacy of fifteen hundred dollars wss left Lundy during his absence, by William Turpin, of New York.—ED.

dollars were received by Thomas Hoge, which, owing to his death, has not been applied to my use, and the persons who have charge of his business profess to know nothing about it!

12th. My health is so far improved that I was able to prepare, to-day, an address, respecting my Mexican plan, for insertion in the "Western Methodist."   16th. My address has been inserted, and our Methodist friends take some interest in my enterprise.   I am now busy in printing the address in handbill form, as also a private letter to my friends, the work having been undertaken by friend Forbes.

June 13th, 1835. From the 16th of May to the present time, I have been detained at Nashville, partly by ill health and partly by business.   During that time, I visited the widow of Thomas Hoge, at Franklin, and obtained the papers which I had left in her husband's care. I also twice visited the family of my friend, Wm. Bryant.

Some coloured people in this vicinity, were lately emancipated by the will of ———— Donnelson, the elder brother of Gen. Jackson's wife; but the court decided that their emancipation was illegal, and that they must be held as slaves by the heirs, unless they would leave the United States.   The acting executor says he is about to send them to Africa.   The coloured people, however, fear to go there, and are apprehensive that the executor will still keep them in bondage, if he can ; they have therefore applied to me, through the agency of a friend, for an opportunity to go to my colony.   I have visited Stokely Donnelson, who has them in charge, and conversed with him on the subject.   He says that he has no objection to their going to my colony, if the Court will agree to it.   My friend Bryant has undertaken to attend to the business in my absence.

I have ascertained that information which I received before my arrival, of the publication of something against me during my absence by Wm. H. Hunt, editor of the Nashville Banner, was correct.   But though I have seen him many times, he has ventured to violence towards me.[*]

Having incurred expenses for printing and otherwise to the amount of near fifty dollars, and hearing no news of my draft on the executors of W. Turpin, I concluded, in order to be enabled to leave Nashville, to avail myself of permission which I had received from Arthur Tappan of New York, to draw on him for a hundred dollars, leaving with friend Graham an order on the executors, for the like sum, to be used if necessary for its repayment.

This evening, in order to reach the mouth of the Ohio river and take passage thence to Cincinnati, I went on board the steamboat Wanderer, which is to start early in the morning for New Orleans, having first taken leave of my kind friends, R. P. Graham and family, who had treated me with the most hospitable attention, ever since my arrival at Nashville, and would listen to no proffers of compensation. Graham had his name entered as the first on my list of colonists. His possessions are supposed to be worth, clear of encumbrance, upwards of ten thousand dollars. Several others also had their names entered, one of whom a very worthy man, has since died of the cholera.

June 14th. The Wanderer left Nashville early this morning, and on reaching Clarksville, 85 miles lower down the Cumberland river, stopped to take in freight; remained there nearly three days for that purpose; and on the morning of the 17th went on again, and in the evening of that day reached Smithland and entered the Ohio river. I kept on down that river, for Paduca, having an object which will be hereafter mentioned. I find on board the Wanderer, a respectable coloured man named Willis Houston, who takes a strong interest in my Mexican enterprise.

18th. Directly after midnight, an accident happened

*The piece alluded to probably contained threats, or inducements to personal violence.—Ed.

to our boat that had nearly proved tragical. We met the steamboat Orleans, which, by some mismanagement in attempting to pass, ran foul of us, and drove her bow through the window of the cabin, on the upper deck, carrying away at the same time, the upper and lower guards of our boat, for several feet. The bow of the Orleans passed but a few inches above a coloured woman, who was sleeping at the time by the window. All on board expected that the Wanderer would sink, and there was a great scramble to convey trunks and clothing to the top of the boat. The captain immediately ordered her to be run on shore, while he and the men examined the damaged part, to see whether it admitted the water. Fortunately, it was ascertained that the boat did not leak; the order to run her on shore was countermanded, and she proceeded on her course.

The Orleans had kept near us to give assistance, in case of need, until it was found that we were perfectly safe.

On reaching Paduca, I left the Wanderer and went to obtain for the widow of my lamented friend Thomas Hoge, a trunk and other things, which he had left at a public house there, a short time before his death. I found them all in the care of C. C. Russell, the landlord, who had now quit keeping the public house. He behaved very honorably in this case. I took the property and went on board the steamboat Splendid, and returned to Smithland, at the mouth of the Cumberland, where I stopped to see that the goods were forwarded to the widow.

20th. Still at Smithland. I was detained here a portion of yesterday in making arrangements to forward the trunk to the widow, and since their completion, there has been no opportunity to take passage up the Ohio.

I have had to-day much conversation with several persons on the subject of my colonial enterprise. Two or three say that they will go out as settlers.

21st. This afternoon I found a passage from Smithland, on board of the steamboat Warsaw, bound up the Ohio.

22d. This afternoon the Warsaw fell in company with the steamboat Rob Roy, and had a real match race with her, for an hour or so. The Rob Roy was the most lightly laden, and burning rosin to increase her speed, she had beaten us by a few feet when we came to Evansville, where we stopped for a short time. I do not like these trials of strength and steam; there is great danger in them.

23d. A number of the passengers and hands, on board the Warsaw, take much interest in my colonial enterprise, and two or three talk of joining it.

24th. We arrived at Louisville in the morning, where the boat remained the whole day to discharge freight, and on account of bad weather.

25th. Before leaving Louisville, this morning, the clerk of the Warsaw made a furious attack on my plan of colonization. He got a few round-shot in return, but was relieved by the captain, who seasonably called him away. At about 9 A. M. we started and proceeded up the river.

26th. We arrived this morning, at Cincinnati. Having tried, without success, to obtain lodging at three boarding houses, I was invited by my friend G. Carey to his house, where I found the most hospitable treatment.

29th. I had a meeting with the coloured people of Cincinnati, which was attended by four or five of the late students of Lane Seminary. I believe they expected to oppose me, but they expressed " nothing objectionable."*

30th. I took passage from Cincinnati in the steamboat Native, bound to Pittsburg, paying my fare as a

---

*The persons here alluded to, were probably a portion of some students who had left Lane Seminary, because the Faculty had prohibited the public discussion of the abolition question by the students, and who, being hostile to the African Colonization Society, were expected also to oppose Mexican colonization.—ED.

deck passenger. The captain, Wm. Bennett, of Browns-
ville, Penna., upon hearing my name, made some inquiries about my residence, &c.   I gave him one of my
addresses, which he took up to the cabin.   Presently
he came to me again, accompanied by John Laughlin, son
of Robert Laughlin, formerly of St. Clairsville, Ohio,
(my old place of residence) and invited me to a *free*
passage in the cabin.   I at first declined the captain's
kind offer, but he would listen to no excuses.   He said
he had long known what I was about, and was now
glad to meet with me.

I accordingly proceeded to the cabin, where I was
introduced to Bishop Soule, of the Methodist denomination, and several other gentlemen ; they were social, in-
quisitive and communicative.   One of them was the
Rev. ———— Eaton, of Portsmouth, Ohio, who is anxious
to obtain more knowledge on the subject of Universal
Emancipation.   I found young Laughlin a very intelligent and philanthropic man, and had much conversation
with him.

July 1st, 1835.   I had, to-day, much talk with persons on board the boat, on the subject of slavery, and
my experimental enterprise.   2d. I became acquainted
with a gentleman from Mobile, Alabama, named S. O.
Butler, who is now on his way to Rochester, N. Y.
where he formerly resided.   He is very friendly to the
whole course of my public proceedings.

3d. The gentleman from Alabama above mentioned,
having learned that I had been sick and detained on
my journey, kindly proposed, if I was short of funds,
to lend me as much as I should wish.   I knew that I
should be short, but told him that I could no doubt obtain, among my acquaintances in Ohio, the small amount
that would be needful, remarking at the same time, that
ten or fifteen dollars would be sufficient.   He replied,
that he had long known and approved my character and
public course, and as he could now assist me without
inconvenience, he preferred to do so.   He then handed
me three ten dollar bank-notes, but I told him that half

that amount was fully sufficient, and I would rather not take more. He then insisted on my taking two of the notes, ($20) and gave me his address at New York, where I might find him any time previous to September next.*

I have seldom met with half so much kindness, under similar circumstances, as I have since coming on board this boat. I trust that my gratitude will be proportionate.

[Here the journal terminates abruptly, but it appears from the subsequent chapter, that Lundy proceeded to Philadelphia, stopping probably on the way, to visit his friends in Ohio and Pennsylvania.—ED.]

CHAPTER XXI.

Lundy's condensed sketch of the preceding journey, and conclusion of his personal narrative.

The preceding account of Lundy's last journey to Mexico, is taken from his journal kept during his absence. The following condensed account of the same journey, and of some subsequent events, was given by him in letters to a friend, and as it states some things not before mentioned, it is thought fit to insert it here.

Having obtained, says Lundy, a little more means, I left Nashville in May, 1834, and returned to New Orleans, intending to go directly to Matamoras, in Mexico. But after waiting at New Orleans nearly two weeks, exposed to the yellow fever, which then prevailed, and in constant danger of being known as an abolitionist, I took the route up Red River, and thence through Texas, by land. While in Texas this time I did not disguise my name, and I several times came near losing my life. But a merciful Providence preserved it for further exertions in the good cause.

---

*Lundy's journal contained an account of all his expenses, so that those who aided him might know how the money was disposed of.

I travelled through the greater part of Texas alone, and at night time generally encamped out, in the woods or plains. I rode a little pony, that carried myself, my bed and provisions. I took but little of the latter, however, and I walked much of the way, leading or driving my horse.

When I reached Monclova again, I found that a law had just passed the Legislature of Coahuila and Texas, forbidding the granting of any more land to citizens of the United States. Thus my two journeys seemed to result in nothing. But I deemed it useless to grieve, and thought that if baffled in one plan, I would try another. In returning to the sea coast from my former visit to Monclova, I had passed through a part of Tamaulipas, and found it a delightful country. I therefore now determined to apply for a grant of land in that State.

I mounted my pony again, and went to Matamoras on the sea-coast, five hundred miles from Monclova. I went alone, the whole distance. Sometimes I did not pass a house for days together. I encamped out every night except two at Reinosa; and during the whole journey I saw but three persons who could speak my native tongue. When I reached Matamoras I had parted with every article of clothing that I could possibly spare, for the purpose of defraying expenses, and had not money enough left to buy a meal for both myself and horse.

I rented a room immediately, at Matamoras, and opened a saddler's shop, although I had no tools but what I took with me to mend my shoes. I succeeded, without the least difficulty, in getting work as long as I wished to stay, and often made five dollars a day, clear of all expenses. Thus I replenished my pockets, and then went south-west two hundred and fifty miles further, to Victoria, the capital of Tamaulipas. There I obtained a grant from the governor, in conformity to a law of the State, of one hundred and thirty-eight thousand acres of land, on condition of my introducing two hundred and fifty settlers with their families. I then returned from Victoria to Matamoras, and went thence to Nashville by way of New Orleans.

At Nashville I was confined again by sickness; and had I been detained there a week longer, I might probably have lost my life by mob violence, as it was shortly after my departure that Amos Dresser received his whipping, and Alphonso Sumner was nearly killed, for their advocacy of abolition sentiments in Tennessee.

While lying sick at Nashville, I learned that William Turpin, of New York, had left me, by will, fifteen hundred dollars. This was cheering intelligence, for my funds were again exhausted. I returned to Philadelphia, and then went immediately to New York, where I received a part of the legacy. I then visited my friends in New Jersey, and afterwards returned to Philadelphia, where I published the result of my journey to Mexico.

I had intended, immediately upon the completion of this publication, to proceed with my settlement in Tamaulipas. A large number of respectable persons, in different states, proposed to accompany me. Among them were our friends David Lee Child, and wife. But the insurrection in Texas, or rather the invasion of brigands from the United States, caused me to defer it a little. I watched for an opportunity of taking passage from New York or Philadelphia, to Matamoras; but none occurred. At length I proposed to D. L. Child, that we should proceed together, in disguise, to New Orleans, and thence to Matamoras. He partly agreed to this proposal; but when Lydia, his wife, was informed of it, she wrote me a long letter, urging me, with the most feeling eloquence, to desist from my hazardous purpose. She said that, very probably, her husband might go in safety; but she was alarmed at the thought of my attempting it. I showed the letter to David, and asked what he thought it would be best to do. He was silent: and I concluded to wait awhile longer, to see how events would turn.

Just about that time, the opportunity presented itself, of exposing, with the co-operation of John Quincy Adams, the vile projects of the Texan invaders. With my proceedings since that time, thou, my dear friend, art no doubt, familiar.*

[Here Lundy's own account of his life terminates.]

CHAPTER XXII.

Events connected with Lundy's life, and the Anti-Slavery cause, up to the close of 1825, not contained in his personal narrative.

Having concluded Lundy's own account of a portion of the events of his life, we deem it fit, before proceeding to a narrative of those subsequent to the year 1836, to return to an earlier period, and record some things which he has either omitted to state, or noticed but partially.

Our materials for this purpose, are drawn principally from his own newspaper or periodical, called the Genius of Universal Emancipation. And here we may observe, that as Lundy was the first, so far as we know, to introduce the system of lectures on the subject of slavery, which has since been so extensively pursued, so he was also the first in the United States, and probably in the world, to publish a periodical work, having for its principal object the extinction of slavery ; a mode of operation which has since so far increased, that the number of journals in the United States, of that character, now (1846,) is believed to be upwards of forty.

At the time of the admission of the state of Illinois into the American Union, Congress had provided, conformably to the ordinance of 1787 which for ever prohibited the introduction of slavery into the territory north-west of the Ohio river, that Illinois might form a constitution, embracing in it such a prohibition. Yet there was a considerable party in the territory at that time, which endeavoured to prevent the introduction of

*The reader will see that this account is taken from letters written by Lundy to a friend.—Ed.

such a clause in the constitution of the new state, their object being to leave settlers from the slave holding states at liberty to bring their slaves with them, and to continue to hold them in bondage. They failed to accomplish this purpose, and the constitution was framed, and the state admitted, with a provision for the perpetual exclusion of slavery.

The party in question, however, not being satisfied with this decision, made strenuous efforts, in the years 1823 and 1824, to obtain its reversal, by means of the call of a convention to amend the constitution ; Lundy, who at that time published his paper at Greensville, Tennessee, took up the question, and addressed some articles of earnest exhortation and argument on the subject to the people of Illinois. He had the satisfaction to see the cause which he espoused triumphant : and to this day the constitution remains unchanged.

In the Genius for February, 1824, Lundy published a letter from Thomas Jefferson, dated January 21st, 1811, five years before the formation of the Colonization Society, in answer to a person who had asked his opinion of " the proposition of *Ann Mifflin*," a member of the Society of Friends in Philadelphia, to procure an establishment on the coast of Africa, to which the people of colour from these states might be colonized, under the auspices of different governments. Mr. Jefferson, in this letter, expressed the opinion that such a measure might be beneficial, not only to the colonists, but also to the people of Africa, in transplanting to that country the useful arts and the seeds of civilization. He stated that in the first year of his presidency, (1801) he had received a letter on this subject, from James Monroe, then governor of Virginia, written at the request of the Virginia Legislature, and that he had, in reply, recommended colonizing at Sierra Leone, if permission could be obtained ; and if not, then that the attempt should be made to obtain leave to colonize in some of the Portuguese settlements in South America. This fact is noticed here, partly as showing,

in some measure, the origin of the American Colonization Society, which was founded in 1816. Lundy, in his
notice of the letter, said he had before expressed his
opinions on colonization, and should not then repeat
them. He expressed his belief, however, that " it is not
impolitic to set the slaves free among us when they are
prepared to enjoy their freedom ;" and he expressed the
hope, that the last will of Jefferson, like that of Washington, would show that he entertained the same view.

About the same time, Lundy published an earnest appeal to the members of Congress, in favour of the abolition of slavery in the District of Columbia.

In his numbers for March and April, 1824, he addressed the people, in reference to the then approaching
presidential election, urging them to select an opponent
of slavery, dwelling on the great influence of the presidential office, and suggesting, as measures that the president might encourage, the abolition of the internal slave
trade, the extinction of slavery in the District of Columbia, and the settlement, " in some place," of slaves,
emancipated for that purpose. He said : " in my view,
the subject of universal emancipation is a *political* one,
in the most emphatic sense of the word, and as I have
heretofore shown, it is exceedingly important. Why?
then, shall we not bring it to bear upon our election of
chief magistrate, as well as any other ?" In the opinion
thus expressed, as to the importance of political action,
abolitionists are probably more united now than they
were when Lundy wrote this address :—indeed they are
unanimous, or nearly so, though they differ widely as to
what is the best mode of political action.

In his number for March, 1824, upon introducing a
letter relative to the Colonization Society, he said :
" Should the Colonization Society unite the work of
Emancipation with their present object of pursuit, I
would instantly raise my feeble voice to applaud, and
extend both hands to aid them ; not that I think it would
be absolutely necessary to send the blacks out of the
country, on account of difficulty in governing them, but

that our prejudice might not operate so strongly as a hinderance to the performance to that great work of justice and righteousness, the total extirpation of slavery from the soil of America. Emancipation, with me, is a primary object, and I cannot for a moment think of joining in any of the colonizing schemes that may be invented, if they shall not have that object in view." He added, that he knew that many active members of that Society were in favour of promoting emancipation, in connection with colonization, but that there were others who took an active and leading part, whom he regarded as rank advocates of slavery, and that in proportion to the influence of the latter class, was his confidence in the successful issue of benevolent exertions, on the part of the Society, lessened. He further remarked that the Society disclaimed emancipation as its object, and aimed only at the removal of those who were already free.

In October, 1823, he had received through John Kenrick of Brighton, Mass., an order from some person at Cape Haytien, for a file of the Genius of Emancipation, with a suggestion of the expediency of sending also a copy, as a present, to Boyer, the then President of the Haytian republic. Lundy sent the file, agreeably to the suggestion, through the agency of Kenrick. He received in return an answer from B. Inginac, the Haytian Secretary of State, conveying President Boyer's thanks for " the excellent work," and assuring him that the descendants of Africa would find a brotherly reception in Hayti, should they choose to come there, and would also receive, each one, a grant of land, suited to the cultivation of coffee. Lundy published this letter in his number of June 1824, accompanied by a suggestion of the great advantages, in respect to economy and efficiency, in colonizing in Hayti, over that in Africa.

The same number contained resolutions, and a nomination of an electoral ticket favourable to John Quincy Adams for President, made at Columbus, Ohio, on the ground of opposition " to the slave holding policy," accompanied by an editorial from the pen of Lundy, in which he opposed the election of Clay, then also a candidate, on the ground of his friendship to slavery. Abolitionists had not then learned, what they have since been taught by the policy of Mr. Adams' administration in opposing the independence of Cuba, lest it should lead to emancipation, and in urging the return by the British and Mexican governments of all fugitive slaves to their claimants—that it is unsafe to presume on the anti-slavery action, when in office, of a man who does not openly declare himself when a candidate; and that his conformity to the habits of his own state, in not holding slaves personally, affords no criterion of his future course as a national officer.

The same paper contained the memorial to Congress, of the Tennessee Manumission Society, dated August, 1833, praying for a prohibition of the internal slave trade, a law that all persons born thereafter in the United States should be free, and that slavery should not be introduced in any State where it did not then exist nor suffered in any States thereafter admitted into the Union.

In the Genius for October, 1824, being the first number published at Baltimore, Md., Lundy commenced a series of articles on " Emigration to Hayti," in which, while he asserted that no man " so long as he conducts himself with honest propriety, can be compelled to quit his native land, by human authority, without a violation of the principles of justice as well as the clearest provisions of the law of nature," he yet expressed the belief, that considering the existing laws and the prejudices in this country, the condition of many of the coloured people and especially of slaves emancipated for the purpose, might be improved by accepting the terms offered them by the Haytian government, viz : the payment of half the passage money, the privilege of citizenship, freedom of religion, and lands in fee simple to be given gratuitously to those who might wish to cultivate them. It may be presumed that these essays had considerable influence in promoting the emigration of several thou sand coloured persons to Hayti, which took place shortly afterwards. In promoting this emigration, Lundy had the co-operation of a number of coloured persons of distinction,: among whom was Richard Allen, of Philadelphia, Bishop of the Methodist Episcopal Church.

In the February number of 1825, Lundy had the pleasure of announcing the emancipation of eleven slaves by David Patterson, a Baptist, of Orange county, North Carolina, and their departure for Hayti, in a vessel sailing from Baltimore : as well as that of publishing a memorial from the North Carolina Convention of Manumission Societies, recommending to Congress the encouragement of Haytian colonization, together with resolutions favourable to such colonization adopted by the then recent Convention of the Tennessee Manumission Societies.

In the March number, of the same year, he announced that he had opened a Haytian emigration office in Baltimore, that he had two more slaves offered from North Carolina, which offer he accepted, and that the President of the North Carolina Society wrote him that there had been a more rapid increase of manumission Societies in that quarter than his most sanguine hopes could have anticipated.

In the April number of 1825, the editor announced, in language of glowing exultation, the passage of a law by the Congress of Central America, the first article of which was in the following words, viz: "From the publication of this law, all slaves, of every age and sex, in every part of the confederated States of Central America shall be FREE: and hereafter shall no persons be born slaves." The law went on to provide for compensation or indemnity, " to the owners of slaves between the ages of twelve and fifty years."

The May number, contained a part of an address delivered shortly before, by George Washington Custis, of Arlington Va., to General Lafayette, on a public occasion at Washington city, with the answer of the General,

which documents, on account of the eloquence and in-.
formation contained in them, are here transcribed.

Extract from Custis' address to La Fayette.

" Would to God, that on your return to our shores, you could
have seen the land of freedom untarnished by the presence of
a slave. Would that you could have seen this fair country, this
great and rising empire, the abode alone of freemen.

Truly, striking must the contrast have been to you, between
the northern and southern sections of our confederation. There,
in the land of steady habits, you beheld the genuine practice of
republicanism in the morality, the industry, and independence
of a people, who would be the pride and ornament of any age
or country.—There you have beheld an unkindly surface,
wrested from its natural rudeness, and made to smile with
plenty, by the labour and economy of a virtuous and hardy population, and fertilized by the sweat which falls from a freeman's
brow. You have seen the benefits of education, the beauty of
moral habits, which form the power and character of a people,
elevated by all which can elevate human nature. You have
said : ' Can this be the nation which I left in the cradle ? Can
this be the country I left hardly emerged from a wilderness ?'
Yet such things are. You left Liberty pluming her youthful
pinions, just ready to take her flight. You find her soaring on
eagle's wings, undazzled by her height, preparing to leave the
favoured regions where the work is done, to skim the ' cloud
capt ' summits of the Andes, and perch in triumph on the banner of Bolivar.

In your tour, General, new and diversified scenes await you,
at every link in the very long chain of the American Con
federation.

You have already reached a more genial clime, a region
more blessed by heaven, but, from the error of our fathers, more
cursed by man.

In the South, our hearts are growing cold : our doors, which
have so often flown open, at the call of hospitality, have rust
on their hinges; our chimnies, in which the blaze did once
' run roaring up,' now emit a feeble smoke, scarce enough to
stain the mid-day sky. Yet generous was the day of our greatness : the social virtues dwelt in our hearts, and under our
roofs the stranger always found a home. Our glory has passed
away; the Ancient Dominion, the seat of talent, of patriotism,
of revolutionary pride, and reminiscence, is falling from her
once high degree : she yields, before the powerful march of
sister states, which were once to her ' as I to Hercules.' 'Tis
true the dreams of fancy still picture the southern proprietor as
reclining on beds of roses, fanned by the Houris of the Maho-
medan paradise ; say rather the unenviable couch of Gautimo-

zin.—The roses which bloom in slavery's clime, soon 'waste their sweetness in its desert air,' and the paths which appear to be strewed with flowers will be found to contain full many a thorn.

But small is the stream* which divides the *Mother of States* from her now mighty offspring.—For nearly two centuries had the parent being, before this 'child of promise' beheld the light; but behold the march of Freedom! for where her progress is unimpeded by the trammels of slavery, hers is a giant's stride. But yesterday, and where this community now flourishes, was a trackless forest: 'tis now enlivened by the 'busy hum of men,' and civilization and the arts have fixed a happy dwelling there; nay more, histrionic talent† has illustrated the words of the divine Shakespeare, where late the panther howled, and

> 'Savage beasts of prey,
> And savage men more savage still than they.'

The axe of the woodman rouses the echoes, which have slept for ages in the silence of nature. The harvest smiles in luxuriance where wild flowers grew of late, and the hymns of praise, heard from the temples of the ever-living God, succeed to the yell of the savage, the signal of despair and death.

Know you of changes like these in the land of the slave? No, my dear General, there, 'like a wounded snake,' improvement, prosperity, and happiness, 'drag their slow length along;' but give to the land liberty, and at once she puts on her seven league boots, and rushes to glory and empire."

Extract from the Remarks of Gen. La Fayette.

"Of the affair of Cayenne, I will briefly state: That on my return to France, in 1785, I formed a plan for the amelioration of slavery, and the gradual emancipation of slaves in the colony of Cayenne. Most of the property in the colony belonged to the crown of France, which enabled me the better to prosecute my plans, being less liable to interruption from the conflicting interests and opinions of various proprietors. The purchase money of the estates and slaves amounted to about thirty thousand dollars, not a very large sum for my fortune in those days, but laid out wholly and solely for the purposes just mentioned. Surely it could not have been desirable for me, in those times of affluence, and interesting relations in France, to cross the Atlantic, and seek adventures for profit, in a distant

---

* The Ohio river which divides Virginia from free States, formerly a part of her territory.

†Cooper playing at Cincinnati, Ohio.

clime. A young man, just returning from aiding in the successful accomplishment of American liberty, I felt such enthu-
siasm in her holy cause, as induced me to wish to see her
blessings extended to the whole human family, and not even
withheld from that injured and degraded race who, lowest in
the scale of human being, have, from their forlorn and friend-
less situation, superior claims to the aid and commisseration of
philanthropy.

Believing that the agents usually employed in the colony,
were not of a sort to further my views, I engaged a Monsieur
B—— at Paris, a man of a firm, yet amiable disposition, and
well calculated for the work in which he was to be engaged.
Furnished with a perfect understanding of my plans and wishes,
B. sailed for Cayenne. Upon his arrival, the first act of his
administration was to collect all the cart-whips and such like
instruments of punishment, used under the former regime, and
have them burnt in a general assemblage of slaves. B. then
proceeded to make and declare laws, rules, and discipline, for
the government of the estates.—Affairs went on prosperously :
and but for the Revolution, which convulsed France both at
home and abroad, the most favourable results were to be expected, and the slaves duly prepared for the rational enjoyment
of freedom.

Poor B. died from the effects of climate, and the proscription
of myself after the 10th of August, followed by the confiscation
of my estates, put a period to this work, begun under auspices
the most favourable, and continued with success : a happy
accomplishment was alone denied by the decree of the convention, which destroyed the whole colonial system, by sudden
and unconditional emancipation, and its consequent horrors in
the colonies of France.

But to the proof. On the La Fayette estates, the emancipated slaves came in a body to the agents, and declared, that if
the property still belonged to the General, they would reassume
their labours for the use and benefit of him who had caused
them to experience an ameliorated condition of bondage, with
the certain prospect of gradual emancipation, and the rational
enjoyment of freedom.''

An editorial of the June number, stated that a gentleman from Virginia had applied at the Haytian Emigration Office for counsel, as to the means of sending
eighty-eight slaves, belonging to him, to Hayti; and that,
with Lundy's assistance, a vessl had been chartered for
that purpose. The July number announced the con-

summation of the "glorious act." The vessel had sailed
with the eighty-eight emancipated beings; and their
emancipator was announced to be David Minge, of
Charles-city County, Virginia, a young man belonging
to the Presbyterian Church, who had inherited the slaves
about two years previously. The whole value of the
slaves, as usually estimated, and of the assistance rendered them, was supposed to be thirty thousand dollars.
The following is an extract from Lundy's account of
Mr. Minge's conduct in the transaction ·

    " After contracting with the ship owner, and purchas-
ing the agricultural implements, aforesaid, he told me
there was something more to be done, for his mind was
not yet clear.   He had applied to the Colonization Society, and to the Haytian Emigration Society of New
York, for assistance in effecting his object, but failed.
He believed, now, that he should succeed;—but, possibly, he might not live to reach home.   " We know
not," he said, " what an hour may bring forth."   He
then gave me a paper, with instructions in what manner
it should be used, which would ensure the delivery of
the slaves to the ship owner, according to contract, in
case of his untimely demise.   He also informed me
that, in addition to the payment of the price of their passage and furnishing them with tools, he should give to
each one clothes, provisions and money.   Accordingly,
I understand that he furnished them with several suits of
clothes, each, gave them provisions, cooking utensils,
and everything of which they would stand in need, on
their arrival in Hayti.   And, to crown the whole, as an
unprecedented act of justice and benevolence, among
American slaveholders, he collected them together on
the beach, when the vessel was in readiness to receive
them, and, ordering them all to be seated in the shade
of a tree, had a peck of dollars brought, and distributed
the shining hoard among them!   Here are thy triumphs,
O Philanthropy!"

    The June number of 1825, contained the commence-
ment, by Lundy, of that series of attacks on the domes-

tic slave-trade, carried on through Baltimore, by A. Woolfolk, and others, which led, some years afterwards, to the beating of Lundy in the streets, the imprisonment of himself and Garrison, and the ultimate removal of both of them from Baltimore.

The July number contained the proceedings of " the tenth convention of the Tennessee Manumission Society," composed of delegates from the several branches of that body. The following resolution, adopted by this convention, will give an idea of the composition and policy of the Society, viz :

" Resolved, That all *slaveholding members* of the Manumission Society, who shall hereafter refuse or neglect to educate their slaves, so far as it is practicable, be excommunicated, and no longer be considered members of this Society."

It appears, from a statement contained in the August number of 1825, that Lundy's paper had more subscribers in North Carolina, a slaveholding State, than in any other State of the Union. The same number of the paper contained the constitution of a new Society, formed in Maryland, under the title of the Maryland Anti-Slavery Society. It was to be composed of as many branches as could be organized. Its President was Daniel Raymond, of Baltimore, and its Secretary, Edward Needles, of the same place. The branches of this Society soon became quite numerous.

The September number contained the constitution of " the Manumission and Emigration Society of Loudoun County, Virginia, formed in August of the same year. The object of this Society was declared to be to expose the evils of slavery, and effect its gradual abolition, and to aid and encourage the emigration of the coloured population to Hayti, Africa, or elsewhere.

It appears, by an article in the same paper, that Daniel Raymond had become " the anti-slavery candidate" for election to the State Legislature from the city of Baltimore, and it was proposed to name candidates for other counties, favourable to a law, such as that by which slavery had been abolished in the State of New York.

The same paper also contained the afflicting intelligence that a subscriber to the "Genius," a young man named Adamson, about 24 years of age, residing in Camden, South Carolina, had been killed by shooting, by a citizen of that place. He was the owner of about 70 slaves, which he had determined to emancipate; and he had been at Baltimore a short time previously, and made arrangements with Lundy for their transportation to Hayti. His untimely death prevented the accomplishment of his plan.

CHAPTER XXIII.

Gleanings and events for the year 1826.

In the fall of 1825, the Genius of Universal Emancipation was changed from a monthly to a weekly publication. We have not been able to obtain a few of the first numbers. Our file commences with the paper of Feb. 11, 1826. It contains a reference to a previous account of an institution which had been commenced in Tennessee, by Francis Wright, George Flower, and some others, with a few slaves whom they had emancipated with a view to test the efficacy of the community system, as applicable to the promotion of emancipation and the improvement of the emancipated. The institution was called "The Emancipating Labour Society of Shelby County, Tennessee," and the place where it was established was called Nashoba. The experiment ultimately proved a failure, and the coloured people at the institution were sent to Hayti.

It was in the fall of 1825, that Lundy made his first voyage to Hayti, from which place he did not return until the close of May, 1826. The paper of March 6th, 1826, contained an account of the sailing from Norfolk,

Va., for Africa of about 50 emancipated slaves, who had been placed under the care of the Society of Friends in North Carolina, together with eleven emancipated for the purpose by the Rev. John D. Paxson, of Prince Edward County, Va.; two by Dr. Webb, near Norfolk, Va.; and one by the Rev. Cave Jones, of New York.

Upon his return from Hayti, Lundy wrote and published in his paper of June 3d, 1826, the following obituary respecting his wife, who had died during his absence.

"O Death! thy keen and fatal dart
Bids anguish wring the sorrowing heart."

"The editor has never made it a practice to insert obituary notices in this work, but he trusts that his readers will hold him excused for occupying a small space in the present number, with the view of paying a tribute to the memory of his late bosom companion, whose untimely demise was noticed a few weeks since, during his absence. Though nothing can be said that will rescue from the power of the grave the friends that we love, after the relentless hand of death hath been laid upon them, still we may be permitted to breathe our last adieu, in obedience to the mandates of true and genuine affection.

Esther Lundy was born in the county of Chester, in the State of Pennsylvania, on the 26th day of the 3d month, 1793. She was the eldest daughter of Henry Lewis, who removed with his family to the State of Ohio, in the early settlement of that part of the country, where he still resides. She had a birth-right in the Society of Friends, which she retained until the day of her death. Since we formed our matrimonial connexion it has frequently been my lot to be from home, for many months at a time. And in consequence of the peculiar duties of my calling, since I have been engaged in a public line of business, I several times found it necessary to change my place of residence. All this must, of course, have occasioned some trials to my wife; and, in addition thereto, she was for several years of the latter part of her life severely afflicted with a rheumatic complaint, that sometimes appeared to threaten her with imminent danger. Yet amidst every difficulty, and under every afflictive dispensation, she evinced an unusual degree of fortitude, for one of her sex. Whenever it fell to my lot to be called from home, and whatever might be the state and condition of her health, she uniformly and cheerfully gave her consent thereto ; observing that she could not find a freedom in urging any thing as a hinderance to the success of my labours in the cause of philanthropy. It may truly be said, that she was actuated by the spirit that directs the Christian in the path of duty; and that the irreparable loss of her numerous friends and relatives, is her eternal gain. She has left five small children in addition to her bereaved husband, to lament her untimely death. In ordinary cases the severance of near and dear connexions by the cold hand of death, is sufficient to out-weigh every other consideration that excites the pang of sorrow and keen regret. Yet when this is attended with peculiarly distressing circumstances, the barbed arrow of grief is doubly pointed, and the mind must suffer all the poignancy of deep and heart-rending affliction. It happened at a time when every relative, except her little helpless children, were absent, that the messenger of death appeared with his awful summons. Yet she was surrounded with Christian neighbours, who spared no exertions to administer the balm of relief in the hour of distress. But alas ! what could they do ? It was the appointed time for her to receive the glorious reward of her many virtues. Her Saviour called—she passed the ordeal of dissolution with perfect calmness and serenity of mind—and her spirit reposes in the mansion of eternal happiness."

In the numbers of June 3d and 10th, 1826, Lundy published his correspondence and arrangement, with the Philanthropic Society of Hayti, and he offered himself as an agent, to aid any slaveholders who were willing to emancipate their slaves on condition of their being sent to that island. The terms were, that the emancipated should labour as redemptioners, on their arrival, in order to repay the cost of their passage, which the Philanthropic Society would advance ; and after the expiration of the apprenticeship, each man having a family would receive a donation of fifteen English acres of land.

This publication was followed by a series of articles, in defence of Haytian colonization, which were written with talent, and with the usual ease of style which belonged to Lundy.

The number of June 10th also contained a series of resolutions for an inquiry into the expediency of abolishing slavery and the slave trade in the District of Columbia, which had been recently offered in Congress by Charles Miner, representative from Chester county, Pa., and which, without a call of the ayes and noes, had been negatived, by an apparently large majority.

The paper of June 24th announced, through a letter from Beaufort, North Carolina, the departure for Hayti, under the arrangement made by Lundy, of 116 slaves belonging to the Society of Friends, and two emancipated, upon condition of going to that country, by John Stafford of Orange county, North Carolina. It appeared, by a statement published two weeks before, that 729 slaves had been given to the North Carolina Yearly Meeting of Friends, for the purpose of being conveyed to lands of freedom, as they could not be emancipated and remain free in North Carolina ; that above 300 had chosen to go to Liberia, 116 to Hayti, 106 to the Western states, 15 to Philadelphia, and that 99 chose to remain in Carolina.

A letter from North Carolina, published in the Genius of July 17th, gave the following account :—" The Manumission Society of North Carolina is now said to contain more than two thousand members. The number is rapidly increasing. A spirit of inquiry is progressing, which does honour to the people of both sexes, and must ultimately terminate in something noble. Several female associations have been formed auxiliary to the Manumission Society of the state."

The number of August 5th, contained the annunciation that Lundy had formed an association with Michael Lamb, for the purpose of supplying, from a store in Baltimore, goods solely the product of free labour, to those who were willing to discountenance the use of the fruits of the unrequited toil of the slave.

The paper for September 2d, contained the address of the Maryland Anti-Slavery Society, upon re-nominating Daniel Raymond as an anti-slavery candidate for the Legislature. It said: "The Anti-Slavery Society of Maryland consists at this time of four respectable branches, with several hundred members, although thirteen months have not elapsed since the first proposition was made for its organization."—"In our sister state of North Carolina, the advocates of general emancipation are increasing, with a rapidity unparalleled in the annals of this nation. It is believed that nearly *three thousand* citizens of that state have enrolled themselves as members of anti-slavery societies, within a period of two years, many of whom are men of the first talents and standing in the community at large, and some of whom are themselves extensive proprietors of slaves."

A letter from North Carolina, published in the same number of the paper, said: "I was at a meeting near the Yadkin river, the past week, where there was an accession of sixty-three new members, and out of nearly 300 that were present, none opposed, but on the contrary all applauded what was done. Many expressed their good will, who did not wish to join at that time. There was not a Quaker among them."

On the commencement of a new volume, Sept. 16th, Lundy published a brief address, in which, speaking of the most expedient course for abolitionists to pursue, he said: "In my opinion we have nothing to do but to go straight-forward, with firmness and resolution, in the road that we have already begun to travel, neither turning to the right nor the left, until we reach the glorious mansion where justice sits crowned with mercy, and where men esteem their fellow men as brethren. For my own part, I never calculate *how soon* the cause of rational liberty will triumph over that of cruelty and despotism, in this country. I have long since resolved to labour for its accomplishment, if health and strength continues, until success shall render my humble exertions unnecessary, or until the lamp of life shall be extinguished."

From an extract contained in the same number, it appeared that the subject of West India emancipation was then much agitated in England, and that some were " for a total abolition, at once and immediately," while others were " for a gradual emancipation."

On October 7th, the " Genius " announced the result of the Baltimore election, giving 974 votes for Raymond, the anti-slavery candidate, which was about one seventh of the whole number of voters, being 350 more than he had received the year preceding. C. S. Walsh, who run as an open opponent of Raymond's views, received but 528 votes. The same paper contained an address issued by a meeting of the Anti-Slavery Society, held two days after the election, in which Raymond was again nominated as a candidate, to be supported at the election of 1827.

The number of November 11th contained information, that in the Ohio Synod of the Presbyterian church, a discussion had taken place on a question which had been before referred to the General Assembly of that church, viz.: Is the holding of slaves men-stealing? and that a large majority concurred in supporting the affirmative of the question. The same paper published a part of a letter of W. H. Fitzhugh, of Virginia, in which he proposed that the national government of the United States should furnish " *pecuniary aid* to the states, for effecting in such modes as they may choose, the extinction of slavery within their limits." In noticing this letter, Lundy admitted that the author was actuated " by the best of motives," and that many friends of emancipation might accord with him, but he entered his own " solemn

protest against the assertion of a principle which would
le:alize the system of slavery by a legislative *purchas*
of slaves. '

The "Genius" of Nov. 25th, 1826, commenced the
publication of the proceedings of "the American Convention for promoting the abolition of slavery, &c.,"
held at Baltimore about a month previous, being the
first session of that body ever held south of Philadelphia.
According to Lundy's account, there were represented
in it, directly and indirectly, eighty-one societies, of which
seventy-three were located in the slaveholding states—
the whole number of societies in the country being
at that time about one hundred , of which there were
forty-five in North Carolina, and more than twenty in
Tennessee. At this convention a resolution was adopted,
with the vote of Lundy in the affirmative, favourable to
the aid of the national government in "the *voluntary*
removal of such slaves as may be *hereafter emancipated,*
to any country which they may *choose* for their residence." This resolution differed from the officially
avowed policy of the Colonization Society ; first in its application to newly emancipated slaves, and secondly, in
leaving the place of migration to the choice of the emigrants; and it also carefully specified that the migration should be *voluntary.*

The number of Dec. 16th, announced the formation
of four new societies, three of them in slaveholding
states.

CHAPTER XXIV.

Events of 1827, and opinions of Lundy, promulgated in the Genius
'of Universal Emancipation.

Lundy's paper for Jan. 20th, 1827, contained his account of the assault upon him, made in the streets of
Baltimore, by Austin Woolfolk, in consequence of the

attack of the Genius upon him, and the domestic slave trade in which he was engaged. The immediate provocation, which Woolfolk alleged, was contained in the paper of January 2d, which gave an account of the execution, at New York, of William Bowser, a slave, for the murder of the captain and mate of the Decatur, a vessel engaged in transporting some of Woolfolk's slaves, to Georgia. The slaves, twenty-nine in number, had risen for their liberty when a few days out from Baltimore, taken possession of the vessel, thrown the captain and mate overboard, and given the command to one of the crew, a white man, upon his promising to carry them to Hayti: but as he knew not how to manage the vessel, she was some days afterwards fallen in with by another vessel, which took her to New York; where the slaves escaped, but Bowser was afterwards apprehended at West Chester, New York, brought to New York city, convicted, and, on December 15th, 1826, executed. Woolfolk was stated to have been present at the execution · and an article, which Lundy copied from the New York Christian Inquirer, stated that the coloured man, at the place of execution, addressed the spectators, and, " as Woolfolk was present, he particularly addressed his discourse to him, saying he could forgive him all the injuries he had done him, and hoped they might meet in Heaven : but this unfeeling soul-seller, with a brutality which becomes his business, told him, with an oath (not to be named,) that he was now going to have what he deserved, and he was glad of it, or words to that effect. He would probably have continued his abusive language to this unfortunate man, had he not been stopped by some of the spectators, who were shocked at this unfeeling, profane and brutal conduct."

Lundy, in remarking on the above, strongly cautioned the coloured people against attempting to obtain their rights by violent measures, and urged upon them " a spirit of forbearance, forgiveness, and charitable brotherly kindness." He added: " The citizens of Balti-

more have now a clue to unravel the character of that
monster in human shape, the Ishmælite, Woolfolk.
The adamantine-hearted creature, knowing *himself* to
be the cause of the death of the captain and mate of the
Decatur, and also of the poor unfortunate Bowser, could,
with a fiend-like assurance, insult him with his out-
rageous profanity, when he was just to be launched into
eternity.   Hereafter, let no man speak of the humanity
of Woolfolk."

It appears, from Lundy's statement, that after the
publication of the above article, as he was going to the
Post Office, Woolfolk accosted him, and charged him
with having called him "a negro stealer," in the columns
of the paper.   Lundy replied that he had not done so.
Woolfolk then asked if he had not published an account
of the hanging of a negro at New York, and of his being
there.   Lundy said he had copied such an account from
a New York paper.   Woolfolk asked him if he did
not accompany that account with remarks of his own,
to which Lundy replied in the affirmative.   Woolfolk
then asked what those remarks were, upon which Lundy
took from his pocket a paper, and offered it to him to
read them for himself.   Woolfolk refused to receive it.
Lundy then declined further conversation and turned
away, upon which Woolfolk stepped up to him, and
said something further should be done whereupon, in
the words of Lundy, " I had scarcely time to observe
to those present that I would not quarrel with him, when
he stripped off his coat, gave it to one of the by-standers,
and took hold of my collar.   Being a much stronger
man than myself, and as I resolved to make no resistance, he found it an easy matter to prostrate my body
on the pavement.   Then with a brutal ferocity that is
perfectly in character with his business, he choked me
until my breath was nearly gone, and stamped me in the
head and face, with the fury of a very demon.   One of
the blows from his heel was given about the middle of
the forehead; with such violence, that it stunned me exceedingly ; and I am confident that had it not been for

a glancing stroke, it must inevitably have fractured the scull, if it had not caused immediate death. As soon as I could release his gripe from my throat, and recover my breath, I called for assistance, and he, was taken from me. It was with some difficulty that I rose on my feet, and my face was literally in a gore of blood. I succeeded, however in getting to a magistrate, and procured a writ for the perpetrator of the outrage ; and then, after engaging a friend to see that it was duly served, I was compelled to take my bed and send for medical aid. So severe were my wounds, that I was confined to my bed more than two days, and to my room nearly a week."

The Genius of Feb. 24th contained the account of Woolfolk's trial before Judge Brice, for the assault on Lundy. "On the part of the defendant several witnesses were produced, from the testimony of whom it appeared, that there was a mistake respecting his being present at the execution of Bowser. One of them stated that he understood his brother was then at New York, instead of himself. Be this as it may," says Lundy, "the extract from the New York paper was given verbatim, and I never heard it contradicted until those witnesses appeared in Court." The counsel for the defendant read at the trial various extracts from the Genius, including those relating to the execution of Bowser. The jury having convicted Woolfolk, Judge Brice sentenced him to pay a fine of *one dollar!* and recommended to Woolfolk to hand the "Genius" to the Grand Jury, with the expectation, probably, that they might indict Lundy for a libel. The jury, however, did nothing in the matter.

The number of March 31st, contained accounts of the formation of twelve new anti-slavery societies, of which six were in Virginia, three in Maryland, two in the District of Columbia, and one in Ohio. The editor remarked, that "there never was a period mentioned in the history of the United States when the tenth part was done (if we except the time when the " Missouri question" agitated the public mind,) relative to the investi-

gation of the subject of slavery that is now doing."
On the 14th April, two more new societies were announced, one in Westmoreland Co., Pennsylvania, and
one in Columbiana Co., Ohio.

On April 28th, the Genius contained the following
announcements, viz:—1. A gentleman, whose statements
may be relied on, informs the editor that Col. Ward, a
resident of Virginia, near Dan River, died a short time
since, leaving about 150 slaves free, by his last will and
testament. He also left them a tract of land, on which
a number of them are settled. The gentleman saw a
large company of them, a few weeks ago, on their way
to Ohio. They were in an exceedingly merry mood,
and appeared overjoyed at the idea of having obtained
their freedom. 2. Robert Cox, a minister of the Methodist Episcopal Church, died in Suffolk Co. Va., on the
10th ult. In his will he made provision for emancipating all his slaves, upwards of thirty, and for giving
each a handsome sum of money. He had offered, during
his life, to transport them to Africa, but they chose to live
with him and receive wages. 3. Mr. Funston, of Fre-
derick Co., Va., by his will requests that ten of his slaves
shall be liberated, with the special desire that they may
be located in the American colony in Africa. He also
appropriates the sum of $1000 for their comfortable
establishment there.

About this time a series of articles, in favour of the
abolition of slavery in Kentucky, by law, was published in the Messenger, printed at Russelville, in that State,
and afterwards copied into the "Genius." Letters
were also received and published, from South Carolina,
Arkansas, and other slaveholding regions, showing an
agitation of the anti-slavery question in those quarters.

The paper of May 5th, contained an editorial, from
which the following is extracted.

" TWENTY YEARS AGO—OR ' TIME'S CHANGES.'

"Twenty years ago, domestic slavery existed in nearly
all the states of this Union, and the foreign slave-trade

flourished, under the sanction of the United States government—now, the shackles of bondage have fallen from hundreds of thousands of slaves, in the different states; the slave-trade, *abroad*, is treated as piracy; the question of totally abolishing slavery in the territory over which the national government exercises the exclusive control, is before Congress, and the measure is advocated by some of the ablest statesmen of which our country can boast.

"Twenty years ago, not a society existed, south of the Potomac, whose sole object was the annihilation of the slave system. Now, more than eighty such societies are organized in the states of Virginia, North Carolina, Kentucky, and Tennessee; and to these may be added, twelve in Maryland and Delaware, and twenty in other states, to say nothing of the numerous Colonization Societies, scattered through nearly every state of the Union.

" Twenty years ago, Mexico, South America, and the whole of the great western Archipelago, with the exception of a single island, were totally enshrouded with the black mantle of negro slavery, and enveloped with the dense vapor of despotism.—Now, the whole of this vast continent, south of the United States, (exclusive of Brazil, which is upon the eve of bursting its chains,) 'stands redeemed, regenerated, and disenthralled,' and there the human mind is emphatically '*marching under the banner of Universal Emancipation*.'

" Twenty years ago, the statesmen of Great Britain dreamed not of abolishing the system of slavery in their West India Colonies.—Now, the Parliament and the Colonial Legislature are at issue on the momentous question ; and more than two hundred societies are said to be formed in England with the view of promoting this great cause of justice and philanthropy.

On May 19th, the Genius commenced the publication of a "Review of the History of Hayti," which was continued through some thirty numbers of the paper.   Of this review, it is designed to insert an abstract at the close of this volume.

On the 4th of July, the Genius published the Constitution of " the Free Produce Society of Pennsylvania," which was formed in the commencement of the year, and which still exists in 1846. It also noticed a similar society which had been established at Wilmington, Delaware, the object being to obtain and encourage the use of the products of free labour, instead of those of slave labour generally consumed. Lundy expressed the opinion that "those movements constitute an important part of the grand system of operations" destined to overthrow American slavery.

From an editorial of the same date, on the commencement of a new volume, we extract the following:

"Probably I might, at this time, indulge a retrospective glance at the past, and compare it with the present state of things.—But I will merely say, that the cause is gaining ground as fast as can be expected, if not as fast as can be wished; and I feel well assured that eventual success is absolutely certain, if the current of enlivening air be not withdrawn that is now directed towards the altar on which the sacrifice of tyranny is destined to be made. I will, therefore, add, that I shall look forward with the hope that my feeble labours may not be entirely unavailing, but that the language of the great Curran may yet be adapted to my natal soil, as follows :—

' I speak in the spirit of the American Law, which makes Liberty commensurate with, and inseparable from, the American soil—which proclaims, even to the stranger and the sojourner, the moment he sets his foot upon American earth, that the ground on which he treads is holy, and consecrated by the Genius of UNIVERSAL EMANCIPATION. No matter in what language his doom may have been pronounced ;—no matter what complexion, incompatible with freedom, an Indian or an African sun may have burnt upon him ;—no matter in what disastrous battle his liberty may have been cloven down : —no matter with what solemnities he may have been devoted upon the altar of Slavery;—the first moment he touches the sacred soil of America, the altar and the god sink together in the dust; his soul walks abroad in her own majesty; his body swells beyond the measure of his chains, that burst from around him, and he stands redeemed, regenerated, and disenthralled, by the irresistible GENIUS OF UNIVERSAL EMANCIPATION."

The same number of the paper announced the arrival, at York, Pennsylvania, of Nathaniel Crenshaw of Hanover county, Virginia, with sixty-five emancipated slaves, which had been liberated partly by himself and partly by his deceased uncle. The latter portion had been emancipated on condition of going to Africa; but they had refused to do so, and were taken to Pennsylvania, in order to prevent their being sold into renewed bondage, under the laws of Virginia.

In the number for July 14th, in noticing a communication from a correspondent, recommending the use of mild language, Lundy said: " Every man is entitled to his own opinion, on this as well as other subjects, but I have always thought, that TRUTH is, or ought to be, so popular, and withal so beautiful, that it stands in no need of decoration. In other words, I have never thought it worth while to study to please the advocates of oppression, nor yet those who are so wilfully blind that they cannot see, with all the light around them, that it is their duty to exert themselves for the abolition of slavery. I cannot find that the best and most successful reformers of other days have left behind them any evidence that such a course would be *politic* in the true sense of the term." He then quoted this remark of Luther[a]: " Almost all men condemn my tartness of expression, but I am of opinion that God will have the deceits of men thus powerfully exposed: for I plainly perceive, that those things that are softly dealt with, in a corrupt age, give people but light concern, and are presently forgotten. If I have exceeded the bounds of moderation, the monstrous turpitude of the times has transported me," &c., &c.

To this Lundy's correspondent, " Wilberforce" replied, in a subsequent number, (August 18th,) that the triumph of Luther's sentiments was not caused by the asperity of his writings; that it appeared from his biography that he had often cause to lament that nature had endowed him with so irritable a disposition : that he refused the appellation of Christian to such of his *protestant* brethren as differed from him in sentiment; that while he entertained a peculiar predilection for the writings of Augustine, he imbibed no portion of the spirit of meekness by which they are characterized ; that he sometimes bitterly lamented his want of self-government ; that he said openly before the emperor at Worms, " I freely confess that I have been led into an asperity of expression, which neither becomes me as a clergyman nor a Christian ;" and that Melanchthon relates, that he heard him confess, with deep sighs and a vast effusion of tears, how intemperate he had been at times, in his language.

In the same number (July 14th) an account was published of a celebration on the 4th, by the people of colour in New York, of the final extinction of slavery in that state, through a law then recently passed, by which the few slaves remaining under the operation of the old gradual emancipation act, were instantly liberated.

The number for July 31st contained an account of the celebration of the 4th, (the anniversary of Independence,) in the Methodist church, at Winchester, Virginia, by the Anti-Slavery Society of that place, which was said to consist of one hundred members. In the notice of this celebration, two clergymen, John Wells and George Reed, are mentioned as participants. The same number of the Genius noticed the formation of a new anti-slavery society in Baltimore county, Maryland.

The number for July 28th, contained the proceedings of the Columbiana County Abolition Society, convened at New Lisbon, Ohio, at which it was resolved : " That this society will not support for any office that may depend upon the suffrages of the people, any person or persons who are not decidedly opposed to the system of slavery, as now tolerated in the United States, and who will not use every lawful effort, both in their official and individual capacities, to remedy the evil by the most speedy and efficient means." It was also resolved to petition Congress, " to take immediate measures for the gradual abolition of slavery, throughout the United States, by passing laws for that purpose."

In noticing the political action thus recommended, Lundy said: " Let the friends of genuine republicanism throughout the United States, act upon this principle, and we shall soon witness a change for the better. It will be said by some, that the people of the free states have nothing to do in this matter. But it is a grand mistake. They *guarantee* the oppression of the coloured man in this country. Let them wash their hands of the crime. They are not yet washed. There is blood on every finger."

The same number gave an account of an experiment, then being made, by Wm. Fitzhugh, of Ravenswood, Virginia, a member of the Colonization Society. He had settled two families of his slaves on farms, which they were to cultivate as his tenants, paying him rent for the farm and for the stock furnished them, but nothing for their own time: all the profits beyond the rent, &c., were to be appropriated to purchasing their freedom, or else to setting out in the world the more deserving among them, whom Mr. Fitzhugh intended to liberate. On a six months trial with one family, it had been found that they were unusually industrious, and showed a laudable pride in keeping the farm in order; and it was intended to pursue the same course with others, if found successful.

On August 11th, Lundy announced " with pleasure," that a manufacturer in Rhode Island had adopted the system of working cotton, produced by free labour, and that the muslins made from such cotton could be had by the bale, of James Mott & Co., in Philadelphia. He

earnestly recommended the encouragement of this enterprise.

The number of August 25th contained the address
of the Rev. Nathan Bangs, of the Methodist church,
delivered before the Colonization Society in New York
city, on July 4th, in which he spoke of the day as a proud
one for new York, by reason of the extinction of slavery,
and stated, that from the very commencement of the
Methodist church the poor Africans had shared in the
labours of the sect, and ever since the year 1768,* a
special effort had been made by it, to raise and exalt
this oppressed people to the rank of Christians.

The same number contained a notice of the continued
and increasing labours, in England, of the female societies, and others, for the extinction of slavery in the
British West Indies; and speaking of Elizabeth Heyrick,
it said : " The patriotic and philanthropic author of a
pamphlet entitled 'Immediate not gradual Abolition
&c.,' has recently published a book in which she dis-
plays the same talent, ingenuity and intelligence, which
so eminently distinguished her former productions."

On September 8th, the Genius commenced the re-
publication of a series of able articles, originally published in the Western Luminary, at Lexington, Kentucky, in the midst of an extensive slaveholding district.
These articles ably advocated the cause of emancipation. This fact indicates the very considerable progress
then made by anti-slavery sentiments in the slaveholding section of the country.

On the 22d, Lundy, having just returned from a journey, cautioned his abolition readers against being
" led away by the din of party strife, and induced to

*Before the Methodist society arose, some members of the
Society of Friends, as well as others, had been acting in opposition to American slavery, but the Methodists were the first society to prohibit their members from holding slaves. They however subsequently relaxed the rule, so as to allow them to hold
them, provided it was not for the purpose of gain :—a regulation
which can evidently be evaded.—Ed.

abandon their ground," at the election which was then
at hand : remarking, that the questions which then agitated the political community (the tariff, and the support
of or opposition to the administration of president Adams,)
were " of minor importance compared with that of abolishing the supreme curse of slavery."

Raymond, the candidate nominated by the abolitionists, had, a few days before, avowed himself favourable
to the tariff and the re-election of president Adams, and
had taken part in a political meeting friendly to those
objects. Lundy, on the 28th, noticed this, and said :
" I am not at all surprised, neither do I *very much regret*, that the anti-slavery candidate for the Legislature,
in this city, has declared his preference for the non-slaveholding candidate for the presidency. "   And he went
on to express his own opinion, in favour of the high tariff
system, as being the non-slaveholding policy.

The election took place on the first of October ; and
on the 6th, Lundy had to announce, that Raymond,
who had been in the field a whole year, as the anti-slavery candidate, had withdrawn his name, by an address
published in the American, on the morning of the election : also, that the Jackson, or opposition candidates,
were chosen. On the 14th, he thus explained the causes
of Raymond's withdrawal.   " As there were three candidates in the field, Raymond, Tyson, and Stricker, in
favour of the national administration, and two only could
be elected, many persons expressed a great desire that
one should withdraw.   But the two last named, having
been elected the preceding year, were of opinion that
they possessed the strongest claim, and positively refused to decline a poll.   It was therefore concluded,
at a meeting of the friends of emancipation held on the
Saturday evening preceding the election, that Raymond
had best withdraw his name, *this year*, with a view of
testing fairly the strength of the parties.   The measure
was not adopted, however, until proposed by himself.
And we have reason to believe that this act of personal
condescension—this evidence of a willingness to sacri-

fice personal consideration on the altar of the public good—will secure him many friends, and that he will, next year, receive the support of the administration party, generally, as well as that of the friends of emancipation."

We shall see, when we come to the history of the next year, how far this expectation was realized.

We now go back to the Genius of September 29th. It contained an account of the first Virginia Convention for the abolition of slavery, which was held in Loudoun county, on the 22d of August; seven local societies being represented. It was resolved at this meeting to establish a permanent annual convention, and that the next meeting should be held in Frederic county, near the centre of the state.

The Genius of October 13th, noticed the American Anti-Slavery Convention, which had just been held in Philadelphia, and at which information had been received, that, exclusive of ten or twelve societies in Illinois, of which no accurate knowledge was possessed, the number of anti-slavery societies in the country, and of their members, were estimated as follows:

Massachusetts, Rhode Island, and New York, 4 societies, 300 members. Pennsylvania (east) 4,—400: Pennsylvania (west) 12,—500: Delaware 2,—100: Maryland 11,—500: District of Columbia 2.—100: Virginia 8,—250: Ohio 4,—300: Kentucky 8,—200: Tennessee 25,—1,000: North Carolina 50,—3,000.—Total 130 societies, 6625 members, exclusive of Illinois. Of the societies, 106 were located in slaveholding states.

The number of November 3d contained a sketch of the state of slavery in Cuba, under the Spanish laws. It embraced the following facts: 1. In every district there is a public officer who is the official protector of slaves, and whose presence is necessary at every legal decision concerning them. 2. Slaves are of two classes, the *venta real*, who may be sold at any price the master can obtain, and the *coartados*, whose slavery is limited, and a price fixed on them, which cannot be increased. This is done by the master's giving the slave a certificate of the price set on him, which is binding on everybody thereafter. This price is generally below the real value.

A slave may become *coartado* by paying a part of his value, and then he is held only for the remainder, and he may, at any time, reduce this sum by additional payments. 3. Slaves may be freely emancipated, either by will, or by a mere certificate of liberation. No security is required that they shall not become chargeable, (as is done in the British Islands, and in some American states,) except in reference to old and infirm slaves. 4. The master will be compelled to perform any promise of emancipation that the slave can prove him to have made : and wills are always interpreted the most favourably for the slaves. 5. Slaves may purchase their liberty : and if they cannot agree with their masters on the price, the master names one appraiser, the protector of slaves another, and the judge the third, and these three fix upon the sum to be given. 6. A master is compelled to sell his slave, if the purchaser engages to emancipate him at the end of a reasonable time. 7. Masters who use their slaves ill, are compelled to sell them at an appraised value. 8. It is the universal custom to liberate those who render services to the government; the government paying the master their value. 9. A slave once emancipated, cannot be reduced again to slavery. 10. Slaves may legally acquire property, either by working on holidays, or by hiring their time and working out : and the master has a right to receive but one real (twelve and a half cents,) per day, for every one hundred dollars of the value of a *coartado* slave, while the slave can earn from four to twelve reals per day. 11. A mother may emancipate her offspring, before birth, for twenty-five dollars : after birth, and before baptism, for fifty dollars : and after baptism, by paying the appraised value. 12. Household slaves are usually taught some trade, by means of which, working in leisure hours, they can easily earn their liberty in seven years : and field slaves are entitled to a certain quantity of land, by the produce of which, and the breeding of pigs and poultry, they often become either *coartado*, or wholly emancipated. The last census, (before 1827,) though not very exact, makes the number of whites in Cuba, 290,000 :

free people of colour, 115,000 ; slaves 225,000.   This
state of things contrasts favourably with that existing in
the United States and in the other West India islands.
[It may be presumed that the majority of *native born*
coloured people in Cuba are free.   A large portion of
the slaves included in the census, were imported from
Africa.]

The same paper stated, that the slaves under the care of
the North Carolina Yearly Meeting of Friends, intended
to be sent to Hayti or Africa, inasmuch as they could
not be liberated at home, exceeded one thousand in
number, inclusive of those already sent away : and that
large donations, to aid their migration and settlement,
had been made by the Yearly Meetings of Baltimore and
Ohio, and by Friends and others, in Philadelphia, New
York, New England, and Great Britain.

On December 3d, Lundy announced, that he was
about to despatch a vessel to Hayti, with emancipated
slaves, and that he could take from fifty to one hundred,
beyond what were already engaged.   Out of the whole
number of slaves under the care of Friends in North
Carolina, who had been consulted as to their wishes, it
was supposed that nearly ninety-five would go to Hayti,
ninety-eight to Africa, ninety-three to Philadelphia, and
nineteen to Indiana : and two hundred and eighteen
preferred to stay in North Carolina. About one hundred
had not yet been consulted.

In the same number of the paper, Lundy, in an article on African colonization, stated, that he had never
changed the views first expressed by him, viz : that if
" too *mach dependance* was not placed on it, and *other
measures* were united with it, then it would aid the cause
of emancipation, but not otherwise : and that the idea
that slavery would be abolished by those means alone
which were pursued by that society, was utterly visionary."

On December 22d, the Genius announced, that several meetings had been recently held in Hartford and
Cecil counties, Maryland, with a view to the formation
of anti-slavery societies.

CHAPTER XXV.

Opinions and events in 1828, collected from the Genius, &c.

About the commencement of 1828, a number of the white carters and draymen of Baltimore prepared and sent to the Maryland Legislature, a memorial, praying that people of colour might be prohibited from pursuing the occupations of carters and draymen within that city. Lundy took up the subject, opposed the measure vigorously, and urged the circulation of counter memorials, which were prepared. The final result was, the defeat of the measure proposed, the Legislature referring it to the city council, and that body declining to act in the matter.

On the 2d of February, the Genius contained a draft of a memorial to Congress, from citizens of the district of Columbia, asking the abolition of slavery there, and on the 9th Lundy announced, that in a few days time, and in Washington alone, upwards of five hundred signers, including all the judges in the District, had been obtained. The paper of April 26th, stated that the petition, which had then been presented, contained one thousand and two signatures, and that some of the signers were slaveholders.

The paper of February 9th, contained a well written memorial, from the Presbyterian Synod of Indiana, to the General Assembly of the Presbyterian church, urging that body to action for the promotion of the cause of emancipation : also a memorial from the American convention of abolitionists, held in Philadelphia, praying congress to abolish slavery in the District of Columbia : and the number of March 15th, contained memorials, then said to be in circulation in New York, addressed to Congress and the state Legislature, in reference to the same object.

In the number for April 26th, after noticing the fact

that the African Observer, published at Philadelphia by Evan Lewis, had been discontinued, for want of patronage, Lundy said: "The ship is not to be given up. The Genius of Universal Emancipation shall, if possible, live at least as long as its present editor does. He has cradled it, and he is now resolved to sustain it, while he has a mind capable of devising the means, and a hand able to work for its support."

On the 1st of May, Lundy commenced his lecturing tour to the Northern states, in the course of which, at Boston, he met and formed an acquaintance with Wm. Lloyd Garrison, as mentioned in his personal narrative. He did not return to Baltimore till fall. In November he went thither again, and proposed to Mr. Garrison to join him in the editorship of the Genius. This offer was declined, at that time, by reason of Mr. Garrison's other engagements.

The Genius of July 4th, speaking of Congress, stated that at the then recent session of that body, there had been presented petitions for the abolition of slavery in the District of Columbia, from three thousand citizens of North Carolina: six hundred of Western Pennsylvania: the Columbiana (Ohio) Society, and the American Convention, in addition to the one thousand names before mentioned, from the District itself. The petitions from North Carolina, also asked aid to the cause of colonization, in addition to the extinction of slavery in the District of Columbia.

The number of August 4th, contained the following account, taken from the Register, published at Raleigh, North Carolina, of an extraordinary slave in that vicinity.

"George M. Horton.—This is the name of an extraordinary young slave, the property of Mr. James Horton who lives in Chatham county, about half way between Chapel Hill and Pittsborough, who has astonished all who have witnessed his poetic talent. He is about twenty-five years of age, and of a mild and humble disposition and deportment. The following account of his beginning and progress in learning, was derived from himself and has been communicated to us by a friend proverbial for his philanthropic feelings. He first learned the alphabet from hearing the school children rehearsing it. He then took the spelling book and became ac-quainted with the form of the letters. Gratified with such employment, he was soon able to spell and read. At this period some person gave him a copy of Wesley's hymns, with which he was delighted, spending most of his leisure hours in reading it, and while at work en-deavouring to make verses in imitation of it. Finding himself at a loss, in properly constructing his verses, he studied grammar and prosody. Being very intimate with the students of the university, who had discovered his extraordinary genius, he delighted to visit them when-ever a Sunday or holiday permitted. He received from them a variety of poetic works, the reading of which constitutes his greatest pleasure. They were in the habit of selecting topics upon which to exercise his poetic muse ; on the following Sunday he would return and have them transcribed. What is very astonishing, he has not only to make his verses, but retain them in me-mory, until he can meet with some one to copy them ; and though he may have four or five sets of verses on different subjects, his memory is so retentive that he has no difficulty in recounting them in turn to his scribe. When an abbreviation is necessary to preserve the metre he will point it out. He has no pleasure in as-sociating with any but those of intelligence, and is al-ways most delighted when he can get an amanuensis to transcribe his verses, and for this purpose will walk every Sunday eight or nine miles to visit the students of college."

The number of the 29th, contained a letter to the editor, from John Murray, of Warren county, Kentucky, of which the following are extracts: "Let the friends of humanity not despair. In 1806, in Kentucky, there was a great stir about emancipation. A goodly number of Baptist preachers, with private members of the Bap-tist denominations, separated themselves from the slaveholders on account of oppression. The 'emancipating preachers,' as they were called, exposed the horrors of slavery. This awoke the people from their stupor. A few joined the chorus : 'the equal rights of all men!—Emancipation.' But a great many woke in rage, and opposed all the emancipators, with all the spleen of which they were masters; and said, these men are not fit to live. Many at that time, thought the emancipators were doing more harm than good, by preaching against slavery; for they could only make the slaveholders mad, and harden them, and cause the negroes to be worse used. But this was a mistake; for they (the slave-holders,) made a pretext that to keep them and use them well was no harm." " Ever since that time, the heaven-born principle—the equal rights of all men,—has been gaining ground in Kentucky." "Now, the people of all classes converse freely on the subject, and, with a very few exceptions, seem willing to free the blacks and colonize them, provided it can be done on our own continent, where the negroes are willing to go, and where the expense of sending them is not great."

The same number of the Genius gave the information, that the new constitution of Peru, South America, promulgated April 19th, 1828, contained this provision : " *No person is born a slave in this Republic : No slave can enter from abroad without being free.*"

The number of September 6th, 1828, being the commencement of a new volume, contained an editorial headed " Ninth Volume," of which the following are extracts :

" More than seven years have now elapsed since the first number of " THE GENIUS OF UNIVERSAL EMANCIPATION " was issued from the press, and sent abroad to take its luck in a fault-finding world, and *stand* or *fall* by its own merits *alone*. No hireling prints were employed to trumpet forth a fame which it never deserved. No associations of wealthy and influential individuals were formed for the purpose of giving it a circulation or popularity which its own character could not sustain or

extend.   Its pecuniary prospects all grew out of BARELY
SIX INDIVIDUAL SUBSCRIPTIONS; and its success, in every
other respect, was left to grow out of its own little self,
with this limited circulation.   But this was not the
only difficulty with which it was doomed to grapple.
Many of the declared friends of emancipation, distrust-
ing its slender hold upon the favour of the people, denounced the attempt as 'wild and Quixotic.'   The
'great mass' looked 'askance' at a project so novel :—
while interested knaves poured forth their vollies of
wrath,' and seasoned their execrations with threats by
no means *creditable* to themselves or flattering to the
editor.   Nothing but a firm conviction of the correctness of our views, the justice of our cause and the rec-
titude of our intentions, could have sustained us in our
undertaking, during the earliest stages of this discourag-
ing conflict.   But the fates have decreed, that ' perseverance in well doing, shall be rewarded.'   Our paper
has worked its way through many opposing difficulties,
and gradually extended and increased its patronage.
And we now have the pleasure to say that it is supported by *many* of the most exemplary and influential
men—both political and religious—in the United States.
The immense pecuniary sacrifices, however, which have
been necessarily made to sustain it thus far, have not
been sufficiently repaired to give it that independent,
firm, and dignified character which its advocates might
wish.

" The difficulties to be encountered in conducting
a periodical like this are numerous and appalling. Each
man who lends his support thinks he thereby obtains an
unqualified right to chalk out the course to be pursued
by its conductor. And as opinions relative to this course
are various and conflicting, we must reject all but our
own, and adopt it as the rule of our conduct. Some of
our subscribers who believe that the condition of the
African race is materially involved in the ensuing Presidential election, urge us to devote a larger portion of
our paper, at this eventful period, to that important sub-

ject;—others, again, when they discover the most distant allusion to a ' *purely political* ' question of this kind very gravely order us to strike their names from our list; and assign for a reason, that we have ' *abandoned our first principles and commenced the publication of a political paper!* ' "

The paper of the 13th, said : "From the African Repository, we learn that a gentleman of Georgia has recently sought aid of the Colonization Society, to remove the whole number of his slaves (43) to the colony of Liberia. The act of giving liberty to so large a number, will deprive this individual of the greater part of his fortune, and leave him unable to do much towards their transportation himself."

The number of the 28th contained an address to the people of Virginia, adopted by the second annual meeting of the Virginia Anti-Slavery convention, which was held openly in the town hall, at Winchester, Frederic county, and continued from the 21st to the 23d of August, 1828. This address was first published in the Winchester Republican. After dwelling on the manner in which slavery had retarded the population and prosperity of the state, it recommended that a provision be made in the constitution, that all slaves born after a certain date should be free at a certain age, and suggested that the then contemplated convention to revise the constitution, would afford an opportunity to accomplish the object. It also expressed approbation of " the colonization of those who would be willing to remove from the country."

The same paper contained an extract from an American traveller's account of Mexico, from which we transcribe the following, as affording interesting information of the state of things in that country, shortly before the issuing of the decree of President Guerrero, which proclaimed immediate emancipation. "The importation of slaves into Mexico was always inconsiderable, and their number in 1798 did not exceed 6,000. Of these many have died, many have been manumitted, and the rest quitted their masters in 1810, and sought freedom in the independent army : so that I am, I believe, justified in stating that there is now hardly a single slave in the central portion of the republic. In Texas a few have been introduced by the North American settlers, but all further importations are prohibited by law, and provision has been made for securing the freedom of the off spring for the slaves now in existence."

Early in October of this year, (1828,) the state election took place in Maryland, and in November it was followed by the presidential election, which resulted in the choice of Gen. Jackson. Nothing was heard during the contest of Daniel Raymond as the Anti-Slavery candidate, who had been withdrawn the preceding year in the hope that at the next election he would "receive the support of the administration party generally, as well as that of the friends of emancipation." The Genius, during the contest, advocated, in occasional articles, the re-election of President Adams, as being a non-slaveholder and a friend of a protective tariff. Lundy was absent from home, lecturing in the Northern states, at the time that most of those articles were published.

In November, 1828, the American Convention for the abolition of slavery sat in Baltimore four days, viz: from the 3d to the 6th, inclusive. Lundy was among the delegates from Maryland. It was there resolved to hold the meetings of the Convention thereafter, permanently, in the city of Washington.

On the 13th of December the Genius announced that petitions for the abolition of slavery in the District of Columbia, were in extensive circulation in the various counties through the states of Maryland, Delaware, Pennsylvania, New Jersey, New York, Massachusetts and Vermont, as well as in parts of other states.

In the number of the same date, Lundy gave an editorial notice of the " Journal of the Times " then recently established at Bennington. The following are extracts from this notice :

"The editorial department of the above mentioned work

is conducted by William Lloyd Garrison, a young gentleman of fine talents, who officiated a few months since,
as editor of the '*National Philanthropist*,' of Boston.
Though he has not the advantage of age and experience,
that belong to the *veteran* members of the fraternity, it
may be truly said that he wields a powerful pen, and
even, (what is deserving of all praise) an *independent*
one. Few, indeed, can claim a title to the latter dis-
stinction; and when we meet with one such, we cannot
withhold the meed of merit fairly due.

"But what more particularly elicits our favourable regard, the editor of this work has shewn a laudable disposition to advocate the claims of the poor distressed
African upon our sympathy and justice; and if he continues to do so, his talents will render him a most valuable coadjutor in this holy undertaking. Greatly, indeed, shall we rejoice, if even *one, faithful*, like 'Ab-
diel,' can be ' among the faithless found,' who, after
having *professed* loudly, have generally abandoned their
post, and left the unfortunate negro to his fate. There
are many who are ready to acknowledge—O yes, they
will *acknowledge*, (good honest souls!) with due frank-
ness and alacrity—that *something should be done* for the
abolition of slavery. They will, also, pen a paragraph
—perhaps an article, or so—and then—*the subject is*
EXHAUSTED!!

"We close this article with the following pithy extract
from the editorial address, accompanying the first number of the 'Journal of the Times.'—There is *nerve* in
it, or we mistake the power of style."

' In the first place, the Journal shall be INDEPENDENT,
in the broadest and stoutest signification of the term; it
shall be trammelled by no interest, biassed by no sect,
awed by no power. Of all diminutive objects that creep
on the face of the earth, that bask in God's sunshine, or
inhale the rich atmosphere of life—of all despicable and
degraded beings, a time-serving, shuffling, truckling editor has no parallel; and he who has not courage enough
to hunt down popular vices, to combat popular preju-

dices, to encounter the madness of party, to tell the truth
and maintain the truth, cost what it may, to attack vil-
lany in its higher walks, and strip presumption of its
vulgar garb, to meet the frowns of an enemy with the
smiles of a friend, and the hazard of independence without the hope of reward, should be crushed at a blow, if
he dared to tamper with the interests, or speculate upon
the whims of the public. Look at our motto—watch us
narrowly in our future course—and if we depart one
tittle from the lofty sentiment which we have adopted
as our guide, leave us to a speedy annihilation.

'Secondly. We have three objects in view, which we
shall pursue through life, whether in this place or elsewhere—namely : the suppression of intemperance and
its associate vices, the gradual emancipation of every
slave in the republic, and the perpetuity of national
peace. In discussing these topics, what is wanting in
vigor, shall be made up in zeal.'

The same number of the Genius announced the passage to a third reading, in the Kentucky Senate, by a
vote of thirty to eight, of a bill for prohibiting the bringing of slaves into that state for sale, and declaring that
all so brought thereafter should be free. This bill became a law, and is still in force : although one or two
strenuous efforts have been made for its repeal.

CHAPTER XXVI.

Events in 1829 and 1830, and gleanings from the "Genius," of those
years.

The Genius of January 3d, 1829, published the official documents, connected with the negotiation with
Great Britain for the mutual surrender of fugitive slaves
and other persons bound to service, which had been
carried on by Mr. Clay, as Secretary of State, under
president Adams, through the agency, first of Mr. Gallatin

and afterwards of Mr. Barbour, as Ministers at London. This negotiation had been undertaken at the request both of the Kentucky Legislature, and also that of the national House of Representatives.

Mr. Clay, in his instructions to Mr. Gallatin, of June 19th, 1826, said that the states of Virginia and Kentucky were peculiarly anxious on the subject, as their slaves were escaping in considerable numbers to Upper Canada. He suggested that the proposed arrangement might be even more advantageous to England than to this country, as, in addition to some slaves escaping from the West Indies, we should surrender Britain's "*military and maritime deserters,*" which would be more numerous than our own. Mr. Gallatin, in his first letter to Mr. Clay, (Dec. 21st, 1826,) stated a conversation with the British Minister, Huskisson, on the subject, in which Mr. Huskisson acknowledged, that the fugitive slaves were " no acquisition to Canada," and made no objection to the *principle* of surrender ; but he spoke of " the difficulties thrown in the way of every thing of that kind, by the Courts, and by the abolition British associations," as obstacles to the arrangement. Mr. Clay, in reply, stated that the measure desired, was embraced in a treaty with Mexico, then (Feb. 1827) before the American Senate for ratification, and expressed a hope, that as the British plenipotentiaries admitted " the correctness of the *principle*," Mr. Gallatin might be successful in inducing them to adopt the suggested arrangement. Mr. Gallatin, on July 5th, 1827, wrote word, that Mr. Addington had informed him, that it was "utterly impossible to agree to a surrender of fugitive slaves:" and on Sept. 26th, he wrote that the reason given for not acceding to the proposition, was, that with respect to British possessions *where slavery is not admitted*, the ministry could not depart from the principle established by the courts, that every man is free who touches British ground; and that " the state of public opinion was such, that no administration could or would make the proposed arrangement."—On June 12th, 1828, Mr. Clay wrote to the new American Minister to England, Mr. Barbour, instructing him to renew the proposition, conformably to a new request from the House of Representatives, and stating that the " evil " was "a growing one." Mr. Barbour replied, Oct. 2d, 1828, that he had conferred with Lord Aberdeen, who stated, " that he would be happy to grant the most substantial remedy, yet, in the present state of public feeling on this subject, which he said might properly be called a *mania*, the application of the remedy was an affair of some delicacy and difficulty : " but he said that Sir George Murray, the head of the colonial department, intended to bring the subject before parliament, when he hoped the evil would be obviated, " as he could not conceive that any people would wish to see their numbers increased by such subjects." This was the last of the documents communicated, relative to a negotiation, which had then lasted about two years and a half. In publishing the correspondence, Lundy strongly expressed his indignation at its contents.

The same number of the paper stated, that great progress was making with the petitions for abolition in the District of Columbia ; that many of the editors of periodical works had endeavored to turn the attention of their readers to the subject, and that upwards of 1,100 signers had been obtained in Vermont.

At about the same period, the Legislature of Pennsylvania, with great unanimity, passed resolutions favourable to the abolition of slavery in the District of Columbia.

We are without any numbers of the Genius, between January 3d, and September 2d, 1829. It appears that

---

*This resolution, which was approved by Governor Shulze on the 23d of January, 1829, instructed the Senators, and requested the Representatives, in Congress, from Pennsylvania, " to procure if practicable the passage of a law to abolish slavery in the District of Columbia, in such a manner as they may consider consistent with the rights of individuals and the constitution of the United States."

Lundy again visited Hayti in the spring of the year, and that the paper was suspended during his absence. Before leaving, he announced that a gentlemen of Maryland was about to liberate his slaves, twelve in number, and send them to Hayti. In the number of September 2d, he stated that they had been safely settled there, having been taken out, as appears from his personal narrative, by himself, and that the person who emancipated them, was Joseph Leonard Smith, a member of the Catholic church. The same number noticed the emancipation, by will, of all the slaves of Gen. Charles Ridgely, formerly Governor of Maryland. The number thus freed, was upwards of two hundred and fifty. Lundy expressed his extreme mortification to find, that the editors of the Baltimore " *American Farmer,*" the Washington " *National Intelligencer,*" and the " *New York Morning Herald,*" had, in their columns, openly condemned this benevolent act.

In the same number, (Sept. 2d,) Lundy commenced a series of articles on " the present state of things in Hayti." He said that he found affairs there much better than when he visited the Island three years before : that emigrants could obtain leases of plantations, with dwellings on them, for seven years, the first two years to be *gratis,* and the remaining five, at a moderate rent : that with respect to religious toleration, no country on earth was more free, and that several congregations of Baptists, Methodists, and others, held public meetings in different parts of the island : that the emancipated slaves taken out by him, had obtained leases for the term of nine years, of land of the richest kind, ready cleared, and had gone to work on it : and that he was ready to make arrangements for the transportation of others who might desire to emigrate thither.

In the same paper Lundy announced the association of Wm. Lloyd Garrison with himself, in the editorship of the Genius, and also that he had obtained the aid of a female editor, who was to have the principal direction of the " Ladies' department." The name of the editor

of this department was not stated, but it is known to
have been Elizabeth Margaret Chandler, the poetess.
Mr. Garrison, in an introductory address, stated, as
he had previously done in "The Journal of the
Times," that the energies of his life should be devoted
to the overthrow of three of the greatest evils which
curse our race, slavery, intemperance and war: that
no man contemplated with more intense and unmingled
satisfaction the colony of Liberia, than he did, it being
the heart and lungs of Africa, "full of generous respira-
tion and warm blood ;" that, as an auxiliary to abolition, colonization deserved encouragement ; but as a
remedy, it was inadequate, and if we depended on the
colonization societies alone, slavery would never be exterminated; that he viewed Hayti with a favourable eye,
as a home for emancipated slaves, and thought it, in
many respects, superior to Liberia : and he stated, in
substance, the following, as his general positions, on the
subject of slavery—namely : 1. That the slaves were
entitled to complete and immediate emancipation : 2.
That the question of expediency had nothing to do with
that of right ; as it was not for tyrants to say when they
might safely break the chains of their subjects: 3. That
even on the ground of expediency, it would be wiser to
set the slaves all free to-day than to-morrow, or next
week than next year : and that to think of removing
them all from the country, was visionary : 4. That the
coloured people, born on the soil, had a right to remain,
and we had no right to compel their removal.

The number of the 16th, contained an appeal, by
Elizabeth M. Chandler, to the Ladies of the United
States, in which she earnestly urged them to enlist in the
cause of emancipation, and particularly in the encouragement of free produce. She followed this piece, by
various others recommending the formation of female
societies, after the model of those in Great Britain, and
discussing other topics, connected with the Anti-Slavery
enterprise.

In the same paper, Lundy announced the receipt of

information, that the government of the United States
was engaged in negotiations with Mexico, for the purchase of Texas; and assuming that, if obtained, Texas
would be a slaveholding territory, he commenced that
strenuous opposition to its annexation, which he continued through his life, and which, at the end of sixteen
years afterwards, proved to have been unavailing.

In the same number, (Sept. 16th,) Daniel Raymond
was again announced by some of his friends, as a candidate at the then approaching election, to represent the
city of Baltimore, in the Maryland Legislature. The Genius
of October 2d, contained an editorial, urging the support
of Raymond, as a champion of universal liberty, and a
warm friend of internal improvements and of "the
American system," or a protective tariff.

On the 9th of October, it published the result of the
Baltimore election, showing but 186 votes for Raymond,
being about one-fifth of the number (viz. 974) that he
had received in 1826, at the election preceding the two
years during which he was withdrawn, in order to unite
the friends of the national administration. Raymond
had issued an address, before the election of 1829, in
which, instead of taking anti-slavery ground, boldly, as
in 1826, he did not mention the subject of slavery at all.
He has since removed to Frederic county, Maryland,
and is said to be now (1846) a holder of slaves.

During a good portion of the autumn, Lundy was absent, either on lecturing tours, or on business connected
with the paper. Some efforts were made at that time,
for the circulation of petitions for the abolition of slavery
in the District of Columbia, but with a seeming diminu-
tion of energy and efficiency. Some of the causes of this
falling short, may be obtained from the following article,
by Lundy, inserted in the Genius of November 20th.

 "SECTARIAN AND PARTY STRIFE.—We are resolved
to have nothing to do with sectarian or party disputation,
in our public proceedings, unless the question of slavery
should appear to be involved in it ; yet we are grieved
to see, in numerous instances, old and faithful labourers

in that sacred cause, abandoning it, simply because others are actively engaged in promoting it, with whom they differ in some religious or political tenet. Great schisms exist in several religious societies, and also in the community at large, respecting the institution of Free Masonry. Many, we are sorry to perceive, refuse to co-operate with individuals of the parties opposed to them, in any measures for the *abolition of slavery*, though they readily admit that the latter subject is all-important. Now this is a deplorable state of things. It is like a civil war in a military camp, when a dangerous enemy is forcing the gates. It is like a family quarrel in which the inmates of a house are engaged, while it is burning over their heads. Why can we not all agree to tolerate the freedom of opinion which our government recognizes, so far as to meet each other on the question of slavery, as on neutral ground, and labour together for its extinction? It is with awful forebodings that we behold this state of things. Who can foresee our inevitable doom?—Shall anarchy rule, and despotism finally overwhelm us?—May God, in his mercy, save us from such a woful catastrophe.' "

On the 27th November, the Genius published the decree of Vincent Guerrero, President of Mexico, countersigned by Laurence (or Lorenzo) de Zavala,* as Secretary of State, dated the 15th of September 1829, by which decree slavery was extinguished in Mexico. The following were its essential provisions. 1. "Slavery is for ever abolished in the republic. 2. Consequently all those individuals who until this day looked upon themselves as slaves, are free. 3. When the financial situation of the Republic admits, the proprietors of slaves shall be indemnified, and the indemnification regulated by law."

* This Zavala was the same who subsequently joined the Texans, in opposition the abrogation of the state governments by Santa Anna. Guerero, after the above decree, was put to death by the consolidation party.—ED.

The number of December 25th, contained a notice of
the session of the American Anti-Slavery Convention,
held at Washington city, commencing on the 8th of the
month, at which convention Lundy was present as a
delegate. A report was there presented and accepted,
which expressed the opinion that it was " easier to per-
suade the majority of the people to pass laws for the
abolition of slavery, than to break off all commercial
intercourse with slaveholders :" that no evidence had
been furnished, sufficient to carry conviction to the public mind, that it was more *profitable* to employ free than
slave labour : but that the evils of slavery, in affecting
the morals and happiness of society, in abridging public
and private enterprise, in promoting idleness end extrava-
gance, and in accelerating the impoverishment of land
were capable of demonstration. It recommended the use
of " temperate and conciliatory language, to illustrate the
inconsistency of bondage with sound political doctrines,
as well as with the obligations of justice and religion ; "
and suggested that appeals to a sense of justice and the
dictates of religion, were means which had effected, in
ancient times, the liberation of serfs in Great Britain
and other European countries, as was shown by the following extract from a quotation, contained in 2 Black-
stone's Commentaries, page 96, viz : "The holy fathers,
monks and friars, had, in their confessions, and specially
in their extreme and deadly sickness, convinced the
laity how dangerous a practice it was, for one Christian
man to hold another in bondage : so that temporal men,
by little and little, by reason of that terror in their con-
sciences, were glad to manumit all their villeins."

Lundy, in his notice of the above mentioned report,
expressed, as he had done in the Convention, his disapproval of what was said in it respecting the compara-
tive pecuniary profit of free and slave labour. He fondly
cherished the hope, that it might be demonstrated, at some
day, that the most profitable course which a slaveholder
could pursue, was to emancipate his slaves, and employ
them as freemen. To test the question of how far this

hope was well founded, was one of his objects, in his attempt at Mexican colonization.

The number of January 1st, 1830, contained a notice of a new paper called "the Eclectic Observer, and Working Men's Advocate," established at Wheeling, Virginia, which came out in strong opposition to the slave system. That of the 15th, noticed the fact, that a bill had been introduced into the House of Representatives of Kentucky, "to provide for the constitutional emancipation of all slaves in the state : " but on its first reading it was postponed indefinitely, by a vote of 18 to 11. The largeness of the minority, indicates the great progress that had then been made in Kentucky, by anti-slavery principles.

From an article of the 26th of February, it appears that a bill had then recently passed the house of Delegates of the Virginia Legislature, for prohibiting the instruction of free negroes, mulattoes or slaves, under severe penalties : and that this bill owed its origin to the circulation of a most injudicious pamphlet, addressed to all coloured people, by David Walker, a coloured man of Boston, in which he incited them to insurrection and bloodshed, as a religious *duty*. The bill ultimately became a law. It is supposed, by some, that the pamphlet of Walker was the cause of the massacre of whites at Southampton, Virginia, which took place in the following year.

The Genius of the succeeding week, copied from a Kentucky paper, a statement, that at Milledgeville it had been accidentally discovered that Burritt, one of the editors of the Statesman, published at that place, had been corresponding with Walker, and had received from him eighteen or twenty of his pamphlets, which were found in Burritt's possession : that he had been arrested, but in consequence of exceptions, was discharged, and had "taken French leave" of the place.

Lundy, in speaking of the above named pamphlet, said : "I can do no less that set the broadest seal of reprobation upon it." "It is a laboured attempt to rouse the worst passions of human nature, and inflame the minds of those to whom it is addressed."

In the number of March 5th, Lundy in speaking of the paper, said, that "in addition to the ordinary difficulties arising from a scanty patronage, others of the most aggravated character have presented themselves. Persecution, in some of its worse forms, has been meted out with unsparing hand. Threats and slanders without number, as well as libel suits and personal assaults, have been resorted to, with the view of breaking down our spirits, and destroying the establishment. In consequence of the limited support that we receive, we are under the necessity of making a radical change in the publication of the work. The partnership (with W. L. Garrison) will be henceforth dissolved, and the paper will be again issued *monthly* by myself, and *confined* to the subject of Universal Emancipation."

The paper for some months preceding this announcement, had assumed a strong political cast, in opposition to the administration of General Jackson and the party supporting that administration, and favouring, in some measure, the cause of Henry Clay as a presidential candidate. Lundy now said; "it will hereafter treat exclusively upon the subject of emancipation."

In speaking of Mr. Garrison, Lundy said, that having been most of the time from home, himself, the conduct of the paper had devolved principally on the junior editor. "In some few instances, as might have been expected, articles were admitted that did not entirely meet my approbation, but I fully acquit him of inserting anything, knowing that it would be thus disapproved; and we have ever cherished for each other the kindliest feelings and mutual personal regard." "It would be superfluous for me to say, that he has proven himself a faithful and able coadjutor in the great and holy cause in which we are engaged." Mr. Garrison, in a parting notice, said: "A separation from my philanthropic friend is painful, yet, owing to adverse circumstances, unavoidable. Although our partnership is at an end, I trust we shall ever remain one in spirit and purpose, and that the cause of emancipation will suffer no detriment.''

At this time a criminal prosecution was pending, which had been commenced by Francis Todd of Newburyport, against Lundy and Garrison, for an alleged libel, consisting of an article written by Garrison, respecting the domestic slave trade, in which Todd was said to be engaged. Lundy, being absent when the writ was issued, was not arrested, and the trial went on against Garrison alone. The Genius for May 1830, announced that the jury had rendered a verdict of guilty, and that Garrison was in prison, for a fine of fifty dollars and costs. Lundy thereupon set to work to effect Mr. Garrison's release, and upon his solicitation, Arthur Tappan of New York paid the fine and costs, and Garrison was discharged, after forty-nine days imprisonment. After Garrison's conviction, Lundy had been required by Judge Brice to give bail to answer the same charge. Before giving it, he remained a few days in prison. A civil suit had also been commenced by Todd against the editors on account of the same publication.

The April number announced that information had been received from Hayti, of the arrival there of Frances Wright, with between twenty and thirty slaves, which she had emancipated, being those previously located at Nashoba, Tennessee. The same number stated, that it appeared, from official documents, that the number of slaves in South Carolina decreased 32,727, in a single year, from 1824 to 1825—the difference being occasioned by the domestic slave trade.*

It also announced the commencement in New Orleans, by Milo Mower, of a daily paper entitled the Liberalist, which openly advocated the rights and interests of the people of colour, and opposed the project then in agitation, of expelling the free coloured people from the state of Louisiana. From a statement in the same number, it appeared that during the preceding ten years, Lundy had expended

*Most of the slaves so removed, went to Alabama, many of the masters removing thither also.

in the Anti-Slavery cause, several thousand dollars of his earnings, had travelled more than five thousand miles, on foot, and twenty thousand in other ways, had visited nineteen states of the Union, held more than two hundred public meetings, and made two voyages to Hayti.

During the latter part of 1829, and the first part of 1830, a colony of several thousand coloured people, mostly from Ohio, was established in Upper Canada, the immediate occasion being the enforcement, in Ohio, of an old law, which was intended to restrain the settlement of emancipated slaves in that State. It appears, from the Genius, that this event excited a strong feeling in Canada, at that time, and the House of Assembly of that Province passed resolutions expressive of its aversion to the settlement, and requested the Governor to apply to the British Parliament, for the future prohibition of such emigration. The application proved unsuccessful, and Canada remained open to coloured settlers. Lundy, who had paid a visit to Canada, encouraged the emigration of free coloured people thither, in case they had previously resided north of 34 degrees latitude, so as to be fitted to endure the climate : and the coloured people of Boston and Philadelphia, formed societies to encourage such emigration.

The May number of 1830, mentioned that forty-nine slaves, emancipated expressly for the purpose, had then recently sailed from Norfolk for Africa, and that thirty-nine more, liberated by Joel Early of Georgia, had arrived at Norfolk, for the same destination.

The same paper announced that Bustamente, Vice President of Mexico, (who had ejected Guerrero from power and put him to death,) had rescinded so much of Guerrero's decree respecting slavery, as provided for the emancipation of the slaves in Texas. The prohibition of the importation of slaves was continued, however, as well as the provision that all persons born thereafter in the country, should be free. Bustamente, who was of the central or consolidation faction, prohibited, at this time, the further settlement in Texas, of people from the United States ; and he was taking measures, according

to the Genius, to govern Texas as a colony, and not as
a state. This project was probably prevented from going
into effect, by the civil war in Mexico, which resulted
in the expulsion of Bustamente from the chief magistracy.

The June number, contained an extract from the New
Orleans Liberalist, which stated, that in consequence
of the recent acts of the Louisiana Legislature, bearing
oppressively upon the free people of colour, a considerable number of that class were about to migrate to Jamaica. The editor of the Liberalist, however, advised
them to remain, in hopes of better times. In the number
of the Genius for September following, it was stated
that the New Orleans Liberalist had been discontinued
for want of support, and that the editor, Milo Mower,
had been imprisoned, on the charge of circulating " a
seditious and inflammatory hand-bill among the coloured
people." The piece so denominated, was an appeal
to the coloured people for support to his publication.

In the number for September, Lundy gave an article
on " National politics, " in which he said : "I now
fearlessly and boldly assert, that the subject of slavery
is no ' state right' matter, but that all the citizens of
this republic are interested in its extinction, and if ever
we abolish it, the influence of *the people and government
of the United States*, must effect it,"

The November number announced the election, in
Guilford county, North Carolina, to the Legislature of
that state, of Amos Weaver, an open emancipationist,
and it gave extracts from an address which he had delivered before the Manumission society of that county,
during the preceding year.

The Genius for December 1830, noticed the decease
of Wm. H. Fitzhugh, of Virginia, whose name has been
repeatedly mentioned in the foregoing extracts. By his
will, he directed the full emancipation, after the year
1850, of all his remaining slaves, being about two hundred in number, and that the expenses of their removal,
to whatever place they might select, should be defrayed.
In addition to this, they were to receive fifty dollars

each, if they should go to Liberia, which course Mr.
Fitzhugh thought the most likely to promote their happiness. Lundy expressed particular regret at the decease
of this philanthopist, as it might interrupt the plan of
culture, adopted by him, as mentioned in the August
number of 1827.

The same paper noticed the rapid increase of anti-
slavery sentiment, among the Presbyterians; and that
the Presbytery of Chilicothe, Ohio, had addressed two
lectures on slavery to the churches under its care. It
also noticed the rapid progress of anti-slavery sentiment
in England, and the fact that, according to the statement
of Brougham, the new election to parliament had shown
an increase of thirty anti-slavery members, making a
difference of sixty, in the relative strength of parties.
It was shortly afterwards announced, that anti-slavery
petitions, in numbers exceeding those of any former period, were flowing into parliament.

CHAPTER XXVII.

Extracts and occurrences for 1831 and 1832.

The January number, of 1831, announced the receipt
of the first number of "*The Liberator*," published at Boston, by Garrison and Knapp: urged every one to sub-
scribe to it who could afford the means, and stated that
subscriptions would be received at the office of the Genius. And, in the next number, Lundy, reverting to the
subject, said, that his limits would not permit him to say
a thousandth part that he "could wish for the encouragement of these noble coadjutors in the cause of emancipation."

The February number mentioned an attempt, made in
the Maryland Legislature, to prohibit emancipation, except on condition of the emancipated leaving the
State. It was not successful.

In the number of March, Lundy said, "The editor of

the Liberator retorts upon me for my critical distinction between "*slaveholders*" and "advocates of slavery." He insists that they are all blameworthy—that "there is none innocent, no not one." I admit they are all guilty, and I have no disposition to extenuate their guilt. But I would observe that there are "degrees of crime,"—&c., &c.

In the same paper, the editor announced "*a glorious movement,*" of which he copied an account from the Western Luminary, of Lexington, Kentucky. That paper stated, that several slaveholders, "under a full conviction that there are insurmountable obstacles to the general emancipation of the present generation of slaves, but equally convinced of the necessity and practicability of emancipating their future offspring, are desirous that a society be formed for the purpose of investigating and impressing these truths on the public mind, as well by *example* as by precept, by placing themselves immediately, by mutual voluntary arrangements, under a well regulated system for gradual emancipation—such a system as they could recommend for adoption as the law of the land." Persons inclined to make the experiment, were requested to forward their names to the publisher of the Luminary, with the assurance that when the names of fifty slaveholders were received, a meeting would be called and a society organized. The next number of the Genius contained the news, extracted from the Luminary, that seventeen slaveholders had already sent in their names as subscribers to the plan.*

The same number, contained the proceedings of a meeting of the coloured people of Baltimore, expressive of

---

*These seventeen names were, Wm. R. Hines, Bardstown; Samuel R. Snead, Jefferson Co.; J. M. C. Irvin, Fayette Co.; Robt. J. Breckenridge, do.; A. J. Alexander, Woodford Co.; Charles Alexander, do.; J. R. Alexander, do.; James McCall, Rockcastle Co.; George Clark, Fayette Co.; John Wallace, do.; George W. Anderson, do.; James H. Allen, do.; James McDowell, do.: Norman Porter, Lexington, do.; Thomas T. Skillman, do.; James Blythe, do.; James G. McKinney, do.

their hostility to the Colonization Society, being the first movement of the kind in that part of the country. The resolutions were said to embrace the sentiments of a great majority of the coloured people of Baltimore. The next number contained the proceedings of a similar meeting in Washington city. The members of the latter meeting, expressed the opinion, that they had " many true and sincere friends" among the advocates of the colonization system, but they declared their disapproval of the action of those friends, and that it would be impolitic, unwise and improper for the coloured people to leave their homes, without the benefits of education.

In the March number of 1831, it was announced that Lundy, being about to leave home for a few months, had engaged Amos Gilbert to superintend the paper during his absence, with the continued assistance of Elizabeth M. Chandler, and that Lundy himself would be an occasional contributor. The journey to be taken was not announced, but it is known to have been first to the northern and eastern States, thence to Canada, and afterwards to Texas. His object in leaving home, was to labour in the cause in the North, solicit aid and collect dues for the paper, and ascertain the relative advantages of Canada and Texas, as asylums for coloured emigrants.

The same number noticed the activity of the Washington Anti-Slavery Society, in preparing and circulating memorials to Congress ; mentioned a report of the execution of one hundred and forty-nine persons in Martinique, for being concerned in a slave insurrection ; and gave an account of the emancipation of twenty-two slaves by Dr. Silas Hamilton, resident near Natchez, Mississippi, who at first offered his slaves to be taken to Africa, but as the Colonization Society had not the means to take them, he removed them, in 1828, to Cincinnati, and not being satisfied with their condition there he went in 1830 and settled them on land in Illinois.

The same paper also contained the following extract of a letter, from the Rev. Jesse Haile of Illinois, formerly of Arkansas.

"I have received a letter from Mr. Rees Alexander, of Arkansas, a gentleman of high respectability, in which he says: 'I must not forget to tell you that the papers (Genius of U. E.) you left with Mother Dixon' (her name is Mary) 'have had a most powerful influence. They have converted her from slavery. She has recently emancipated all her slaves. She employed the best attorney in the Territory to attend to the business for her, in order that there might be no future advantage taken. She has recorded a bill of emancipation of all her slaves, at her death; and also has made a will, bequeathing to them two-thirds of all her property of every description: which will is also recorded.' Would to God that all who hold them, would do likewise!' 'Then would their light break forth out of obscurity,' and their darkness would become as the noon-day.'

'You will understand that, when I left the Territory, I deposited the Genius of Universal Emancipation with the above named Mary Dixon who is an aged widow. She has six slaves."

The May and July numbers noticed the emancipation, by Elizabeth Greenfield, of Philadelphia, of all the slaves on a plantation in Mississippi where she formerly resided. The number of slaves is not mentioned, but it is stated that she was offered the sum of ten thousand dollars for them. She had at first provided, by will, for their settlement on lands which she had purchased for them in Ohio. But when the persecution of the coloured people in Ohio arose, she, at the age of eighty years or upwards, journeyed to Mississippi and back, a distance of over four thousand miles, and induced her former slaves to emigrate to Liberia.*

The July number announced that Amos Gilbert after a brief trial, could not reconcile himself to the state of things at Washington, and had retired from his connexion with the editorship. Hence the paper would revert to the care of Lundy and his female assistant. It appears from a private letter which Lundy wrote about this time, that he printed the paper at whatever place

---

*One or more of them afterwards returned to the United States.

he happened to be, and to find a printing press which he could use, and funds to defray expenses, in the course of his journey.

The paper for August stated, that in Kentucky, the required number of fifty slaveholders to form an Anti-Slavery Society, had been made up, and it was expected that the society would soon go into operation.

The August and September numbers gave full accounts of the insurrection of about fifty slaves which took place in Southampton county, Virginia, on the 3d Sunday of August, 1831. The insurgents were headed by a fanatical preacher, named Nat, Turner, who professed to be inspired, and assured his followers that a peculiar appearance of the sun, some days before, presaged their success. They possessed themselves of horses, and of guns, and other weapons and began an indiscriminate massacre and destruction of property. Thus they proceeded from plantation to plantation for a distance of twenty miles, slaughtering men, women and children, to the number in all of sixty three, as it was stated. On the first assault, two of Turner's followers shrunk from his command to take life, and he commenced the work himself. The attack began before day-break, at the house of Travis, the master of Turner, and the insurgents were dispersed early in the afternoon. Some thirty of them were put to death without trial, by the exasperated whites.

About the same time an extensive plot for an insurrection, was discovered among the slaves of several counties in North Carolina. One of the participants in this plot, was likewise a preacher, by the name of David, and was said to be a very intelligent man. Between fifty and one hundred blacks were arrested and put in prison, in Sampson and Duplin counties, and several were executed. There were also rumors of plots in Delaware and other parts of the country.

These occurrences were very unfortunate for the anti-slavery cause, as they confirmed in their opinions, those who were opposed to the education of the coloured people, as well as to emancipation unless accompanied by expatriation. They also created a strong feeling in the South, against the circulation of anti-slavery newspapers and tracts, and were probably among the prominent causes which ultimately rendered it impracticable for Lundy to continue his paper at Washington city. The southern papers attributed the origin of the plots, to the Genius and the Liberator, especially the latter, which it was said had been circulated in the South in large numbers. It is probable, however, that the conspiracies were instigated chiefly by the before mentioned pamphlet of David Walker, if in fact they owed their origin to any publication whatever.

From the time that these events occurred, Anti-Slavery Societies in the South ceased almost entirely to be formed, and those previously established, soon sunk into disuse. They have not, to this day, been resuscitated.

The Genius of September said, " we regret every attempt to use force, in violation of law, not only because of the ill feeling it creates, or the individual distress it may occasion, but also on account of the insurmountable obstacles it invariably throws in the way of our future progress. Nothing can be more fatal to our hopes— nothing better calculated to retard our philanthropic operations, than such silly, phrenzied, anti-christian proceedings, on the part of the coloured people. And it is gratifying to perceive, that not a single free person, or one of intelligence, among them, has yet been certainly implicated in the horrid proceedings under consideration." And in the December number, it was said that " since the unfortunate movements among the slaves of Virginia, &c., some of our friends have evinced a disposition to let the subject rest, though that very circumstance should have been considered the strongest proof of the necessity of speedily putting an end to the system of oppression which is productive of such disastrous results."

The number of September defended the Liberator against the charge of being published for " the avowed purpose of inciting rebellion in the South," and other like accusations, which had been made in the National

Intelligencer and various other papers; and it quoted
from the Liberator, these words : " We have circulated
no papers extra in any part of our country. We have not
a single subscriber south of the Potomac. We have no
travelling agent or agents. It is not the real or '-avowed
object' of the Liberator to stir up insurrections, but the
contrary."

The October number gave the information that the
Attorney General of North Carolina, had submitted a
bill of indictment against Garrison and Knapp, for publishing the Liberator, to the Grand Jury at Raleigh, who
had returned it a true bill: and that in several other
places, it had been made penal for a coloured person,
bond or free, to take the Liberator from the Post-office :
also that a movement and petition was in progress, in
Virginia, to obtain a law for the removal of the free
blacks, and to prevent emancipations, except on condition of the emancipated being sent out of the country.

The Genius for December, announced the presentation to Congress, by John Quincy Adams, of 15 memorials, asking for the abolition of slavery in the District of Columbia. In presenting them, Mr. Adams complimented
the signers, but stated that he should not give the proposed
measure his support: that " whatever might be his opinions of slavery, in the abstract, in the District of Columbia, he hoped it would not become a subject of discussion in that house: " and that " the most healing medicines, when unduly administered, become the most
deadly poison." This version of Mr. Adams' remarks
was taken from the New York Whig. The editor of
the Genius stated, that he had seen another version,
which was " much more explanatory."

In the same paper it was stated that the Georgia
Legislature had offered a reward of five thousand dollars for the arrest and conviction of the publishers of the
Liberator : and that a respectable and intelligent coloured
preacher of the Baptist persuasion, named Raymond, had
been compelled, by a mob, to abandon his residence at
Norfolk, and migrate to New York. He was sus-

pected of participating in the Southampton plot; and it was with difficulty that some respectable persons prevented the mob from taking his life. The same paper also contained the confession of Nat Turner, made before his execution, from which it appeared that his own master, Travis, was the first person that he murdered. He denied any connexion with the North Carolina plot, and professed to have had a revelation that he should do " the great work," when warned by a sign in the heavens, and that he should conceal it until the first sign appeared : and in his own words, that " on the appearance of the sign I should arise and prepare myself and slay my enemies with their own weapons." He said that when the first sign appeared, (an eclipse in February,) the seal was removed from his lips, and he communicated the revelation to the four persons in whom he had most confidence : that many schemes of action were then formed and rejected, until the sign appeared again, (a strange appearance of the sun in August,) when he determined to wait no longer. From this circumstance, little doubt of his insanity can be entertained. The pamphlet of David Walker, which he had probably seen, had professed much religious zeal, and urged insurrection on the alleged authority of the New Testament.

The same number of the Genius stated that four hundred coloured persons had arrived at New York on their way to the Canada settlement, having left their homes on account of the fiery persecution which was raging against them by reason of the slave plots and insurrections : that twenty-two had been sent in the same direction, for the same reason, by the Friends in North Carolina, and that upwards of three hundred, many of whom were liberated slaves, had sailed from Norfolk, Virginia, in a vessel bound to Africa.

In a supplement to the December number, the Report made in Congress by Mr. Doddridge, Chairman of the Committee on the District of Columbia, relative to the petitions for abolition in that District, was published. The report expressed the opinion that as the District was composed of cessions from Maryland and Virginia, it would be unwise and impolitic in Congress, if not unjust to the adjoining states, to interfere, while slavery existed in them : and that if such interference were proper, at any time, the present moment was inauspicious for its consideration. This report was made on the 19th of December, shortly after the commencement of the session, with a view, probably, to discourage the further signing and presentation of memorials. Lundy accompanied the publication of this report with comments, in which he inquired if it was "*unwise*" or "*unjust*" for Pennsylvania to abolish slavery within its limits, or for Congress to prohibit it in Ohio, &c., before it had been abolished in the adjoining states of Maryland and Virginia.

The same paper noticed, that in the Virginia Legislature a memorial from the Yearly Meeting of Friends, and one from citizens of Hanover County, both recommending the abolition of slavery, had been presented ; that a motion to reject them had been made and lost : that the memorial of the Friends had been referred, and that the celebrated debate of 1831, in that Legislature, on the subject of slavery, had commenced. This debate ultimately terminated in a refusal to act upon the subject, either of colonization or emancipation ; and from that time to the present, the question has been at rest in the Virginia Legislature.

In the month of January, 1832, Lundy made a visit to the Wilberforce settlement, in Canada, travelling on foot much of the way, and encountering many hardships. A letter which he wrote, giving an account of this journey, is lost: but the following has been furnished by the relative to whom it was addressed, as the substance of an account contained in it of a striking incident.

Lundy stated that he came, one afternoon, to a stream of water, swelled high by the rain, the foot-log, for crossing, being partly swept away, and the current deep and strong. The country was thinly inhabited, if at all. There was snow on the ground, and he feared to be out all night. He saw on the opposite side of the stream, a tree blown down, the top of which lay in the water, so near to the foot-log, that he thought he could jump from the one to the other.   He made the attempt, and reached the tree, but the limbs were not strong enough to bear him, and he plunged almost entirely into the water.   He caught the branches of the tree, however, and by their assistance, climbed out and got on shore.   It was now near night, no house was in view, and he knew that if he did not get warm he must perish. He recorded in the letter, many of the thoughts which passed through his mind on this occasion, which showed that he held his life as a sacrifice in the cause of emancipation : and that whether he fell in the lone wilderness, on the bosom of the stormy deep, or under the hot sun of Hayti or of Mexico, it was the same to him.   He walked on in a cow path, through the wood, but becoming weary, and being wet, cold and in pain, he sat down on a log.   He believed that he might not be able to quit the place : but then he thought of his children, and his friends, of all the ties of this life, and of the enslaved millions to whom life is a burden, and it seemed to him that his work was not yet ended.   His mind was quiet and serene, and so far as he was concerned, he was resigned to die, but he mourned for the living.   His spirit reached forth in desires for the happiness of mankind, and it seemed to him that he was sent to do them good.   This feeling became so strong, that he resolved to make an effort to prolong his earthly existence : and looking around him, he saw, at some distance, in the woods, the light of a candle.   He endeavoured to reach it ; and being unable to walk he crawled to a hut, obtained permission to enter, and having become warm, he found his vital energies restored.   At that time, he felt that if life be brought into peril, in the prosecution of duty, it is our reasonable obligation to offer it up.

In the month of March following, Lundy gave a description of the Wilberforce settlement of coloured people, situated nearly west from Albany, N. Y., on the Au-Sable river, about twelve miles from London, in Upper Canada. It had been established for about twenty months, and consisted of thirty-two families, comprising in all about one hundred and sixty persons. Near two thousand coloured refugees had visited the place, but for want of means of employment, they had left and gone to other parts of Canada. The settlers were sober, industrious and thrifty. They had two schools, two churches, one being of the Methodist, and the other of the Baptist sect: and a temperance society. There were settlements of coloured people in other parts of Canada ; one at Lake Simcœ, in the northeast part of the province; one at Woolwich, on or near Grand river, some thirty-five miles from the head of Lake Ontario; another at Chatham creek near the river Thames, sixty-five miles below London; and another near Malden, not far from Lake St. Clair. This last was said, at that time, to consist of about four hundred persons.

In subsequent numbers of the paper, Lundy inserted his journal of travels in Canada, from which we make the following brief extracts.—"*Queenstown, U. C., Jan.* 13*th*, 1832.—We had some difficulty in getting into the ferry boat, but at length found ourselves safely on the Canada shore. I had scarcely put my trunk down, at the stage office door, when a man of quite an ordinary appearance, stepped up to it, and giving it a jerk one side, abruptly said, in a tone of authority : ' *open that.*' I understood him—he was the Custom House officer —and it was his business to see that travellers do not smuggle goods, under the appellation of baggage, to defraud the revenue. Although I had nothing to sell, except a few incomplete volumes, or files of my periodical work, this expounder of the revenue laws (he was a deputy) exacted about seven dollars, for duties and fees on a few books and pamphlets, with a little writing paper. I was afterwards told that the demand was illegal : but I had not, then, leisure to contest it." * * *January* 14th. * * * "After a few hours' ride, we came to the thriving village of Brantford. This place is situated twenty-five miles west of Hamilton. It takes its name from *Brant's Ford*, across Grand River, immediately in the neighborhood of the town. Here is a large settlement of the Mohawk Indians. They are quite a civilized people. They have a village, about two miles to the east of this place, where there is a Meeting for worship, at which an Episcopal Clergyman regularly officiates. It is called the ' Mohawk Parsonage.' This place is the residence of the celebrated *Brant Family*, one of whom was, a short time since, returned as a member of the Provincial Parliament. It appeared, however, that a few illegal votes were given for him, and his seat was denied him. But I heard several *white* persons remark, that if he offers again, as a candidate, he will, no doubt, be fairly elected. He is a full blooded Indian, well educated, and, as the white people say, ' very much of the gentleman.' Until now I saw very few of the *African race* in Canada. A considerable number of them reside in Brantford. There appears, also, to be a good deal of *mixture* of American, European, and African blood (but especially the two first) in this section of country.

January 15th. This being the first day of the week, the places of business are closed, and all is still and quiet. On our arrival, yesterday, many Indians were in town, and a few of them staid about the tavern pretty late in the evening. Some of them, as well as the blacks and whites, drank quite freely ; and I learn, this morning, that a fracas occurred in our landlord's barroom, among the heterogeneous assemblage there. Having retired early, I knew nothing of it. The blame was thrown upon the '*negroes*,' by the bar-keeper, who was a ' Yankee' of ' high pressure ' prejudice, but it did not amount to much ; and, to-day, very few Indians or blacks are to be seen in the public places.

By the way, it might not be amiss to observe, that the white emigrants, from the United States, retain all the prejudices, here, that they formerly held against the

coloured people in their native country. And the latter,
being admitted to equal privileges with them, under this
government, are accused of being 'saucy.' Perhaps
there is some ground for the charge ; for when we reflect that the coloured people are now released from the
shackles of degradation, and yet frequently provoked by
the taunts, and gibes, and supercilious treatment of the
'Yankees,' we need not wonder at their indulging their
resentment, sometimes, too far, and even behaving with
impropriety. But when the whites, themselves, clear
their skirts of the guilt of being 'saucy,' in their deportment towards the blacks, I apprehend that we shall hear
little more of this kind of complaint."

The Genius for January, 1832, copied an article from
the New York American, recommending, as Rufus King
had done in Congress some years before, that the surplus proceeds of the public lands should be applied to
the purchase of slaves, with the consent of the states
wherein they might be owned, and to their transportation out of the United States, with a proviso, that after
a certain period, slavery should no longer exist within
our Republic. Lundy, in commenting on this proposal,
said : "So anxious are we for the extinction of that ' supreme curse,' the system of slavery, that we hail this
proposition with pleasure." " Let the government pay
any reasonable sum (in the way of compromise) for the
slaves, upon the express condition that all shall certainly
be emancipated in due time ; but never- sanction the
principle that man can be rightfully considered the
property of man, by the purchase of a single one, without this irrevocable stipulation."

An editorial contained in the same number, stated that
Governor Roman, of Louisiana, alarmed at the act of
the Virginia Legislature in banishing from that state
certain slaves suspected of being concerned in the Southampton insurrection, and fearful that they might be introduced into Louisiana, had called a special session of
the Legislature, and recommended the passage of a law

for prohibiting, entirely, the introduction of slaves into
that state, for a certain number of years, as the only
method of avoiding the existing danger of the introduction of slaves guilty of crime committed in other states.
The Legislature, however, contented itself with prohibiting the introduction of slaves from other states, except by emigrants actually coming to reside in Louisiana and by citizens purchasing for their own ' use, and
holding them for five years after their importation : and
providing further, that in case of such importation, by
citizens, for their own use, the slaves should not be obtained from the adjacent states and territories of Alabama, Mississippi, Arkansas or Florida. All slaves introduced in violation of this law, were to become free,
and be removed from the state. The law also prohibited
under penalty of death, the circulation of all pamphlets,
&c., having a tendency to produce either discontent
among the free coloured population, or insubordination
among the slaves : the use of language of a like tendency,
under penalty of imprisonment for each offence, of from
three to twenty-one years ; and the teaching of slaves to
read or write, under penalty of imprisonment from one
to twelve months.

The same paper contained news from Brazil, of an
insurrection of the blacks on the island of Cobras, in that
Empire, and an attempt made by them to take Rio Ja-
neiro : " but the disturbance was soon quelled." It also
contained the proceedings of a meeting held at Leesburg,
Loudoun county, Va., at which the Mayor presided, and
at which resolutions were adopted favourable to the
gradual emancipation and removal of the slaves held in
that state, together with a memorial to the Legislature,
recommending that measure. It had likewise, an account of the mobbing, at Petersburg, Va., of H. D.
Robinson, an English vender of books and pamphlets,
who, upon a report that the negroes were approaching
the town, had marched, with others, to defend a bridge
in the vicinity ; but upon the subsiding of the panic, he
had remarked, that " the blacks, as men, were entitled

to their freedom, and ought to be emancipated." The next day, as he was about to leave the place, he was seized, taken into the woods, stripped and severely whipped, and was then informed that it would not be safe for him to appear there again. The same paper mentioned the mobbing, at Macon, Georgia, of John Lamb, for taking the Boston Liberator. He was tarred and feathered ; then hot oil was poured on his head and set fire to; he was then carried on a rail, to a river and ducked, and afterwards tied to a post and whipped. The letter which gave the account, said : " Northern men who reside among us, are more violent against the Liberator than our native Georgians."

In the February number of 1832, the editor expressed his high gratification to find that Wm. Swaim, formerly assistant editor of the Genius, and at that time editor of the Patriot, at Greensboro', North Carolina, still ventured to write against slavery, although the Legislature of that state had passed a law intended to muzzle the press.* Swaim, died, however, shortly after the passage of this law, and it may be presumed that his paper was discontinued, or changed in its character. The same number of Lundy's paper, contained an account respecting the slaves that were taken from the coast of the United States, on board the British squadron, during the war of 1812. They were settled in Trinidad, in 1816, to the number of seven hundred and seventy-four; and in 1824, they had increased to nine hundred and twenty-

---

*The law of North Carolina, here referred to, imposed the punishment of imprisonment, pillory and whipping, for the first offence of circulating seditious pamphlets, and death for the second offence : also a fine of two hundred dollars for teaching a coloured person to read or write, or selling him books or pamphlets. Slaves might be emancipated by the existing law, only on giving bond in one thousand dollars, that each slave so emancipated, should leave the state within ninety days, and never return. If a slave neglected or failed to leave the state within the time prescribed, he was to be sold again into servitude.

three, being an increase at the rate of about two-and-a-half per cent. per annum, while the slaves in the same island were decreasing at the rate of two-and-three-fourths per cent per annum.   The liberated slaves from the United States had maintained themselves, and were industrious, comfortable and orderly.

   The March number contained the information that the Legislature of Alabama, alarmed by the Southampton insurrection, had passed a law prohibiting the introduction of slaves into that state for sale, as well as the immigration of free coloured persons, under penalty of being sold as slaves.

   The same paper contained an account written by the venerable Moses Brown of Providence, R. I., which went to show, that so far as was known, Rhode Island was the first country in the world which had passed a law against African slavery.   The following is a copy of the law :

   " At a General Court, held at Warwick the 18th of May, 1652.
   Whereas there is a common course practised among English men, to buy negroes, to that end that they may have them for service or slaves for ever ; for the preventing of such practices among us, let it be ordered that no black mankind or white being shall be forced by covenant, bond or otherwise, to serve any man or his assignees longer than ten years, or until they come to be twenty-four years of age, if they be taken in under fourteen, from the time of their coming within the liberties of this Colony—at the end or term of ten years to set them free, as the manner is with English servants.   And that man that will not let them go free, or shall sell them away elsewhere, to that end that they may be enslaved to others for a longer time, he or they shall forfeit to the Colony 40 pounds."

   In the April number, Lundy, who was then absent from Washington, gave this account of the contents of a letter from a friend residing in that place, viz :   " He informs me that the Grand Jury have made out a bill of indictment against me ; that the Marshal has been in search of me ; that the spirit of opposition to every thing like emancipation runs high ; that the Abolition Society has not met for some time ; that consternation prevailed every where, at the period of the Southampton insurrection, &c., &c." The same number contained an abstract of two laws, then recently enacted by the Maryland Legislature, one of which prohibited the coming into the State of free people of colour, and the bringing of slaves into it for sale; the other made an appropriation for the transportation of emancipated slaves, or other free people of colour, to Liberia or elsewhere, with their own consent. It also mentioned the presentation, some weeks before, to the Virginia Legislature, of a petition signed by 215 ladies of Augusta county in that State, asking the passage of a law to effect emancipation. And it likewise mentioned that Dr. J. Bradley, of Oglethorpe county, Georgia, had recently emancipated 49 slaves, and sent them to Liberia. It also gave accounts of a recent insurrection in Jamaica, which had been quelled, and in which it was estimated that about 36,000 slaves had been engaged, and "more than 2000 had been killed or executed, hung up by scores, and without much ceremony, or shot down at sight." One hundred and fifty estates had been laid waste by fire, the damage being at first estimated at fifteen millions of dollars; and the value of slaves had depreciated three-fourths or upwards. These statements were probably exaggerated. The official estimate of the damage was four millions of dollars.

The publication of the Genius was suspended from May to November of this year, (1832.) During this interval, Lundy went to Nacogdoches in Texas, by way of New Orleans and the Red River, travelling *incognito*, as in the then excited state of the public mind, he deemed it unsafe to be publicly known in that part of the country. He mentions, in a letter to a friend, that he travelled 320 miles of the way on foot, and alone, through the wilderness, carrying a knapsack on his back. He reached Nacogdoches on the first of July, and left on the 7th, having forwarded to the government a petition for a large tract of land, for the settlement of people of colour, and having received assurances from a number of

Mexicans of probable success, in case he should persevere in his application. He expressed, in the Genius,
after his return, the opinion, that Texas was far better
suited than Canada, for the residence of coloured emigrants from the Southern States ; an opinion which has
been most amply confirmed by subsequent experience
of the evils to which persons necessarily improvident
from previous habits, and with a constitution inherited
in some measure from the climate of Africa, are exposed in the frigid atmosphere of the extreme north.

In the November number (1832) on the commencement of a new volume, Lundy said : " The primary
object of this work has ever been to show that justice,
like charity, should begin at home—that no dependence
can be placed on a system of foreign operations *alone*,
in the abolition of slavery. The total failure of the
" African Institution" in England, and the waning popularity of the Colonization Society in the United States,
may be adduced in proof of the correctness of this
axiom." " The former has given place to a patriotic
congregation of West India emancipators, and the latter
is destined to be superceded by something of a more
philanthropic nature."

The December number contained Lundy's animad-
versions on the course of John Quincy Adams, before
mentioned as occurring on the presentation by him of
abolition memorials, at the preceding session of Congress. Lundy stated, that he had an interview with
Adams, while the Pennsylvania memorials were in his
possession, and that he then made no objection to their
presentation to Congress. We were, therefore, said he,
astonished at his remarks in the House of Representatives. To this statement, Lundy subjoined Mr Adams's
explanation, as made to Evan Lewis, in which "he expressed very explicitly his abhorrence of slavery, and his
willingness to use all his talents and influence for its abolition whenever he conceived he had a right to do so.
But he did not think he had a right to legislate for the
District of Columbia, on any subject, at the suggestion

of the citizens of Pennsylvania, or of any other State."
"What must we say," remarked Lundy, "of the solidity
of this argument, when the fact is stated that a petition to
the same purport had a short time previously been presented to Congress from the District of Columbia, signed by more than 1000 of its inhabitants?"

In the same number, Lundy copied from Garrison's prospectus for the third volume of the Liberator,
his explanation of "immediate, not gradual emancipation," and remarked : " He urges nothing impracticable,
nor in the least degree dangerous to the peace and
welfare of the community at large. The utility and
safety of measures, such as are here proposed, have
been often tested and fully sustained." The plan thus
spoken of, was stated to be, not that the slaves upon
being immediately emancipated, should be turned loose
upon the nation, to roam as vagabonds or aliens; not
that they should be instantly invested with all political
rights and privileges," &c., but " that they shall be
placed under a benevolent and disinterested supervision,
which shall secure to them the right to obtain secular
and religious knowledge, to worship God according to
the dictates of their conscience, to accumulate wealth,
&c., &c."

CHAPTER XXVIII.

Events and gleanings for the years 1833 and 1834.

The January number of the Genius for 1833, noticed
the presentation to Congress of an anti-slavery petition
from Tennessee, as well as that of one from the District
of Columbia, which latter contained upwards of three
hundred signatures, being but about one-third of the
number that had been obtained in that District some
years previously. The February number of that paper,
noticed some additional petitions, including one from

Bullitt county, Kentucky, which was signed by upwards of four hundred citizens. Lundy said, the question would " no doubt receive the ' go by' at the present session :" but he added " we shall assuredly succeed in time if we hold on." " To insure success in this undertaking, the electors *must instruct their representatives;* and in order to accomplish this, or at least to make a beginning, let memorials and petitions be forwarded to both Houses of Congress, from every section of the Union. Let the tables, the seats and the very aisles of their halls, be stowed with them." The same number of the Genius said of John Quincy Adams : " This gentleman continues to pursue an *extraordinary* course. We have not had leisure to attend any of the sittings of the House of Representatives, but we learn that on the morning of the 4th instant, he indirectly opposed any action of Congress upon the proposal to abolish slavery in the District of Columbia; it will be remembered, too, that the *people of that District* have again petitioned for the enactment of a law to that effect."

The January number contained a statement, from the African Repository, that one hundred or more slaves had been offered their freedom on condition of removing to Africa. It also stated, that in the Maryland House of Representatives, on motion of Mr. Johnson, the committee on the coloured population had been instructed to inquire into the expediency and practicability of designating a day, after which all slaves subsequently born should be free at a certain age, upon condition of removal to Africa, or some other place of safety, beyond the limits of the United States. It does not appear whether this committee reported on the subject or not.

The February number gave the following list of anti-slavery periodicals, existing in the United States, set down in the order of the time of their commencement : viz.: The Genius of Universal Emancipation, Washington, D. C.; The Greensborough Patriot, Greensborough, North Carolina ; The Western Luminary, Lexington,

Kentucky; The Miscellaneous Repository, Mount Pleasant, Ohio; The Friend, Philadelphia, Pennsylvania;
The Friend, or Advocate of Truth, do.; The Genius of
Temperance, New York City; The Liberator, Boston,
Massachusetts; The Abolitionist, do. (by the same publishers;) The Morning Daily Advertiser, New York;
The Palladium, Bethania, Pennsylvania. Total eleven.
The March number contained the prospectus, and a
commendatory notice of that well known anti-slavery
paper " *The Emancipator*," which had just been commenced at New York by Charles Dennison, a minister
of the Baptist denomination : also a list of some anti-
slavery papers which had been omitted in the former
account, viz.: The Christian Monitor, Brooklyn, Connecticut ; The Courier, Northampton, Mass.; The Telegraph, Boston, Mass.; The Christian Soldier, do.;
The Telegraph, Brandon, Vermont; and The Christian
Mirror, Portland, Maine : making 'in all eighteen.
Some of them were not devoted especially to emancipation, but they advocated it frequently and earnestly.

The Genius for March, 1833, proclaimed " the gratifying news," that the British ministry had resolved to
recommend to Parliament the total and unconditional
abolition of slavery in the American colonies, to be
completed in three years, by which eight hundred thousand slaves would be set free.

The April number contained a notice, by the editor
of the Cincinnati Chronicle, who had just returned from
a tour in Kentucky, of the condition of the slaves and
the state of public opinion in that Commonwealth. The
slaves were better fed and clothed, and their condition
generally much ameliorated, compared with that which
existed ten years before; and there was a growing sentiment that " neither the pecuniary interest, the comfort,
nor the personal safety of the white population, is en-
hanced by slavery." It also copied, in order to give an
idea of southern feeling, an article from the Raleigh
(N. C.) Register, which predicted that if the contemplated
emancipation took place in the West Indies, " the white

population of those Islands would be compelled to abandon them, and we should have, in our immediate vicinity, independent negro sovereignties, whose contagion would rapidly spread into the southern States." It asked if our government could look quietly on, and see such a measure consummated.

The same number of the Genius, announced that Lundy had left home, to be absent some four or five months; that he would write for the paper occasionally, but that it would be chiefly under the charge of a few friends, who had given proofs of their capability to manage it well, and of their devotion to the cause. The journey here alluded to, was Lundy's second visit to Texas, and first to Monclova, in Mexico.

The number for May, contained accounts of the affair relative to Prudence Crandall, which had occurred at Canterbury, Connecticut. She had announced her intention to open a school at her own residence, for the instruction of colored females, and had engaged about twenty pupils, when a town meeting was called, to be held on the 1st of April, 1833, for the purpose of adopting measures to prevent the establishment of the proposed school. At this meeting, by request of Miss Crandall, the Rev. Mr. May, of Brooklyn, Conn., and Arnold Buffum, agent of the New England Anti-Slavery Society, appeared and requested to be heard, in explanation and defence of the contemplated seminary. They were refused a hearing; and resolutions were adopted expressing a determination that the school should not be established in that town : also, a resolution for the drafting of a memorial to the Legislature, deprecating the bringing of the people of colour from other towns and states, for any purpose whatever, "and more especially for the purpose of disseminating principles and doctrines opposed to the benevolent colonization system." Miss Crandall having persisted in her plan, the July number said : "The citizens of Canterbury have resolved to hold no intercourse with her—to sell her no article of necessity:—when she appears in the street she is insulted,

hooted at—horns blown and pistols fired, not at her
we admit, but in derision." "Her father and siste.
have been threatened with fine and imprisonment, if
they visit her. Eggs have been thrown at the house; the
windows have been broken by brick-bats; and to crown
all, she has been incarcerated in a prison, and confined
in the same cell which had been the abode of a murderer." The Connecticut Legislature having passed a
law to prohibit the instruction within that State, of coloured youth from abroad, the August number of the
Genius gave an account of the trial of Miss Crandall,
for the violation of that law. Her defence was that the
citizens of each State were, by the constitution, entitled
to all the privileges of citizens in other States, to which
it was asserted, in reply, that coloured persons were not
citizens within the meaning of that provision. The jury
could not agree, five being for acquittal and seven for
conviction.—The Genius for September, mentioned
that Andrew T. Judson, who had taken a leading part
against Miss Crandall, had since been appointed an
agent of the Colonization Society. The school was continued till September or October, 1833, when Miss Crandall was tried again, and convicted by the jury. Shortly
before this period, the editor of the Liberator, in passing
through Brooklyn, Connecticut, was served with notice
of five indictments for libels alleged to be contained in
the comments published in that paper, of March 16th,
1833, on the conduct of the five prominent actors in the
opposition to the school of Miss Crandall.

The Genius for June, 1833, contained resolutions of
the Maryland Colonization Society, declaring their desire, " so far as they can, to hasten the arrival of that
period when slavery shall cease to exist in Maryland,"
and expressing the opinion that " this can be best done
by advocating and assisting the cause of colonization,"
and that it was " proper to use every means in their
power to raise Maryland to the rank of a free state;"
they therefore resolved to establish, forthwith, " a settlement at a suitable point on the Coast of Africa," and

designated Cape Palmas as a proper spot.   This was
the origin of the Maryland colony at that place.   The
Genius (in Lundy's absence) condemned much of the
reasoning of the Society, but expressed gratification that
it had at length decided to act as an anti-slavery society,
though not in the most effective manner.

About this time a convention of free people of colour
was held in Philadelphia, to which a letter was forwarded by Lundy, dated at Nashville, May 28th, 1833,
in which, after contrasting the condition of the African
race on the American *continent*, fifty years before, with
the great advance existing at that time, when he estimated that 4,350,000 had acquired freedom, and
3,100,000 of them were invested with every civil and
political privilege, he stated that his primary object for
the fifteen years that he had laboured in the cause, had
been the total and unconditional abolition of slavery,
and to elevate the colored people to a perfect equality
with the whites: that he thought slavery would be
abolished before many years ; that few of the coloured
people, comparatively speaking, would ever be removed
from this land, and that attention to education and improvement at home, was a thousand fold more efficacious
in extinguishing prejudice, than all foreign schemes.
But as some of the victims of oppression were anxious
to change their location, and could obtain their civil and
political rights at once by doing so, Lundy felt it to be his
duty to assist them ; he had therefore turned his attention to Canada, Texas, and Mexico, to ascertain the
most suitable place for making settlements.   He believed
that in such settlements, the coloured people could demonstrate their capability of improvement and self-government, and thus abate the prejudice against them,
which was the great desideratum at that moment ; and
he thought that by similar means a great effect had been
wrought in England.   Thus he hoped to rouse the
nation, *en masse,* and that the irrevocable mandate would
be ushered forth "through the potent medium of the
ballot box, that slavery shall exist no longer."

The convention to which this letter was addressed, returned to Lundy a vote of thanks.

The Genius of April, 1833, announced the joyful news that the bill for the emancipation of the slaves in the British colonies had passed both houses of Parliament

The number for January, 1834, contained an address from Evan Lewis, upon assuming the sole charge of the editorship of the paper until Lundy should return, and changing the place of its publication, avowedly to Philadelphia. For some time before, it had been dated at Washington, but generally not printed there. The new editor stated that he had been forty-five years an opponent of slavery, and twenty-eight years before had become a member of the oldest abolition society in existence : that the principles of abolition were not new, but a new impulse had been given to them : and that he had, from the commencement, considered the influence of the Colonization Society more injurious to the cause of emancipation than all other causes combined.

The same paper contained the constitution and declaration of sentiments of the American Anti-Slavery Society, which was passed at Philadelphia on the 6th of December, 1833.

The February number of 1834, mentioned that Wm. Goodell, previously editor of the Genius of Temperance, &c., had taken the editorial charge of the "Emancipator," at New York. It also contained a sketch of some proceedings in the Maryland Legislature. An order having been passed in the House of Representatives, directing a committee to inquire into the expediency of repealing or modifying the severe laws which had been passed in 1831, relative to slaves and people of colour, Mr. Mann, of Washington county, then moved that the same committee be directed to "inquire into the propriety of fixing some distant day, after which all the issue of slaves born within the state should become free and be removed out of the United States." The reading of the motion by the clerk, was the signal for a scene of unusual excitement in the house. Messrs. Merrick, of Charles county, and Day, of Prince George, denounced the proposition with great vehemence, when Mr. Mann, finding that the subject was unpalatable to the whole house, asked leave to withdraw his motion. Messrs. Pratt and Merrick opposed the leave to withdraw, wishing an expression of the sense of the house on the motion. Others deprecated agitation and discussion, and finally, after a warm debate, leave to withdraw the motion was granted.*

The Genius of March, 1834, contained extracts from an address issued by the "Kentucky Gradual Emancipation Society." It did not state when the Society was formed, nor when the address was issued. It is probable, however, that the Society was the one commenced by the fifty slaveholders before mentioned.

The April number contained an obituary notice of the late acting editor, Evan Lewis, who had then recently deceased. He was a native of Delaware county, Pennsylvania: he joined the Pennsylvania Abolition Society in 1804, at the age of 22 years: he afterwards removed to Wilmington, Delaware, joined the Abolition Society at that place, and for several years was one of the delegates of that Society to the National Anti-Slavery Convention. In the year 1831 he obtained the prize offered by Ebenezer Dale, of Hallowell, Maine, for the best essay on " The duty of ministers and churches of all denominations, to avoid the stain of slavery, and to make the holding of slaves a barrier to communion and church membership." He resided at Philadelphia at the time of his decease. The Genius announced that his place, as temporary editor, was filled by Dr. Edwin P. Atlee

The same number contained a letter to the editor of the Emancipator, from H. Lyman, at Lane Seminary,

---

* Mr. Pratt, one of the violent opponents of the motion, is now governor of Maryland. Another, Mr. Merrick, was recently United States Senator.

near Cincinnati, dated March 4, 1834, giving an account of a discussion held by the students for twenty
evenings, on the following questions, in substance, viz:
" Ought the slaveholding states to abolish slavery immediately; and ought the Colonization Society to receive the patronage of the Christian community." The
first question was determined unanimously in the affirmative, though two were not prepared to vote: the
second in the negative, with one dissenting voice. An
Anti-Slavery Society was formed among the students
on the 9th of March. Six of the officers were from
slaveholding states. The paper for May contained interesting details from T. D. Weld and Augustus Wattles of these proceedings, for which we have not space.

The number of May, 1834, copied from the Cincinnati Gazette, a statement furnished by Lundy, who had
just reached Cincinnati, from Monclova, in Mexico. He
thought that the government of Mexico had " settled
down upon a liberal and permanent basis: the President, Santa Anna, was popular, and had a third time
retired to his farm. He was said to have publicly declared his intention to pattern after Washington.
Newspapers were rapidly multiplying on the liberal
side, and they had for some months past been filled with
articles criticising the conduct of the priesthood, and
demanding the free toleration of the protestant religion.
The great mass of the citizens, and even many of the
Catholic clergy, were decidedly in favour of this measure.
The executive branch of the general Government* had
recently corresponded with those of the several states,
relative to the immediate adoption of measures to amend
the constitution for that purpose, and there was little
doubt of the amendment being speedily accomplished.
They were preparing to establish the right of trial by
jury in Coahuila and Texas.

The law of 1830, forbidding the settlement in Mexico

* Presumably through Gomez Farias, the Vice President, a
more stable friend of liberty than Santa Anna.—ED.

and Texas, of citizens of the United States, was repealed, prospectively, to take effect on May 21st, 1835. The
introduction of slaves was prohibited, except those
bound by indentures for only ten years.   Stephen F.
Austin had been the bearer, to Mexico, of a constitution
for Texas, as a separate state from Coahuila, to be submitted for the approbation of the general government.
The unsettled state of affairs at that period, prevented
immediate attention to his application.   In his anxiety
for a speedy sanction of it, he gave offence to the Vice
President.   At length, finding that he would probably
be unsuccessful, he wrote to the *Ayuntamiento* (council
or municipality) of Bexar, recommending the institution
of a correspondence with the other local authorities, and
the formation of a state government, without the consent
of the general Congress, or of the other states.   The
Ayuntamiento disapproved his course, and gave information of it to the Governor of Coahuila and Texas,
who forwarded it to Santa Anna.   When the news
reached Mexico, Austin had left for Texas. A "*force*"
was instantly despatched after him.   It overtook him at
Saltillo, arrested him, and took him to Mexico for trial,
on a charge of disobedience to the constitution and laws.*
The general Congress, when it took up the question,
disapproved the proposed Constitution of Texas, and the
proposition for a separate government for that state. The
reasons for disapproval were said to be, that the convention which framed the constitution was organized
in an illegal and informal manner: that many substantial settlers were opposed to the measure, as premature :
that the proposed constitution contained no prohibition
of slavery, and that it was "pretty well understood "
that the new state would endeavor to re-establish the
slave-system.   It was expected that Austin's proceedings would not produce any commmotion in Texas. The
foreigners in that state, it was said, generally condemned

* He was imprisoned about a year and a half, and then discharged without being brought to trial.

his conduct, and of the few settlers willing to join in his movement, " the principal part were persons of little character or responsibility."

The Genius for July, 1834, contained an account of a riot which took place in New York city, at Chatham street Chapel, on the 4th of that month, being the Anniversary of American Independence. The "*friends of human liberty*" (or opponents of slavery) had assembled at the chapel to celebrate the day. After a prayer by the Rev. G. H. Ludlow, the singing of five verses of a hymn written by J. G. Whittier, the reading of the Declaration of Independence by Dr. Stephen Brown, and that of the Declaration of Sentiments of the American Anti-Slavery Society, by Lewis Tappan, which was interrupted towards its close by clamour and hisses, David Paul Brown of Philadelphia, who was the selected orator of the day, attempted to address the assembly. But it soon became apparent, that a mob had assembled with a determination to drown his voice by clamour; and after several ineffectual attempts by him and the Rev. Dr. Samuel H. Cox, to obtain a hearing, amid exclamations of " Treason! Treason ! Hurrah for the Union," the remaining five stanzas of Whittier's hymn were sung, and the meeting quietly dispersed without the delivery of the oration. The New York Commercial Advertiser, as well as the Courier and Enquirer, of the next day, expressed its approbation of this mob.

The same number also contained an account of another riot directed against the abolitionists, which took place in New York city, on the nights of the 9th and 10th of July. The mob broke the doors and windows of the house of Lewis Tappan at midnight of the 9th, and carried his furniture into the street and set fire to it. It was then proposed to set fire to the house, when a message was dispatched for the Mayor, who soon came with an additional force of police officers, and commanded the mob to disperse. " He was answered with three cheers for James Watson Webb of the Courier." But the crowd was finally dispersed, several rioters having been arrested. During these riots the doors and windows of Dr. Cox's Presbyterian church were broken; also the windows of Zion's church, belonging to a coloured Methodist society; those of an African Baptist church in Division street; the doors and windows of Dr. Ludlow's house; and the doors, windows, and furniture of Dr. Ludlow's church in Spring street. St. Phillip's African Episcopal church was nearly destroyed, including a fine organ. An African school house in Orange street was destroyed; and a number of dwelling houses, inhabited by coloured people, were totally destroyed, and a number greatly injured.

There was also a mob at Newark, New Jersey, on the 11th of July, which disturbed an Anti-Slavery meeting and did some injury to the meeting house in which it had convened. These riots were attributed by many, partly to the influence and publications of the colonizationists, between whom and the Abolitionists a very hostile feeling had at that time arisen.

The same number of the paper, also contained an address from Lundy to the patrons of the Genius, dated at New Orleans, 6th mo. 1834, he being then at that place on his return to Mexico. After a brief sketch of his preceding journey to that country, and of its soil, climate, and productions, he said: "I am satisfied that the government is as well calculated to secure to its citizens religious and political freedom, as any in the world. The restrictions heretofore operating against persons professing the protestant religion, are soon to be entirely done away: and the people, en masse, are resolutely determined that the system of slavery shall never be re-established in the republic." Lundy concluded this address with a eulogium on the virtues and talents of Evan Lewis, and a commendation of Dr. Atlee, the new editor.

The same number of the Genius likewise contained a disclaimer, signed by Arthur Tappan and John Rankin, on behalf of the executive committee of the American A. S. Society, of a hand bill which had been then recently circulated in New York city, inciting people to resistance to the laws made in respect to slavery, as well as a disclaimer of any desire either to encourage intermarriage between white and coloured persons, to dissolve the Union, to violate the constitution and laws of the country, or to ask Congress to transcend their constitutional powers, " which the abolition of slavery by Congress, in any state, would plainly do."

At this time the publication of the Genius was suspended by Dr. Atlee, for want of adequate support. We continue, however, a brief sketch of events, gleaned from other papers. In this month (July,) it was announced that James G. Birney of Kentucky, had abandoned the Colonization Society, and become a convert to the doctrines of the American Anti-Slavery Society. He liberated his slaves, and published, in an extra of the Lexington (Ky.) Intelligencer, the letter containing the reasons for his change of opinion.

On the night of the 13th of August, 1834, a series of anti-abolition riots, which lasted three nights, commenced at Philadelphia, in the southern suburbs of the city. They were principally directed against the coloured people, and the houses occupied by them, or in which they worshipped ; but the houses of several white abolitionists were menaced, and in fact owed their protection to the police. Those of Dr. Atlee and Arnold Buffum, are mentioned in the papers. The number of houses injured or destroyed, was forty-four, being mostly of small value. Among them was an African Presbyterian church. The coloured people were pursued and beaten, one of them to death, and another lost his life in attempting to swim the Schuylkill, in order to escape his pursuers.

It was mentioned, in the Emancipator of October 23d, 1834, that Dr. Hawes, of Virginia, had liberated one hundred and ten slaves by his will, and given to the Colonization Society twenty dollars each, for the purpose of transporting them to Africa.

On the 6th and 13th of October, 1834, the Trustees

of Lane Seminary, Ohio, adopted rules for that institution, which were intended to prevent the discussion of the Anti-Slavery question by the students. These rules forbade the formation of any societies among the students, without the approbation of the faculty, as well as the holding of meetings by them, except of a devotional character, or connected with their studies, and ordered the discontinuance of both the Anti-Slavery Society and the Colonization Society, which had been formed among them. In about a month afterwards, these rules were modified, so as to be far less objectionable than at first.

About this time, or shortly before, the celebrated English lecturer on Slavery, George Thompson, arrived in this country, and was engaged in delivering lectures in the state of Maine, by which a good deal of excitement was produced. Some of his meetings were disturbed : but perhaps the most of them were peaceable.

It was also at about this period, that the celebrated John Randolph of Roanoke, Virginia, died in Philadelphia, having first made his will, by which about three hundred slaves obtained their freedom. This will was about ten years in litigation, before it was finally confirmed. By it a sum of money was left to purchase land for the freed men. The purchase was made in Mercer county, Ohio, in 1846, but the owners were prevented, by threats of violence, from settling on it, and, in consequence, sought and obtained employment in another part of that state.

In November, 1834, in was announced that the newly organized Colonization Society, had sent one hundred and twenty-eight emancipated slaves to Bassa Cove, Africa, of whom 110 were those liberated by Dr. Hawes.

In the same month, Gerrit Smith of Peterboro, New York, who had previously been distinguished as a member of the Colonization Society, commenced the publication of letters addressed to the Abolitionists, in which he took a ground intermediate between that occupied by most of the respective members of the two hostile societies.

On the 15th of December 1834, fifty-one of the late students of Lane Seminary, published an address containing a full statement of the reasons which had induced them to dissolve their connection with that institution. Those reasons were found in the course pursued by the faculty in reference to restraining discussion and action on the subject of slavery.

CHAPTER XXIX.

Events and gleanings for the years 1835 and 1836.

During the first two months of the year 1835, nothing of particular interest occurred in connection with the anti-slavery movement, except notices of lectures by George Thompson and by the agents of the American Society and its auxiliaries, and the presentation to Congress of numerous abolition memorials, with speeches in that body favourable to the object, made by Mr. Dickson, representative from Rochester, New York, or its vicinity, and Mr. Phillips, from Salem, Massachusetts.

The Emancipator of March 31st, contained the "cheering news" from Kentucky, that on the 19th a convention from different parts of that state, assembled at Danville and formed the "Kentucky Anti-Slavery Society," auxiliary to the American Society, to attend the approaching meeting of which body, James G. Birney was appointed a delegate. The subject of a convention to amend the Constitution of Kentucky, had then recently been agitated in that state, the discussions involving the question of the abolition of slavery, and it was believed that considerable progress was making in public sentiment on the subject.

On the 12th of May the second annual meeting of the American Anti-Slavery Society was held at New York. A resolution was adopted, recommending the raising of thirty thousand dollars for the use of the society during the year.   Of this sum fourteen thousand five hundred dollars were subscribed on the spot.

On the 24th of July, a public meeting on the subject of abolition was held at Richmond, Virginia, Dr. John Dove in the chair, and George W. Dixon Secretary. A committee was appointed to report to an adjourned meeting on August 3d, at which time sundry resolutions were reported and adopted. These resolutions declared that the citizens assembled, would hold any attempt by Congress to impair the right of property in slaves, as guaranteed by the constitution, or to regulate the sale of slaves from one state to another, "as a wanton violation of our political compact, destructive of our whole frame of government:" that they had a just claim on the non-slaveholding states for the enactment of laws to put down "all incendiary and seditious associations whose avowed purpose is to disturb our peace and excite insurrection among our slaves;" that the existing laws of Virginia, respecting incendiary publications should be revised; that the captains of steamboats and other vessels coming from the North, be requested to use vigilance in detecting any emissaries of the abolition societies who should be on board their vessels, or should use them for the dissemination of incendiary papers among the inhabitants, either white or black; that the Post master General be requested to exert all his lawful power to repress the transmission by mail and delivery at the post offices, of tracts, &c. calculated to excite a spirit of insubordination or insurrection; and that the Legislature the magistrates and police, of the state and city, as well as a committee of vigilance appointed by the meeting, be requested to aid in accomplishing the objects specified.

At Charleston, South Carolina, on the 29th of July, it became known soon after the arrival of the mail from New York, that a large quantity of abolition tracts had come in it.   This fact, being published in the Courier of the next morning, caused a great excitement.   On the succeeding evening, between 10 and 11 o'clock, a number of persons assembled forcibly entered the post office by wrenching open a window, and carried off the packages "containing the incendiary matter," as it was called. Arrangements had been previously made by the Post Master of Charleston, to detain the tracts until instructions should be received from Washington, as to forwarding them or not to the several places in the South to which they were directed. On the succeeding evening, " according to full notice published, (said a Charleston paper,) the pamphlets, &c. were burnt at 8 o'clock, P. M., opposite the main guard house, three thousand persons being present. The effigies of Arthur Tappan, Dr. Cox, and W. L. Garrison, were at the same time suspended. At 9 o'clock the balloon was let off, and the effigies were consumed by the neck, with the offensive documents at their feet." The number destroyed, according to the Emancipator, was about one thousand, consisting of "the Emancipator, the Anti-Slavery Record, and the Slave's Friend." On the 3d of August, a large public meeting, called by the city councils, was held in the same city. It appointed a committee of twenty-one to take charge of the U. S. mail, and to report at a future meeting the means best adapted to put down the abolitionists. At the head of this committee, which was composed of the most prominent men of the city, was ex-United States Senator Hayne.

On the 4th of August, Amos Kendall, Post Master General of the United States, wrote to the Post Master of Charleston, that he had " no legal authority to exclude newspapers from the mail, on account of their character or tendency, real or supposed : " but he was " not prepared to direct him to forward or deliver the papers" spoken of in his letter of July 29th : that the post office was created to serve each and all the United States, and not to be used as the instrument of their destruction : " that none of the papers having been forwarded to him, he could not judge of them for himself; but he was informed by the Post Master of Charleston, that they were " most inflammatory and incendiary, and insurrectionary in the highest degree." He added, that

by no act of his, would he knowingly give circulation to
papers of that description : that " we owe an obligation
to the laws, but a higher one to the communities in which
we live, and if the former be perverted to destroy the
latter, it is patriotism to disregard them:" and that with
these views he " could not sanction, and would not condemn" the steps taken by the Post Master of Charleston ;
but his justification must be looked for in the character
of the papers detained and the circumstances by which
he was surrounded. A copy of this letter was transmitted
to the Post Master of Richmond, Va., in answer to one
from him on the same subject.   Mr. Kendall also
wrote, on the 22d of August, to S. L. Gouverneur,
Post Master at New York, who had detained some abolition tracts destined for the South, that the Post Master
General had no authority to order the exclusion of such
papers from the mail, but if he possessed it, he would
exercise it, as to the Southern states. He intimated that
each deputy Post Master must decide for himself as to
his course; and that one might be punishable for delivering such papers in a state where the laws forbade their
circulation, though it was perfectly proper to deliver
them in other states.

On the 21st of August, Amos Dresser, a former student
of Lane Seminary, and a member of the Anti-Slavery
Society established at that institution, was arrested at a
Methodist camp meeting ground, near Nashville, Tennessee, on a charge of having in his possession, and
distributing incendiary abolition publications.   He had
left Cincinnati on the 1st of July, with the " Cottage
Bible," and some other religious books for sale, and had
also taken some Anti-Slavery publications, the most of
which he had left at Danville, Ky., where an Anti-Slavery Society existed.   On his arrival at Nashville, he
sent his barouche to be repaired, inadvertently leaving
in the box some anti-slavery tracts and other pamphlets.
The workmen employed on the barouche, found and examined the tracts, one of which was a number of the
" Anti-Slavery Record," containing a print of " a

drove of slaves chained, the two foremost having violins on which they were playing—the American flag waving in the centre, while the slave-driver with his whip was urging on the rear." In was then reported that Mr. Dresser had been "circulating incendiary periodicals among the free coloured people, and trying to excite the slaves to insurrection." To this report it was soon added, that he had been posting up hand-bills about the city, inviting an insurrection of the slaves. Having obtained the return of the pamphlets left in the barouche, and explained that they were left there by accident, he locked them up and continued the sale of his Bibles for several days, the excitement in the mean time constantly increasing. On the 21st, by order of J. P. Erwin, Mayor of Nashville, he was arrested and taken, together with his trunk, before a committee of vigilance consisting of sixty prominent citizens who had assembled at the Court House, the Mayor having previously asked him if he was ready for trial, to which he had replied in the affirmative. Being then interrogated as to the contents of the trunk, he replied by requesting the committee to examine it themselves. They did so, and found some few anti-slavery publications, as well as the journal of Dresser, and some private letters, several of which were from abolitionists, and alluded to slavery. The journal and letters were read aloud, and it was shown that a number of the Emancipator, used as a wrapper to a Cottage Bible, had been left on the counter of Nashville Inn, with the Bible, at the time of Dresser's arrival. In answer to questions put to him, he stated, that he had distributed no anti-slavery tracts in Tennessee, except a copy of "Rankin's letters" which he had sold in Sumner county, and that he had showed none, except the number of the A. S. Record, before mentioned, which he had read to a Mr. Cayce, at his own request. He was then shown a handbill, and asked if he had ever seen anything of the kind, to which he replied that he had not. Being called no for his defence, he avowed his anti-slavery sentiments; declared that he sought the good both of the master and the slave; contemplated emancipation through persuasion; and that in his few interviews with slaves he had recommended to them quietness, patience, and submission. The committee having deliberated, found him guilty:—1. Of being a member of the Ohio Anti-Slavery Society. 2. Of having in his possession, periodicals published by the American Anti-Slavery Society; and thirdly they declared that they believed he had circulated those periodicals, and advocated the principles inculcated in them. They therefore sentenced him to receive twenty lashes on his bare back, and to leave the place in twenty-four hours. He was then taken to the public square, it being near midnight; and the punishment was inflicted by Mr. Braughton, the principal police officer, with a heavy cow-skin, in the presence of a large circle of spectators. One of the spectators moved to remit the punishment. The motion being seconded excited a great commotion, which was suppressed only by the commencement of the stripes. The excitement continued so great, that Mr. Dresser thought it necessary to quit the place in disguise the next morning, leaving behind him his property, which he afterwards sold at a considerable sacrifice.

About this time an article published in the Richmond (Va.) Whig, speaking of the abolitionists, said : " The people of the North must go to hanging these fanatical wretches, if they would not lose the benefit of the Southern trade, and they will do it." "Depend upon it the Northern people will never sacrifice their present lucrative trade with the South, so long as the hanging of a few thousands will prevent it."

A meeting held in Glynn county, Georgia, Sept. 4th, 1835, requested Gov. Lumpkin, of that state, to call upon the President of the United States for the arrest, in conformity with the 4th article of the constitution, of either Garrison, Thompson, the Tappans, Cornish, Cox, Jocelyn, Rankin, Leavitt, Goodell, or Elizur Wright, " for an attempt to excite domestic violence." And on Sept. 17th, the Louisiana " Constitutional and Anti-

Fanatical Association," offered a reward of five hundred dollars for the conviction of any abolitionist(of the violation of the laws of Louisiana against instigators of sedition among the slaves.

In the month of September, 1835, Webster Southard, of Boston, Mass., published an "Anti-Slavery Almanac," for 1836, being, it is supposed, the first publication of the kind made in this country. Since that time Anti-Slavery Almanacs have been published every year.

It appeared from various articles in the papers at this period, that the agitation throughout the South was attributed in a great degree to the pictures with which some of the anti-slavery tracts were headed.

On account of the extensive excitement on the subject of these publications, the Executive Committee of the American Anti-Slavery Society, issued an address through the Emancipator of October, 1835, in which they declared that they did not desire Congress to abolish slavery within the states, nor believe that it had any right to do so; but that they did hold to the right of Congress to abolish it in the District of Columbia, and to that of the State Legislatures to do so within their own limits: that they had sent no agents to the Southern states: that they had sent no publications to the slaves; that their tracts were not intended to excite insurrection, nor did they think them calculated to produce that result; and that they had uniformly deprecated all forcible attempts on the part of the slaves to recover their liberty.

On the 10th of October, the Female Anti-Slavery Society of Boston issued a notice, that it would hold its annual meeting in the New Jerusalem church, in that city, on the 14th of the month, and that George Thompson was expected to deliver an address on the occasion. But in consequence of apprehensions of a riot, the proprietors of the church gave notice that they would not open it unless $20,000 were deposited in bank, as security against its suffering injury. The place of meeting was therefore changed to Congress Hall, and notice of the change given from some of the pulpits on Sunday the 11th. On the morning of the 14th, several of the papers of the city published inflammatory editorials, hostile to Mr. Thompson and threatening lynch law if he should make his appearance. In consequence of this, the lessee of the hall gave notice in the papers of Tuesday evening, that the meeting could not be held in it, and warned all persons not to assemble there at the time appointed. The meeting therefore was not held, but numbers of persons called "genteel and respectable" assembled about the hall, threatening violence to Mr. Thompson.

A notice was then published in the Liberator of the 17th, that the meeting, which had been postponed, would be held at 3 o'clock on the 21st, at number 46 Washington street, and that "several addresses" would be delivered on the occasion. On the morning of that day, inflammatory articles appeared in some of the papers. A placard was circulated, stating that "the infamous foreign scoundrel Thompson," was to address the meeting: that it would afford "a fair opportunity for the friends of the Union to snake him out;" and that a purse of one hundred dollars had been raised "by a number of patriotic citizens to reward the individual who should first lay violent hands upon him, so that he might be brought to the tar kettle before dark."

At the hour of meeting, about twenty members of the Female Anti-Slavery Society assembled at the appointed place, being the front room of the building in the back part of which was the office of the Liberator. A mob assembled at the same time, which soon increased to thousands, and was said to be composed, in a good measure of what were called "respectable and influential" men, "gentlemen of property and standing." The mob entered the hall and raised shouts for Thompson. The Mayor then appeared and informed them that Thompson was not in the city, and would not be present at the meeting.

The disturbance however continued, insomuch that

the society adjourned to another place, and the members left the hall. The mob then demanded that the sign of the office should be taken down, and the Mayor ordering the request to be complied with, it was done, and the sign was boken to pieces. The mob then vociferously demanded Garrison, when, by the advice of his friends, he left the office by a back window, and went to a carpenter's shop in the vicinity. He was pursued thither, discovered, and about to be violently dragged away by a rope which was put around his body, when some persons friendly to him seized him and took him to the Mayor's office. That officer committed him to prison as a breaker of the peace, alleging that it was the only means of insuring his safety, the mob having pursued him and surrounded the office. He was accordingly taken to prison in a carriage, by a circuitous route, the mob making several attempts to stop the carriage, and blocking the direct course. The next day he was discharged, on examination before Judge Whitman, and left the city for a few days, until the violent excitement of the people had abated.

A convention to form a State Anti-Slavery Society for New York, had been called to be held at Utica on the 21st October, 1835. In consequence of this call, three meetings of citizens of Utica, hostile to the holding of the convention there, were held, one on the 8th, one on the 17th and one on the 21st. That of the 8th protested against the holding of the convention at Utica as being repugnant to the wishes of its citizens. That of the 17th protested against the resolution of the Common Council to grant the court room in the Academy for the sitting of the convention, and resolved to re-assemble at that place on the 21st, to prevent the Convention from being held. That of the 21st, on hearing that the Anti-Slavery Convention had convened at the Bleeker street Presbyterian church, despatched a committee to require it to disperse, which was accordingly done. The members of the Convention complied with the request, having completed the organization of a state society, just as the

summons to disperse was received. Among the prominent actors in these proceedings were Joseph Kirkland,
Chester Hayden, Samuel Beardsley, Wm. G. Tracy,
Ephraim Hart, Wm. C. Noyes, Rudolph Snyder, and A.
G. Dauby, the first named being Mayor, the two next
members of Congress, and some others holding seats in
the State Legislature, or other public stations. They informed the Abolitionists that they did not intend violence
themselves, but intimated that others would probably
resort to it if they did not disperse promptly.

About this time Wm. Goodell retired from the editorship of the Emancipator, the official organ of the American Society, and was succeeded by A. A. Phelps, who
was some months subsequently succeeded by Joshua
Leavitt.

The Northern press was at this period generally hostile to the Abolitionists. The New York Evening Post
and the New York American, of opposite politics, came
out, however, openly and decisively in favour of the right
of free discussion. The Cleveland Whig avowed itself
in favor of abolition, and of the dissemination of Anti-
Slavery arguments among the slaveholders, as a proper
means to attain that end.

On the 12th of November, 1835, Gerrit Smith addressed a letter to A. L. Cox, Secretary of the American Anti-
Slavery Society, desiring him to enrol his name in the list
of members, not because he approved entirely either of
the constitution or the proceedings of that Society, against
both of which he still entertained the objections which
he had before made public, but because he considered
the society so far identified with the right of free discussion, that if the society should fall, that right must fall
with it.

In November, 1835, Lundy, having returned from his
last journey to Mexico, issued a number of the Genius
of Universal Emancipation. In it he said: "A number of
state societies and annual conventions, with several hundred auxiliaries, have been recently established in the

United States, having in view the abolition of slavery
and the improvement of the condition of the African
race.   There are also a large number of periodicals devoted wholly or in part to the cause.   The good work
has progressed with a rapidity unparalleled, within the
space of a few years."

In an article headed "What should Abolitionists do?"
he said : " In advocating the cause of emancipation, a
high degree of circumspection, and the entire command
of our own tempers, are requisite.   Though it is difficult
for human nature calmly to endure the obloquy which
is heaped upon us, and the malice and violence with
which we are assailed, yet it becomes us to restrain our
indignant feelings, and appeal to the reason and judgment, instead of the passions of others, particularly when
their minds are fully awakened.   The language of cutting retort or severe rebuke is seldom convincing, and
it is wholly out of place in persuasive argument."   He
also expressed his disapproval of the policy of those, who
on account of the violence of the persecution, were disposed to suspend their labours, at least for a season.

In the same number of the Genius, Lundy noticed
the insurrection in Texas against Santa Anna, which
had then recently commenced, and expressed the conviction that a desire to re-establish the system of slavery
was a prominent motive with the Texans for resisting the
consolidation of the government of the Mexican states,
and that even if that change had not been attempted,
they would soon have declared themselves independent
of the Mexican Republic.

The same number also stated, that Andrew Donelson
of Tennessee, brother-in-law of President Jackson, had
died a few months before, emancipating unconditionally
by his will, twenty-one slaves ; that a gentleman from
Virginia had brought four slaves to Philadelphia to
emancipate and send to Liberia, but applying to Dr. E.
P. Atlee for deeds of manumission, he had been induced
to change his mind, and leave them free on their natal
continent ; and that a southern philanthropist, who did

not wish his name published at that time, was preparing to liberate more than one hundred slaves, whom he intended settling in Hayti, Tamaulipas and the western parts of the United States.

The same number contained an obituary notice, by Lundy, of Elizabeth Margaret Chandler, the poetess, who had been several years assistant editor of the Genius; and an announcement that her poems, accompanied by a biographical sketch, would be soon published. She died in Lenawee county, Michigan, the 2d of November, 1834, aged 24. The same paper also contained an address to philanthropists respecting Mexican colonization, which stated that a considerable number of coloured persons, a portion of whom were slaves that were to be emancipated on condition of migrating, had made application to become settlers in the proposed colony, to which it was intended to send the first expedition from Philadelphia in February 1836, unless the disturbances in Texas should extend to Tamaulipas, so as to prevent it. In this article, Lundy returned his acknowledgments to those who had aided in furnishing a portion of the funds which he expended in his travels, and in obtaining the grant of land; and stated that he was prevented from publishing their names only by the refusal of a part of them to consent to it. After that number, the publication of the Genius was suspended for a period of nine months.

In December, 1835, President Jackson, in his annual message to Congress, invited the attention of that body " to the painful excitement produced in the South, by attempts to circulate through the mails inflammatory appeals addressed to the passions of the slaves, in prints and in various sorts of publications, calculated to stimulate them to insurrection, and to produce all the horrors of a servile war." He urged the necessity of maintaining, in good faith, " those compromises of the constitution upon which the Union is founded;" said that the Post Office department, being " designed to foster amicable intercourse and correspondence between all

the members of the confederacy," should not be " used
as an instrument of an opposite character;" and recommended the passage of such a law as would " prohibit,
under severe penalties, the circulation in the Southern
states, through the mail, of incendiary publications intended to instigate the slaves to insurrection." In reference to this recommendation, the Executive Committee
of the American Anti-Slavery Society addressed a protest to the President, in which they denied that they had
ever issued any publications with the design which
they conceived he had imputed to them. The subject
of the proposed restriction on the mails was afterwards
agitated in Congress, but no act was passed in relation
to it.

In January, 1836, Wm. L. Marcy, Governor of New
York, in his annual message, stated that he could conceive of no objects that the abolitionists had in view, in
their operations in New York, but to embark the people
" in a crusade against the slaveholding states, for the
purpose of forcing abolition upon them by violence and
bloodshed;" and he recommended the enactment of a
law for punishing those who should be guilty of " acts
calculated and intended to excite insurrection and rebellion in a sister state." Of course, the abolitionists,
denied that they had been guilty of any such intentions.
No law of the kind proposed by the Governor was
passed. Not far from the same time Governor Everett
of Massachusetts made a suggestion of the expediency
of prosecuting the abolitionists, somewhat similar to that
made by Governor Marcy.

At the same time Governor Marcy communicated a
correspondence with Governor Gayle of Alabama, by
which it appeared that the Grand Jury of Tuscaloosa
county in that state, had indicted R. G. Williams of New
York, publishing agent of the American Anti-Slavery
Society, on a charge of attempting to produce " conspiracy, insurrection and rebellion among the slave
population of that state, by publishing the ' Emancipator'
containing these words: ' God commands and all nature

cries out that man should not be held as property. The system of making men property, has plunged 2,250,000 of our fallen creatures into the deepest physical and moral degradation, and they are every where sinking deeper.'" Governor Gayle demanded of Governor Marcy the surrender of Williams for trial on this charge. Governor Marcy refused to comply with the requisition, on the ground that Williams had not been in the State of Alabama, and that a compliance with such demands would enable one State to legislate for the entire government of the citizens of another.

Numerous petitions for the abolition of slavery in the District of Columbia having been presented to Congress, that body, on motion of Mr. Pinckney of South Carolina, made February 8th, 1836, resolved by a vote of 201 to 7, that "Congress possesses no constitutional authority to interfere in any way with the institution of slavery in any of the States of the confederacy; and also, by a vote of 163 to 47, that "Congress ought not in any way to interfere with slavery in the District of Columbia."

On the 6th of March, Martin Van Buren, then a candidate for the Presidency, being called on for his opinions by some of the citizens of North Carolina, wrote to them that he thought Congress had constitutional power to abolish slavery in the District of Columbia, but that Maryland and Virginia would probably not have ceded that district had they anticipated such a measure, and he therefore thought that the power "ought not to be exercised against the wishes of the slaveholding states."

In the same month, eighty-three emigrants sailed from Richmond, Virginia, for Liberia, most of whom were formerly slaves and had been emancipated on condition of emigrating. Some weeks afterwards forty-five persons of the same description sailed from New Orleans for the same place.

From the annual report of the Executive Committee of the American Anti-Slavery Society, made to the meeting of that body on May 10, 1836, it appeared, that there were then five hundred and twenty-six anti-slavery

societies known to exist, of which three hundred and
twenty-eight had been formed during the preceding year.
The number of members in two hundred and fifty-four
of the societies was 27,182.   The number in the remaining societies had not been reported.   The Society
had expended, during the year, $25,866, being an in-
crease of 150 per cent on the preceding year.   It had
employed thirteen lecturing agents during a good portion of the time, and had printed upwards of one mil-
lion of copies of various tracts, including the Emancipator.   Among the agents, were the names of Allen,
Alvord, Birney, C. C. Burleigh, Gould, Lyman, George
Storrs, Streeter, Thomas, Tyler, Wattles and Weld.
Of the anti-slavery societies reported, only two were
mentioned as being in slaveholding States.

On the 26th of May, the House of Representatives of
Congress adopted a resolution "that all petitions, memorials, resolutions and propositions relating in any way,
or to any extent whatever to the subject of slavery, shall,
without being either printed or referred, be laid on the
table, and that no further action whatever shall be had
thereon."   The vote was ayes 117, noes 68.

On the 8th of June the bill before the national senate,
for restraining the transportation of abolition documents
by mail, was rejected : ayes 19, noes 25.

On the 5th of July 1836, forty-seven coloured persons
from Kentucky and Tennessee, left New York for Liberia.   The number was originally sixty-five, of whom
fifty were emancipated slaves that had been liberated on
condition of emigration.   Of these, ten escaped at Pittsburg, and eight at New York, preferring to remain in
this country.

In the same month, a mob at Cincinnati, Ohio, consisting of fifteen or twenty persons, entered in the night
time the office of Mr. Pugh, printer of the Philanthropist, an anti-slavery paper edited by James G. Birney,
took the press to pieces and carried off parts of it, and
destroyed the sheets of an impression of the paper which
had been partly stricken off.   Shortly afterwards, Mr.

Birney went to board at the Franklin House, in that city, during the absence of his wife who was on a visit to Kentucky.   Seventeen out of about fifty boarders in the house, then wrote Wm. Johnson the landlord, that if he permitted "Mr. Birney, the abolitionist," to remain, they would leave the house.   He disregarded the threat, and twelve of the boarders, mostly clerks, quitted the house, but their places were directly filled, or nearly so, by others.   In the same city, on the 22d of July, a large meeting was held at the lower market house, at which resolutions were passed threatening violence, if the publication of the Philanthropist was not discontinued, and a committee was appointed to wait upon " Mr. Birney and his associates and request them to desist from the publication of their paper," and to warn them that if they persisted, the meeting could not hold themselves " responsible for the consequences." Mr. Birney and the Executive Committee of the Ohio Society, having declined to comply with this request, a large mob assembled on the evening of July 31st, proceeded to the office, broke the windows and furniture, scattered the papers and books, and burned many of them, and took out the press, drew it down to the river, broke it to pieces and threw it into the stream.   They then went to the houses of Birney and his friend Donaldson, with a view, apparently, of personal violence; but finding neither of them at home, they proceeded to several houses inhabited by coloured people, and tore them down.

On the third of August 1836, Lundy commenced a new Anti-Slavery paper at Philadelphia, under the title of "the National Enquirer," which was published weekly.   In the same month he resumed the monthly publication of the Genius of Universal Emancipation. During its suspension, he had communicated to the National Gazette of Philadelphia, several articles, under the signature of Columbus, relative to the affairs of Texas and Mexico. They were copied into various other prints. He afterwards devoted a considerable portion of his time to the same subject.

The Enquirer of August 17th, contained an account of the manumissions in the French colonies, in the year 1835, giving the number as follows: In Martinique, 16,341 : In Guadaloupe 7,682 : In Guiana 1,162 : In Bourbon 1,965. Total of slaves set free in one year, 27,150.

The Genius for September, contained tables of the produce exported from the British colonies òf Demerara and Berbice during the first quarter of each of the last three years of absolute slavery, and the corresponding quarters of the three first years of the apprenticeship system, showing an increase in the latter period of nearly fifty per cent.

The "Enquirer" of October 8th, contained "an appeal to the Christian women of the South, on the subject of slavery, by A. E. Grimke, a native of Charleston South Carolina, who had emancipated her slaves and removed to the North. The same paper announced the resumption of the publication of the Philanthropist, at Cincinnati, since the destruction of the press by the mob. The Enquirer of the 15th, contained the proceedings of a meeting of coloured people in Philadelphia, expressive of their sentiments on the decease of Thomas Shipley, who had long been known in that city as one of the most indefatigable labourers in the cause of freedom.

The number for December 17th, contained extracts from the message of Governor Ritner to the Pennsylvania Legislature, in which he declared that among the cherished doctrines of Pennsylvania, there had heretofore been opposition to slavery at home, opposition to the admission of new slaveholding states into the Union, and opposition to slavery in the District of Columbia: and he recommended that these doctrines should be maintained unshrinkingly and fearlessly.

The number of December 31st, contained a suitable obituary notice of Dr. E. P. Atlee, who had edited the Genius during a part of Lundy's last tour to Mexico, and who had been a constant and earnest friend of the anti-slavery cause. It also noticed the result of the first

Anti-Slavery fair ever held in Philadelphia. It had been instituted by the Female Anti-Slavery Society. The proceeds were upwards of three hundred dollars—a sum small in comparison with those derived from recent exhibitions of the kind ; but it was then deemed of considerable importance.

CHAPTER XXX.

Gleanings and occurrences in 1837 and 1838.

The Enquirer of January 7th, 1837, contained a notice from Lewis Tappan, assistant Treasurer of the American Anti-Slavery Society, that the Executive Committee had appointed seventy agents to labour in the free states. This was a greater number than the Society was found able to keep in the field for any considerable length of time.

The number for January 21st, contained a new law, passed by the Legislature of Maryland, which subjected to imprisonment for a period not less than ten nor more than twenty years, all persons who should print, engrave or circulate, any pictorial representation, pamphlet, handbill or newspaper, tending to create discontent among the people of colour and stir them up to insurrection.

The number for January 28th, mentioned the forwarding, by the editor, of a petition for the abolition of slavery in the District of Columbia, signed by five hundred and twenty-two inhabitants of Salem county, New Jersey, the signatures having been procured by a lady, " one of the most indefatigable abolitionists in the nation : " and that a like memorial had just been forwarded from Philadelphia with five hundred and twenty names, " principally obtained by a most worthy young female philanthropist." Lundy remarked, that he would gladly mention the names of these ladies, but their modesty forbade it.

The number of abolition petitions presented to Congress having been very large, the House of Representatives adopted on the 18th of January, by a vote of about two to one, a resolution offered by Mr. Hawes of Kentucky, that all such petitions should lie on the table, without being read, and without any action on them whatever.

The Enquirer of February 11th, contained the proceedings of an Anti-Slavery Convention held at Harrisburg from the 31st of January to the 2d of February inclusive, for the formation of a Pennsylvania State Anti-Slavery Society. Lundy had been very active and zealous in promoting the call and the assembling of this convention, and had published in his paper the signatures to the call, amounting to upwards of 1,200. He was one of the delegates, and as chairman of a committee, made a report, accompanied by a petition to Congress, adverse to the recognition of the independence of Texas and its annexation to the United States, which were adopted. At this meeting the constitution of the present Anti-Slavery Society of Pennsylvania was adopted, and the Society organized. The convention also adopted the following resolution :

"Whereas, the self-denying zeal, and untiring efforts of Benjamin Lundy, by which he sustained the "Genius of Universal Emancipation" for eight years of general apathy on the subject of slavery, when no pecuniary embarrassment, no privations of society, no cold neglect or indifference to his warning voice could dissuade him from his fixed principles of duty; but finally the attention of many was roused by it throughout the land : therefore, Resolved, that Benjamin Lundy receive the thanks of this Convention."

On the 11th of February, in consequence of John Quincy Adams having informed the House of Representatives, in Congress, that he had received a petition purporting to come from slaves, that body, on motion of Waddy Thompson, of South Carolina, and Joseph R. Ingersoll of Pennsylvania, resolved : "That this House cannot receive said petition without disregarding its own dignity, and the rights of a large class of citizens of the

South and West, and the Constitution of the United States." The vote was, ayes 160, noes 35.

On the 4th of March, the newly elected President, Martin Van Buren, was inaugurated In his address on that occasion, he declared, that no bill for the abolition of slavery in the District of Columbia, if passed without the consent of the slaveholding states, could ever receive his constitutional sanction. To this course he was pledged by his public declarations made before his election.

On the 18th of March, 1837, the Pennsylvania Anti-Slavery Society assumed the pecuniary responsibility of publishing the "National Enquirer," its editorship remaining, as before, in the charge of Lundy.

The number for April 1st, contained an address to Abolitionists, signed " Mentor," in which were these words: "let us then organize and try our strength at the ballot-boxes: not as a distinct party, but as the preponderating weight, which shall be the means under Providence, of saving our country." Of this proposition Lundy remarked, that whether the views of the writer were " strictly correct or not, we must have more political action."

The number of April 8th, announced that the Senate of the state of Massachusetts had adopted, unanimously, a resolution in favour of the abolition of slavery in the District of Columbia: and with one dissenting voice a resolution against the admission of any new states into the Union, unless its constitution should prohibit slavery.

The Enquirer of May 6th, gave an account of the proceedings of a convention in favour of the " Integrity of the Union," which was held at Harrisburg, Pa., on the 1st and 2d of the month, and consisted of near one hundred members coming from different parts of the state. It adopted resolutions declaring that the United States government has no constitutional power over slavery within the several states of the Union; that it ought not to legislate for abolition in the District of Columbia, as to do so would impair the harmony and might peril the integrity of the Union ; that attempts by citizens of one state to denounce the' institutions of another, were unwarranted; and that African colonization should be encouraged, as tending to the ultimate abolition of slavery, the elevation of the African race, and the civilization of Africa. The greater portion of the state was unrepresented in this convention, and it was the last anti-abolition convention formally assembled in the state of Pennsylvania.

The numbers of the Enquirer of May 12th and 19th, noticed the meeting of the American Anti-Slavery Society held at New York, commencing on the 9th. It appeared from the annual report, that the society, during the year, had received into its treasury thirty-six thousand dollars, being an increase of ten thousand dollars on the preceding year; it had issued 669,387 impressions of anti-slavery publications, of all sorts; and the number of societies auxiliary to it was one thousand and six, of which four hundred and eighty-three had been organized during the preceding year. Of the seventy agents appointed, sixty-five had rendered service, and the aggregate of their labours was deemed equal to that of thirty-two persons constantly employed. The number of coloured persons in Upper Canada was stated in the report at about ten thousand, composed mostly of fugitive slaves. A convention of American Anti-Slavery women was held at New York at the same time, being the first national meeting of the kind. Lundy had been zealous in encouraging the holding of this convention.

On the 3d of June, Lundy published another editorial on the subject of political action. He said: " We have nothing more to do than to unite in a firm phalanx and hold the balance at the polls. Let us lay aside all political party dissentions, all individual preferences, all minor considerations, and take a determined stand on the ground of patriotic philanthropy." On the 29th of the month, an election to fill a vacancy in Congress took place in the third district of Pennsylvania, which was composed of the northern part of Philadelphia county.

The candidates were Charles J. Ingersoll and Charles Naylor. The "National Enquirer," and the abolitionists generally, who had stood aloof at the last preceding election in the district, now took sides with Naylor, on the ground of assurances contained in a private letter from him, and he was elected, according to the Enquirer, by the votes of abolitionists. What the assurances were which his letter gave, is not well known; but it is certain that during his subsequent sitting as a representative, he never made a speech or a motion, or gave a vote in favour of abolition.

The Enquirer of August 17th, announced the publication of the second edition of a pamphlet entitled the "War in Texas," written by Lundy, with a view to prevent the acknowledgment of the independence of Texas, and its annexation to the United States. At the time of the publication of the second edition, the independence of that country had been acknowledged : but Lundy continued to labour in opposition to its annexation, occupying much of his paper with the subject. His writings had attracted the attention of John Quincy Adams, and led to an acquaintance and some correspondence between him and Lundy.

The same paper noticed certain questions which had been put by the abolitionists of Rhode Island to the candidates for Congress in that state, and the reception of favourable answers. Lundy remarked : "The question of abolishing slavery, wherever it may be acted on, must be finally settled at the ballot box. Let this ground be taken in every election district immediately, when we ascertain that we have votes enough to hold the balance between the parties."

The Enquirer of Sept. 7th, contained an account of a mob at Alton, Illinois, on the 21st of August, which broke into the office of the Alton Observer, an abolition paper published by Elijah P. Lovejoy, and broke the press to pieces and scattered every description of materials found in the office through the streets. While the mob was at its work, one of the abolitionists rung the bell of one of the churches, "and three or four hundred of the citizens of the town collected on the spot, but they evinced no disposition to interfere in the affair."

The paper for September 28th, gave the number of Anti-Slavery Societies in each state, as estimated to exist in the month of May preceding. They were as follows : Maine 33 societies : New Hampshire 63 : Vermont 89: Massachusetts 145: Rhode Island 25°: Connecticut 39: New York 274: New Jersey 10: Pennsylvania 93: Ohio 213: Indiana 2: Illinois 3 : Michigan 27: being all in the non-slaveholding states. The oldest of these societies was the New England, established January 1st, 1832. The above account included only those known by the name of "Anti-Slavery" Societies. The Pennsylvania Abolition Society, organized in 1784, was then and still is in existence. Whether any other of those called abolition or manumission societies, organized prior to 1832, remained in active existence, was not stated. The whole number of members of the above societies was estimated at upwards of one hundred thousand.

The number of October 12th, contained the result of the Philadelphia city election for Assembly, from which it appeared that Joseph Mc'Ilvaine, who had been zealously opposed by Lundy in the Enquirer, had received five hundred and forty-two votes fewer than the highest candidate on the same ticket, and five hundred and seventeen fewer than the lowest of the remaining candidates. The ground of opposition to him was that he had opposed a bill providing jury trials for persons claimed as fugitive slaves, and had also opposed, in a speech, the granting of the Legislative Hall for the delivery of an anti-slavery lecture.

The Enquirer of October 19th, stated that in Belmont county, Ohio, where the abolitionists had sufficient numbers to turn the political scale, and the Whigs were supposed to have the majority, the candidates of that party for Assembly, having failed to give satisfactory answers to questions put them by the abolitionists, and one of the

Van Buren (or democratic) candidates having answered favourably, the whig abolitionists had in part abstained from voting, and some had voted for the favourable candidate on the other side. The result was the loss of the entire whig ticket, and the candidate who answered satisfactorily stood highest on the list of the chosen. Lundy remarked : " This was nobly done. A few such lessons will teach politicians something like respect for our principles."

The number for November 23d, 1837, contained the account of the mob of Nov. 7th, at Alton, Illinois, in which Elijah P. Lovejoy, editor of the Alton Observer, was killed. The press on which the Observer was printed having been twice destroyed by previous mobs, and Mr. Lovejoy being resolved to persevere in the publication of the paper, a new press was purchased and landed at Alton late in the evening of the 6th, and conveyed under the eye of the Mayor of the city to the warehouse of Godfrey, Gilman & Co , where about fifty friends of the editor were armed and secreted in one of the rooms, to be ready to aid the Mayor in case of a mob, such as had been threatened. There was, however, no attack until the next night at about 10 o'clock, when a mob assembled, repaired to the warehouse, and gave some indications of an attack. W. S. Gilman, one of the owners of the building, then appeared at a door in the third story, addressed the rioters, and urged them to desist, informing them that those within the building were prepared, and should defend their property. The mob replied that they did not wish to injure any person, but were determined to destroy the press, which they demanded for that purpose. Mr. Gilman replied that it would not be given up. The mob then repaired to the north end of the building and attacked it, by throwing stones and other missiles, continuing their violence for fifteen or twenty minutes, until a gun was fired from one of the windows of the warehouse, and one of the mob, named Lyman Bishop, from Gennessee county, New York, was mortally wounded. He was carried to

a surgeon's office, where he died in about half an hour,
most of the mob having dispersed upon his being shot.
This occurrence having increased the excitement, a
much larger mob soon assembled, and requested the
Mayor to go and inform those in the house, that they had
assembled to destroy the press, and would not desist till
the work was accomplished, but they would retire until
the Mayor returned with an answer. That officer complied with their wishes, they retiring in the mean time.
He was informed by those in the warehouse that they
had assembled to protect their property against lawless
violence, and were determined to do so. The mob now
increased, being armed with guns and other weapons.
The Mayor commanded them to desist: they listened,
but would not regard the command. A rush was made
to the warehouse, amid cries of "fire the house," "burn
them out," &c. The house was accordingly set on fire :
and "the firing of guns soon became fearful and dangerous between the two contending parties," "scenes
of the most daring recklessness and infuriated madness
followed in quick succession. The building was surrounded and the inmates were threatened with extermina-
tion and death in the most frightful form imaginable.
Every means of escape by flight was cut off. About the
time that the building was set on fire, the Rev. E. P.
Lovejoy, as he was standing near the door of the warehouse, received four balls in his breast. Two others of
the party in the warehouse were wounded. Several of
the persons engaged in the attack were severely, though
not dangerously wounded. When the contest had raged
for an hour or more, the persons within intimated that
they would abandon the house and press, if suffered to
depart unmolested. The doors were then thrown open,
and they retreated down Front street. Several guns
were fired on them while they were retreating, and a
ball passed through the coat of one of them, near the
shoulder. A large number of the mob now rushed into
the warehouse, threw the press out on the wharf, broke
it to pieces, and threw the fragments into the river. One

of the spectators then courageously extinguished the fire on the roof of the building, which was but little injured, and the mob dispersed without further violence."

The above statement is mostly taken from an account of the transaction published by the Mayor, John M. Krum. Another account stated that a volley of stones was thrown through the doors and windows, before Gilman addressed the mob :—that his speech was answered by another volley: that two guns were fired by the mob, the balls whistling through the windows, before the shot was fired from the house which killed Bishop, it being fired by consent of all within the building; that on the second attack of the mob, one of its number ascended the roof by a ladder and set it on fire; that in the mean time a detachment of four or five, one of whom was Lovejoy, was sent out to defend the property, and one of them fired upon the man on the ladder and wounded him. One of the mob then took deliberate aim at Lovejoy and shot him, as he was standing by the foot of the ladder. He fell, but jumped up and ran into the counting-house, exclaiming "I am shot, I am a dead man," and expired in a few minutes. Those within, seeing the building on fire, then proposed to capitulate, and received a promise that if they withdrew and left their arms, not one of them should be molested. Yet as they went out the door and turned the corner, almost every one of them was fired at. Mr. Ruff received a ball in one of his legs, his clothes were perforated with holes, and one shot entered his nose near the eye, causing a profuse bleeding. Mr. Weller, of the firm of Gerry & Weller, also received a ball in the leg, and several others had their clothes perforated by balls. As they retreated, they were pursued and fired after in every direction, till none of them could be found.

The Enquirer of November 30th, 1837, announced that the raising of the Pennsylvania Hall, to be "dedicated to Freedom and the Rights of Man," took place in Philadelphia on the 25th of that month.

The number for December 28th, contained the ayes

and noes on the motion on Mr. Patton of Virginia, for the re-adoption, by the newly elected House of Representatives of Congress, of the so called gag rule; which forbade all debate and action on abolition petitions. The vote was ayes one hundred and twenty-two, noes seventy-four, showing a gain of twenty-seven votes to the side of the right of petition, since 1836, when the vote on Pinckney's resolution was one hundred and sixty-three ayes to forty-seven noes. On the passage of Patton's resolution there was one representative from a slaveholding state, viz. John J. Milligan, of Delaware, among the noes. Lundy in speaking of this decision, said: "If the halls of Congress are to be closed and the avenues barricaded to the ingress of our petitions, we must find another channel through which they can be conveyed. That channel may be found through the ballot box. Let it be sought and pursued, while our rallying cry is, political abolition."

The same paper stated that upwards of sixty persons, mostly coloured mechanics and agriculturalists of good property, were about to migrate to Hayti from Georgia and Florida. The expedition was fitted out under the auspices of —— Kinsley, of Florida, a wealthy planter, a Scotchman by birth, whose mulatto son and his family were among the emigrants.

The Enquirer of January 25th, 1838, contained the decision of the Pennsylvania Convention, then sitting at Philadelphia, on the question of excluding coloured persons from the right of suffrage under the amended constitution. The vote was, for exclusion seventy-seven: against it forty-five. Judge Fox, of Bucks county, had previously decided that coloured people were not entitled to the right of suffrage under the old constitution; and the Supreme Court of the state made the same decision before the vote was given by the people on the adoption of the amendments. The soundness of these decisions was doubted by many.

The same paper contained a sketch of the proceedings of the annual meeting of the Pennsylvania Anti-

Slavery Society, held at Harrisburg on the 16th Jan., at which Lundy, as chairman of a committee, reported a memorial to Congress against the annexation of Texas, which was adopted by the society.

The Enquirer of February 22d, 1838, mentioned that the Legislature of Louisiana had recently passed a law, prohibiting the migration of free persons of colour into that State, and also prohibiting the return of those who should at any time leave it.

On the 9th of March, Lundy retired from the charge of the Enquirer, which had been for some time published as the organ of the Pennsylvania Anti-Slavery Society. He was succeeded by John G. Whittier, and the name of the paper was changed to " The Pennsylvania Free-man." Lundy, in his valedictory, declared his perfect satisfaction with the choice made of his successor, and that it was his own intention to remove to another field of action, in some part of the Western country, and to resume there the publication of the Genius of Universal Emancipation. In the same number of the Enquirer, the Executive Committee issued a brief address to the public, in which they expressed their regard for Lundy " as one of the earliest and most unflinching friends of the man of colour," and " as one who has been largely instrumental in arousing an anti-slavery feeling in Pennsylvania, and in promoting an effective organiza-tion," &c.

In the same month, several numbers of the Literary and Religious Magazine, published at Baltimore by Robt. J. Breckenridge, having arrived by mail, at Pe-tersburg, Virginia, the post master of that place detected in them some articles which maintained that slavery, as it exists in the United States, is inconsistent with the Holy Scriptures. He forthwith addressed a letter to General Pegram, chairman of the Petersburg Commit-tee of Vigilance inquiring whether the incendiary docu-ments ought not to be burned, conformably to the Act of Assembly of March 23d, 1836. The general decided the question in the affirmative, and the magazines

were accordingly " burned in the streets, by order of the
Recorder, and in the presence of some of the most respectable citizens;" to use the language of the Petersburg Intelligencer.

In the month of April, the House of Representatives
of the State of Maine, passed, by a vote of sixty-nine to
sixty-two, a resolution favourable to the Abolition of
Slavery in the District of Columbia; and the Legislature
of Massachusetts shortly afterwards adopted resolutions
favourable to that measure, as well as to the abolition of
of the slave trade, and against the admission of any additional slaveholding States into the Union.

The Pennsylvania Hall which had been built at Philadelphia by abolitionists and others, was opened on the
14th of May, and various free discussions and public
meetings, among which was that of an Anti-Slavery
Convention of American Women, were held during that
and the two succeeding days. A great and constantly
increasing excitement prevailed in the city during this
period, occasioned partly by previous hostility to abolition; partly by the managers not assigning separate
seats for the people of colour; partly by expressions made
use of by some abolitionists within and about the building, and greatly heightened and inflamed by exaggerated and unfounded reports of what was said and done
in the Hall. On the 17th, early in the evening, the
managers, at the request of John Swift, Mayor of the city,
closed the Hall and delivered the keys to him—he
having advised the abstaining from holding an evening
meeting, as a necessary means for ensuring the safety of
the building. A large mob was assembled and was
every moment increasing. The Mayor having taken
the keys, addressed the crowd in deferential language;
and recommending to them to go home and go to
bed, as he intended to do, he wished them " a hearty
good night," and left the ground amid the cheers of
the assemblage. About half an hour afterwards, the
doors were forced by the mob, and the Hall was set on
fire, with little apparent resistance from the police.

The fire engines of the city repaired to the spot, and by their efforts protected the surrounding buildings. Many of the firemen were not disposed to extinguish the fire in the Hall, and some who attempted it were deterred by threats of violence. The Hall, which had cost upwards of thirty thousand dollars, was consequently consumed—the wall only being left standing.

Lundy, who attended the meetings during the three days, had in contemplation of his journey to the West, collected the little property that he possessed, and placed it in one of the rooms of the Hall, then occupied as the Anti-Slavery Office. It was there consumed in the flames.

The following extract from a letter which he wrote to a friend the next morning, will serve to show his feelings on the occasion :

"I thought last evening, that I should be able to call this morning about nine o'clock, but I have not had it in my power to get away from my friends, until now—nearly the middle of the day. Well! my papers, books, clothes—every thing of value, (except my journal in Mexico, &c.) are all, *all* gone—a total sacrifice on the altar of Universal Emancipation. They have not yet got my *conscience*, they have not taken my *heart*, and until they rob me of these, they cannot prevent me from pleading the cause of the suffering slave.

'The tyrant [may even] hold the body bound,—
But knows not what a range the spirit takes.'

I am not disheartened, though every thing of earthly value (in the shape of property) is lost. Let us persevere in the good cause. *We shall assuredly triumph yet.*"

CHAPTER XXXI.

Removal of Lundy to Illinois—Publication of his paper there—His illness and decease: with notices of matters not contained in the foregoing pages.

In the month of July, 1838, Lundy left Philadelphia for Illinois, where his children then resided. On his way, he became acquainted with a young woman of Chester county, Pennsylvania, a member of the Society of Friends with whom he afterwards corresponded and contracted a matrimonial engagement. From his correspondence with this young woman, the personal narrative of his life contained in the foregoing pages, is extracted, with the exception of the portion which relates to his travels and residence in Texas and Mexico, which is taken from his journal kept at the time.

While on this journey to Illinois, he wrote to his friends that his health was excellent, and that he felt happy in being clear of the crowded city. He did not reach Illinois until September, 1838. A letter written by him on the 19th of that month, dated Putnam county, says: "I am here among my children, at last—this is emphatically one of the best and most beautiful countries that I have ever seen. You shall hear from me ere long, through the Genius of Universal Emancipation." A postscript dated seven o'clock, P. M., says " since writing the above I have attended the (Anti-Slavery) Convention at Hennepin. Ir was a fine large meeting, composed of intelligent men and women. It passed a unanimous resolution to encourage the circulation of the Genius, and a large number of subscriptions was immediately obtained."

Having been disappointed in several attempts to purchase a press and types at Hennepin, where he intended to settle, he received a proposition from some inhabitants of Lowell, La Salle county, Illinois, to establish his paper there. He removed thither in the winter of

1838-9 ; his son Charles accompanying him, and his other children following in the spring. A letter from him dated 2d month 3d, 1839, says : " I have purchased a printing office, and established it at a new town called Lowell ; but we have no post office here yet, and the G. U. E. will be published awhile at Hennepin. I have found great difficulty in getting my printing done, but am now prepared to go on regularly as soon as I receive paper, for which I have sent to St. Louis."

Lundy built a house and printing office at Lowell, and in the spring purchased a tract of land about four miles distant. His paper was printed irregularly for want of funds, he having, for a portion of the time, no other assistance than his two sons, one of whom attended to the farm. In the fore part of August he was attacked with a fever prevalent in that part of the country, but was not then confined to his bed, nor thought to be dangerously affected. On the morning of the 21st he worked in his printing office, and wrote a note to one of his children, stating that he had been quite unwell but was now better. In the afternoon of that day, however, he was seized with severe pains, and retired to bed at the house of his friend Wm. Seely. The next day he continued to grow worse and to suffer much pain, until 10 o'clock in the evening, when the pain ceased, and he became easy and comfortable. Being then told by his physician that his end was probably approaching, he replied that he felt better; he felt as if he were in Paradise. At 11 P. M. he calmly breathed his last last, without groan or struggle. His remains, attended by a number of his friends, were removed on the 23d to the house of his son-in-law, Isaac Griffith, near Magnolia, Putnam County, whence, on the following day, they were removed, and interred in the Friends' burying ground, on Clear Creek in that county.

Thus terminated the earthly existence of one of the most self-sacrificing and indefatigable of reformers.

Having resolved, twenty-three years before his decease,

to devote his energies to the relief of the suffering slave, and the oppressed man of colour, he persevered to the end, undeterred by difficulties and undismayed by dangers, undiscouraged by disappointments and unsubdued by sacrifices. Alone, often on foot, he encountered fatigue, hunger and exposure, the frost and snows of winter, the rains and scorching sun of summer, the contagion of pestilence, and the miasmatic effluvia of insalubrious regions—ever pressing onward toward the attainment of the great object to which he had dedicated his existence.

He was the first to introduce the publication of anti-slavery periodicals, and the delivery of anti-slavery lectures, and it is believed that he was also the first to induce the formation of societies for the encouragement of the produce of free labour. Although he presumably, from the commencement of his labours, believed, in common with a large portion of the abolitionists of this country, in the safety and prosperity of immediate emancipation, and encouraged it in all individual cases, yet it may be supposed, that like most of them, he was discouraged, by the seeming greatness of the pecuniary and other obstacles, from urging instant liberation as a measure of national or local legislation. But on the appearance of a pamphlet written by Elizabeth Heyrick, of England, entitled, "Immediate, not Gradual Abolition," he at once adopted its views, and issued proposals for its re-publication in this country. But the friends of the anti-slavery cause were not prepared, at that time, to give it the necessary encouragement.

From the commencement of the agitation of the question of colonizing a portion of the free people of colour, with their own full consent, he was favourable to it, not as a principal, but as a secondary and subordinate means of promoting both emancipation and the elevation of the African race—being always careful to caution the people against recommending or anticipating the removal of the whole coloured population. Hence he naturally looked with a favourable eye upon the formation of the American Colonization Society, and upon its operations, a number of years subsequently, as evinced by the extracts contained in the foregoing pages: yet when the spirit of hostility had arisen between the Colonization and Anti-Slavery Societies, and some of the prominent branches and members of the former became active in proscribing those who attempted the education and elevation of the coloured people on their native soil, as well as in opposing their enjoyment of political rights, and recommending laws for their compulsory migration, he became openly hostile to that society, and declared that its existence had been only productive of evil.

Benjamin Lundy was slightly under the middle size, of a slender form, light and rather sandy complexion and hair, a sanguine temperament, and a cheerful and sprightly disposition. His manners were gentle and very unassuming. He was afflicted with considerable difficulty of hearing, the probable cause of which is mentioned in the early part of these memoirs. The following extracts from a letter respecting Lundy, written after his decease, by his half-sister, will doubtless interest the reader :

"My first recollection of Benjamin was when young, he having returned from Ohio to visit his parents and family. The year I cannot remember, but it was shortly before his marriage.

His kind disposition and engaging manners soon won my attachment, and I received many demonstrations of kindness from him—and though he left us while I was yet young, my recollections of him were always so gentle and tender, that I could not bear to hear a word said in disapprobation of him. This attachment was strengthened by years and a repeated correspondence after I arrived to womanhood, and I doubt not but to this fact I owe much of that fervor of zeal, which I feel to devote my existence to the anti-slavery cause.

My youthful recollections are, that he was of gentle and mild manners, yet quickly perceptible of the views and intentions of others, and always prepared to meet them in the way he thought best suited to them; of a studious habit, he seldom sat without a book in his hand, and always embraced every opportunity for improvement. So great was his desire for mental cultivation, that in the little time he was in New Jersey, he got up in the neighbourhood, where he resided, an association for mental improvement, similar to the lyceums of the present day. It was composed of the most enterprising young men in the neighbourhood. Several pieces of his composition for presentation to this association, I once had in my possession, but not now. The energy of his active mind (though somewhat impeded in usefulness by a deficiency in hearing, supposed to be caused by over-exertion in boyhood,) breathed animation in those around him. Wherever he was, and while he remained in New Jersey, he was forward in all research, investigation, and improvement; but when he left, the literary ssociation soon became lukewarm, and finally became inactive and extinct.

He was much grieved that the advocates of the cause of emancipation seemed not to enter into the view of Elizabeth Heyrick respecting immediate emancipation, as he did. He talked much to me about it, and lamented it; for, said he, the view was a sound one. But having for many years stood the buffeting of pro-slavery in free and slave States, having endured the more offensive feeling of the apathy of those calling themselves abolitionists, and having seen many fall from their zeal, and colonization render the heart callous with the spirit of caste, he gradually became weary of new adventures, and preferred the paths of experience; and hence he has sometimes been represented as opposed to the measure of immediate emancipation. This I believe was not true.

When he kept a free produce store in Baltimore, he met with a loss by robbery. He told me that he had reason to believe that some evil minded persons stirred up a black man to rob the shop, expecting he would prosecute him, and then they would appeal to the fact as a refutation of his doctrine that coloured persons were fit for freedom. He said he thought the coloured man less to blame than some others, and hence would not enter process against him.

This kind of annoyance he often met with. When he lived in Tennessee, he told me they had a coloured child, a girl, they intended to bring up, but envious persons put all sorts of mischief into her head, and she became so unmanageable that they were obliged to send her home to her parents.

While he published the Genius, and was not the printer himself, he laboured industriously every day, and wrote nights and First days; and all his hard earnings, after a frugal support of his family (in which his wife gave much assistance until she became a cripple with the rheumatism,) he spent in support of the Genius. I repeat it, there is much cause to regret the loss of many specimens of his beautiful compositions in early life, both in prose and verse. Soon after the birth of his second daughter, having informed us of it, and of their conclusion to call her "Elizabeth," he proceeds thus :

> Hear let me pause—the muse in accent clear,
> Repeats a name that memory holds most dear ;
> My mother, it was thine—blest spirit see,
> Thy son—thy only son, remembers thee.
>
> It n'er shall be forgot till this fond heart
> Lies motionless—or till the fatal dart
> Sings through the air and quivers in my breast,
> Bidding me seek the realm s of peace and rest.
>
> Nor even then, for while the parting soul,
> Rising aloft shall view the distant goal,
> Hope whispers—and in language soft and sweet,
> Fortells that kindred spirits there shall meet.

There was more of it, but my memory will not serve me further.

His three eldest children were born in Ohio. The two youngest were born in Baltimore, he being from home on a sea voyage. He had gone to Hayti with some liberated slaves, and was detained there I think for want of a conveyance. Just as he embarked for the port of Baltimore, he received information of the decease of his wife, and of her having left twins only a few hours old. From his detention he had feared that some great inconvenience might arise ; but this was a shock for which he was unprepared. He thought of the want of his kind attention to his dying wife, though he did not doubt but all was done for her that could have been to make her comfortable, (and in acknowledgement of the kind sympathy of their friends of Baltimore, it is due to say this was the case.) but the heart and hand most near, and consequently most bereft, was not there. He thought of the five infant minds, of which he was now the sole sustainer and guide, and of their destitute condition, and his heart almost fainted within him. Had he been with her who was now no more with him in his earthly pilgrimage, and witnessed her serenity, her rejoicing in hope, and how solemnly and sweetly she commended him and them to the protection of that being who p esides over the destinies of men, how all earthly ties were severed from around her, and how strong was her belief and prayer for their preservation in the paths of inno cency and uprightness, he might have had something of outward de-monstration that his great loss was her happiness. But in all this deep affliction the consciousness of having been absent in the prose-cution of a work of love to men, and hence of reverence to God, soothed his agonized soul, even on the mighty deep; and when he re-turned and found his house vacated. his infant babes, some in one place and some in another, and she that until then had greeted his return from peril and danger, gone, forever gone, his firmness in the doctrine of our duty to God being our highest interest and happiness, was severely tested; yet, even his manly spirit, bending not to the ignorance and pride which despises the laws of our nature, when grief became so relaxed as to admit it, found relief in a flood of tears.

He wrote to our parents and us of his situation, and thought it best not to keep house, if he could avoid it, or get his little ones more under care such as he desired. Our father and mother, in accord-ance with our warm desire, soon concluded to bring the three eldest children to our home, and they continued with us until they were nearly grown. He supported the twins with nurses and at board, until they were three years old, and then our father was willing to take them, but a sister-in-law in Ohio, who had lost nearly all her children, insisted upon having them, and came with her husband to Baltimore for them. They have since removed to Illinois, and the children I believe are yet with them. Benjamin was now again a lone one in the world, stripped of home and the social enjoyment and composing influence of his innocent children, and all this that he might labour for others. What a sacrifice ; what disinterestedness was here !

He visited his children occasionally, and frequently made them presents of clothing and books. He had the peculiar, happy manner of making them greatly rejoice to see him, even to the shedding of tears, and yet to become willing for him to leave them again. Thus a strong, deep attachment grew up in their minds for him, though he was seldom with them."

The following extracts of a letter written by Lundy from the house of his father, at Ancocus, N. J., in March 1836, to his children residing in Illinois, may serve to illustrate his peculiar views and character.

"Since I last wrote you, my time has been so incessantly occupied with matters of business, and in corresponding with persons who wish information concerning my colony, that I have not until now found leisure to commune with you as freely as I intended to do. And even at present, I must be brief—as I have much to attend to of a public nature, connected with the great cause of suffering humanity—which I desire *you*, my dear son and daughter, also to *bear in mind*, as long as your Heavenly Father permits you to exist in this world.

I need not repeat to you what I have endeavored to make you fully acquainted with before : that I do sincerely regret our long separation. You are *dear* to me—often do I think of you —fervently do I pray the Father of mercies to preserve you from the dangers of vice, the temptation of the world, the snare of the wicked. But *everything depends on your own conduct.* He *will* so preserve you, if you are obedient to his holy requirings. He has given you faculties and powers of mind, to enable you to resist the allurements of vice; but if you do not exercise those faculties, and exert those powers, he will leave you a prey to the corrupting passions and propensities, and the strong temptations of a sinful world. You are now both of a suitable age to think and reflect for yourselves, and to judge of what is necessary to secure your own peace and happiness.— And yet you are at the precise time of life when temptation is the strongest—when the mind is most fickle—your hearts most susceptible of impression. In short, *now is the day*, my dearly beloved, in which you stand the most in need of the advice of the good, and the instruction of the experienced. Look around you and see *who are they* that live the most respectably—are spoken the best of by good men and women—who possess the most influence in preserving good order in society, both religious and moral—who, in fine, appear to be the most happy and useful members of the community at large. Endeavor to become acquainted with such as these—listen to their admonitions—imitate their conduct—(for you will be sure to imitate the conduct of *some*, as you are now mere learners—*apprentices* in the *moral* business of the world) and as you become experienced in life yourselves, though your judgment may direct you

to pursue a course somewhat different from theirs, the example
which you will have witnessed, and the information and instruction received, will be of great benefit to you. In matters
of Religion, I would not wish to see you either rigidly sectarian,
or inadvertent as to its sacred duties.

A religion which consists in mere *profession*, or *formality* of
outward appearance and action, is nothing but mockery of God—
while on the other hand, those who are careless and indifferent
respecting the duties which they owe their Maker and Eternal
Preserver, seldom enjoy peace in this life, the respect of mankind, or the anchor of hope for happiness here or hereafter.
There is too much profession, and too little practice of religious
duty, among the greater portion of men—too much ostentation
and pride mingled with their *public* devotion. A regular atten-
dance of religious meetings, is both profitable to ourselves and
others, *provided* we turn our eye inward; direct our thoughts to
God, and in truth and sincerity worship Him while there. I
therefore enjoin it upon you my dear children, to attend your
religious meetings as regularly as you can. But do not go there
merely for the purpose of *seeing others*, or *being seen yourselves.*
Go there " *to worship your Father which is in Heaven.*"   Let not
the vanities and pleasures of juvenile amusements, nor yet the
cares of worldly ambition or gain, influence or even occupy
your minds beneath the roof of the solemn sanctuary. Be willing to listen to the admonitions of those who offer their advice
upon such occasions. But *remember*, listening to others, or imita-
ting the conduct of others, is no part of the performance of duty.
The worship of God consists in the humble contrition of heart—
the turning our thoughts wholly unto him—and waiting on him
with perfect willingness to be obedient to the manifestations of
His will.   And let me impress it upon your tender minds—
never indeed forget this solemn injunction from your *earthly*
parent who feels deeply concerned for your welfare, and loves
you as he loves his own life :—*Always think of your Heavenly
Father with reverence.*   When you are assembled in the house
of devotion—when you are engaged in the various occupations
of life—when you are amidst the circles of social acquaintance—
or in the lonely silent walks of meditation—whenever the idea
of His existence occurs to your minds—*Think of Him with reverence.*   This is the *performance* of religious duty.   While we
reverence our Maker, we love Him, and are willing to be obedient to all his requirings. We then feel our passions and vain
desires subjected to the principle of virtue—we feel them re-
strained by the calming and softening influence of Heavenly
Grace; and we wish well to all the creatures God hath made.
This also leads us to reflect on our situation in life. We call
to mind the duties we owe to each other, as members of the
great human family : and as we manifest a willingness to act
in obedience to the will of the Almighty, we shall " learn of

Him," through his teachings in our own hearts, and through many other channels that, to secure happiness in this life, we must act justly towards each other. We must wrong none—deceive none—be kind to all—charitable to all—in short you must " Do unto others as you would they should do unto you." This is not only the " golden rule," but it is one of the safest rules by which to regulate our conduct towards each other. Let these admonitions sink deep in your minds my beloved ones. Do not forget, nor disregard the advice of your absent Father. He loves you with all a parent's fervor. It is impossible that he should recommend to you, what his own experience tells him would not be for *your own* good. Be wise, my dear children, and lay the foundation for your future happiness before your passions become strong and lead you astray—before prejudice erects his empire in your hearts, and warps your judgment—before vice triumphs over you, and the punishment of evil doers awaits you, to destroy your temporal, and perhaps, eternal peace. The spring time of youth will soon be past. Beauty will fade,—and vivacity give place to the cares of life. All gaiety is transient tinsel. Trust not in the evanescent joys of youthful amusement. The time is not far distant when you must assume the direction of your own affairs altogether. You will then think of choosing more intimate and confidential companions for the rest of your lives. This will be to you a matter of extreme importance. Take the most guarded care, in this particular. Look not too much to worldly honor, on the one hand, nor be careless of genuine comfort and virtuous principle on the other. Study not to *please* others, so much as to *deserve* their esteem by doing well yourselves. Be genteel and polite in your manners, decent in your appearance ; modest and liberal, yet unaffected and intelligent in your conversation. And if you study to improve your minds, acquire habits of industry and economy, and make yourselves happy and virtuous; you will thus *command* the notice and respect of others in a far greater degree than you ever will by any efforts or arts to enlist their esteem. I have now, my dears, written much more than I intended—yet I scarcely know how to stop. Dearly do I love you. Remember my words—bear in mind what I have told you before—and read these lines often. Not only read but often *reflect* upon what I have said to you ; I speak in familiar terms the more readily to meet your youthful comprehension. Finally—so conduct yourselves, as to become useful members of society, ornaments to your country, benefactors of the human race, sincere followers of Christ, and acceptable servants of the Most High God.

From your ever affectionate Father,
BENJAMIN LUNDY.

Elizabeth Shotwell Lundy.
Charles Tallmage Lundy.

APPENDIX,

Being a brief notice of the revolution in Hayti, condensed from an elaborate account published in the Genius, during the year 1827.

In the year 1789 the number of slaves in Hayti was 480,000, the free people of color 24,000, and the whites 30,831, according to the estimate of Edwards: but the estimate of Alcedo made 600,000 slaves, 44,000 free people of color, and 42,000 whites.

On the 20th of August 1789, the French National Assembly, in framing a constitution for France, adopted, as a part of it, the declaration, that "all men are born and continue free as to their rights." This declaration, taken in connexion with the existence in Paris of an Anti-Slavery Society, called "*Amis des Noirs*" (friends of the blacks), of which the prominent liberals in the Assembly were members, created a great ferment in Hayti, where it was supposed to be a prelude to a general emancipation.

The planters on the reception of this news, threw off in a good measure their submission to the authority of the mother country ; and they never afterwards fully returned to it. They proceeded, of their own mere authority, to elect three provincial assemblies for the northern, southern and western parts of the island, respectively. They afterwards chose a general assembly, which convened at St. Marc, April 15th, 1790. The mulattoes (or free people of color) resolved to claim at once the enjoyment of equal rights; but their demand being rejected, they collected in large bodies under arms. They were, however, soon overpowered, and the few whites who had favored them were cruelly persecuted. One of them, a magistrate named Ferrand, was put to death by a white mob.

The fear that the whites of the island would declare its absolute independence, induced the National Assembly to decree, on the 8th of March 1790, that the Constitution of France should not be applied to the colonies. A civil war nevertheless broke out between Peynier, the French governor, and the colonial assembly, which was only terminated on the 8th of August, 1790, by the departure of the majority of the assembly for France, with a view to justify their conduct to the National Assembly. That body however condemned their proceedings, and declared their acts null and void.

The National Assembly of France, although it had disclaimed the idea of liberating the slaves, had nevertheless directed, by a decree adopted March the 28th, 1790, " that every person of the age of 25 or upwards, possessing property or having resided two years in the colony and paid taxes, should be permitted to vote in the formation of the colonial assembly." This of course embraced the free mulattoes, but the planters would not so construe it. A mulatto named James Ogee, who had been educated in France, raised about two hundred followers, and wrote to the governor demanding that the provisions of the *Code Noir* (or black code) which had been enacted by Louis the 14th, for the protection of the slaves, should be enforced, and the privileges enjoyed by the whites extended to the mulattoes, of whom he declared himself the protector, by force of arms if necessary.

A force was sent against him, which killed or captured a portion of his followers, and dispersed the rest, who took refuge in the Spanish part of the island. They were demanded thence, and being delivered up, Ogee and his lieutenant, Chavane, were broken on the wheel, and twenty of their adherents were hung.

The news of the execution of Ogee, who was a person mild in manners and enthusiastic in principle, and who had demanded a compliance with laws which those who put him to death violated, caused great indignation in Paris, insomuch that for a time the planters there dared not appear in the streets. About the same time, deputies from the mulattoes of Hayti arrived to ask an explanation of the decree of March the 28th, 1790. The subject was brought up in the national assembly by Gregoire, who advocated the rights of the mulattoes: Robespierre exclaimed, " perish the colonies rather than sacrifice an iota of our principles:" and on the 15th of May, 1792 the assembly enacted, that the people of color, born of free parents,, should be entitled to all the privileges of citizens.

This decree excited the utmost rage and indignation among the planters and their party, who could not brook it that the mulattoes should be placed on a political level with themselves. They refused the civic oath, trod the national cockade under foot, threw off all subordination to France, and elected deputies to a new assembly which met on the 9th of August, 1792. To appease them, Blanchelande. the nominal French governor, wrote to France urging the repeal of the decree, and to the Haytien assembly promising to suspend it of his own authority.

The mulattoes, alarmed at these proceedings, began to collect in large bodies, without hindrance from the whites, whose attention was occupied with their newly chosen assembly. A slave insurrection, probably instigated by the mulattoes, commenced in the north, about nine miles from Cape Francois, on the night of the 22d of August, 1792, and spread rapidly to the surrounding plantations, most of the white inhabitants being massacred. The whites marched from the Cape, and defeated 4,000 of the rebels; but they were soon obliged to retreat by the constant increase of their opponents: and the mulattoes and blacks having joined their strength, attacked and forced two camps of the whites, and speedily overran the whole neighboring country. It was estimated that in the course of two months, 2,000 white persons of all conditions and ages had been massacred: 180 sugar plantations, and 900 coffee, cotton and indigo settlements destroyed, and the buildings on them consumed; 1200 families reduced from opulence to beggary; and that 10,000 of the insurgents had perished by the sword or by famine, and some hundreds by the executioner.

A rebellion now broke out in the west, where 2,000 mulattoes were joined by 600 negro slaves. Having defeated a force sent against them, they proceeded to ravage the country to an extent of 30 miles, and at length approached Port au Prince with intent to burn it. It was saved from destruction only by a treaty, called the *concordat*, which was effected on the 11th of September, between the mulattoes and the white inhabitants of Port au Prince, by which the latter agreed to suffer the decree of the French assembly to go into effect.

This treaty was ratified by the general assembly on Sept. 20th, 1791, and the rebellion abated for a time.

But it soon burst out afresh with increased energy, in consequence of news from France that the National Assembly had, on September 24th, 1791, repealed its decree in favor of the rights of the mulattoes. This class attributed the repeal to the influence of the planters, and declared that one party or the other must be exterminated. The war now became sanguinary : one-third of Port au Prince was burned ; and the prisoners taken on both sides were put to death with savage tortures. On the 4th of April, 1792, the National Assembly again retraced its steps, by declaring that the free blacks and people of color should have the same rights as the whites : and it despatched three commissioners, with 8,000 troops, to enforce its will. These commissioners endeavored to subdue the revolted slaves, while they sustained the political rights of the mulattoes.

In June 1793, a civil war broke out at Cape Francois between the commissioners on the one hand, and the planters and M. Galband on the other, in consequence of the commissioners denying the eligibility of Galband to the office of governor. The commissioners, being hard pressed, offered pardon, and it is said the plunder of the city also, to the rebel negroes, if they would join them. The negro generals, Jean Francois and Biasson, rejected this offer ; but, on June 21st, after several combats between the whites, a negro chief named Macaya, entered Cape Francois, at the head of 3,000 revolted slaves, and began an indiscriminate massacre of the whites, putting all to death who could be found, and consuming more than half the city by fire. The whites of both parties who escaped, took re uge on board the shipping in the harbor.

On the 19th of September, 1793, a British force arrived from Jamaica and occupied Jeremie, according to previous arrangement with the planters, who had been for a considerable time engaged in soliciting the British Government to take possession of the island. On the first news of this invasion, the French Commissioners, Santhonax and Polverell, with a view to gain strength, changed their policy from that of suppressing slave insurrections, to that of proclaiming the immediate and total abolition of slavery and the enjoyment of political rights by the emancipated. It is said that over 100,000 slaves embraced this offer of liberty, and withdrew to the mountains, where they formed a savage republic. In the north, 40,000 revolted slaves still remained in arms.

The war went on between the British and the planters on the one side, and the commissioners and their adherents of all complexions on the other, till June 1794, when the commissioners returned to France and received the approval of the National Assembly. They had left Hayti chiefly in the hands of a mulatto general named Andrew Rigand, and a negro chief named Toussaint L'Overture, who, from the condition of a slave, had risen to exhibit talents and estimable qualities, such as are rarely found combined in one of the human race. In March, 1797, Toussaint was appointed general-in-chief of the French armies in Hayti, the French government thus ratifying an authority which he had for a long time actually enjoyed.

In the summer of 1788, the British forces evacuated the island, after five years of vain efforts to subdue it to themselves and the planters.

Toussaint now turned his attention to the promotion of industry, the restoration of decayed agriculture, and the amelioration of the laws: In 1801 he procured the adoption, by the people, of a constitution for Hayti, which was formally proclaimed to be an independent neutral power.

At the close of that year, peace being made between France and England, Bonaparte, first consul of France, dispatched his brother-in-law, Le Clerc, to Hayti, with a military force, to bring the island under his dominion. Both he and Le Clerc made solemn promises, of continued liberty to all who had acquired it, and offered the post of second in command to Toussaint. The colored chiefs resisted, however; but their adherents deserted them so rapidly, many of them joining the French troops, that by the middle of March, 1802, the French had acquired possession of all the principal towns, and the country along the coast. Le Clerc then ventured on a proclamation restoring to the planters their former authority over the negroes upon their estates. This act of perfidy roused the people, and they so flocked to the standard of Toussaint, that the tide of success changed ; and by the middle of April, Le Clerc was besieged at Cape Francois.

He now again changed his tactics, and on the 25th of April, 1802, proclaimed " liberty and equality to all the inhabitants without regard to color," subject to the approval of the French government. This measure was so successful in gaining over the blacks, that their chieftains,' commencing with Christophe and Paul L'Ouverture, and terminating with Toussaint and Dessalines, thought fit to submit on condition of an amnesty to their troops, and the retention of their rank by themselves and their officers. The French sovereignty was then recognised throughout Hayti.

About the middle of May, 1802, Le Clerc sent a force which surrounded the house of Toussaint, in the dead of the night, seized him and his family, and conveyed them on board a frigate, which carried them to France. Toussaint there died in a loathsome dungeon, in April, 1803. His wife and children disappeared about the same time, and were never afterwards heard of. Le Clerc excused the arrest of Toussaint on the pretext that he had engaged in a conspiracy, but no proof of such a fact was ever furnished.

The abduction of Toussaint roused the blacks again to resistance, their confidence in the French commander being destroyed. The war was renewed, and accompanied by the most barbarous treatment of prisoners on both sides. The loss of the French in the year 1802 by the sword and by disease was estimated at 40,000. Success continued favorable to the Haytiens, until November 1803, when the French troops under Rochambeau, (Le Clerc being deceased) capitulated to Dessalines, and left the country.

In April 1804 a general massacre of the remaining French inhabitants took place by the instigation of Dessalines, a sanguinary tyrant, who had assumed the chief authority, and who charged the French with plotting against his government. Since this period the independence of Hayti has remained undisturbed.

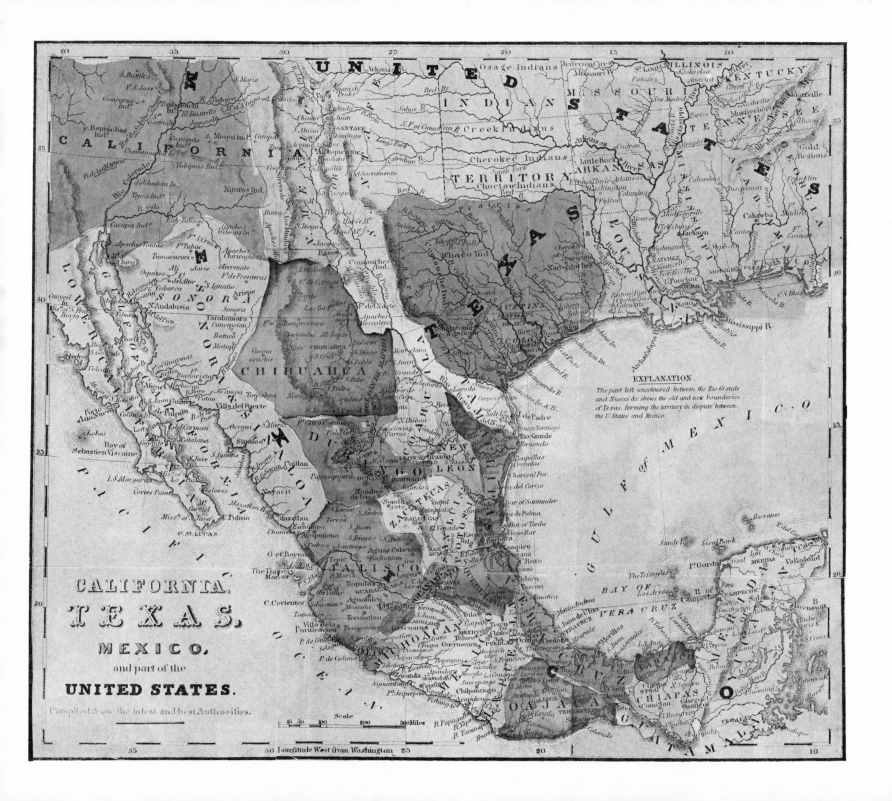

CALIFORNIA, TEXAS, MEXICO,

and part of the

UNITED STATES.

Compiled from the latest and best Authorities.

EXPLANATION.

The part left uncoloured between the Rio Grande and Nueces &c. shows the old and new boundaries of Texas, forming the territory in dispute between the U. States and Mexico

Scale

25 50   100   200   300 Miles

Longitude West from Washington